THE **LAW** OF
BITCOIN

THE LAW OF BITCOIN

PAUL ANNING
LORNA BRAZELL
MARK BRAILSFORD
JERRY BRITO
MATTHEW J. CLEARY
JILLIAN FRIEDMAN
STUART HOEGNER
MICHAEL TAYLOR
RYAN J. STRAUS
CHRISTOPH-NIKOLAUS VON UNRUH

THE LAW OF BITCOIN

Copyright © 2015 Gaming Counsel Professional Corporation
Author Credits: Paul Anning, Lorna Brazell, Mark Brailsford, Jerry Brito, Matthew J. Cleary, Jillian Friedman, Stuart Hoegner, Michael Taylor, Ryan J. Straus, Christoph-Nikolaus von Unruh

All rights reserved. No part of this book may be used or reproduced by any means, graphic, electronic, or mechanical, including photocopying, recording, taping or by any information storage retrieval system without the written permission of the publisher except in the case of brief quotations embodied in critical articles and reviews.

The information, ideas, and suggestions in this book are not intended to render legal advice. Before following any suggestions contained in this book, you should consult your personal attorney. Neither the author nor the publisher shall be liable or responsible for any loss or damage allegedly arising as a consequence of your use or application of any information or suggestions in this book.

iUniverse books may be ordered through booksellers or by contacting:

iUniverse
1663 Liberty Drive
Bloomington, IN 47403
www.iuniverse.com
1-800-Authors (1-800-288-4677)

Because of the dynamic nature of the Internet, any web addresses or links contained in this book may have changed since publication and may no longer be valid. The views expressed in this work are solely those of the authors and do not necessarily reflect the views of the publisher, and the publisher hereby disclaims any responsibility for them.

Any people depicted in stock imagery provided by Thinkstock are models, and such images are being used for illustrative purposes only. Certain stock imagery © Thinkstock.

ISBN: 978-1-4917-6868-6 (sc)
ISBN: 978-1-4917-6867-9 (e)

Library of Congress Control Number: 2015908857

Print information available on the last page.

iUniverse rev. date: 06/17/2015

CONTENTS

Acknowledgements xi
Foreword xiii

What is Bitcoin? 1

Canada 17
    1. Anti-Money Laundering & Counter-Terrorist
    Financing Rules 19
        1.1. The Criminal Code 19
        1.2. The Proceeds of Crime (Money Laundering)
             and Terrorist Financing Act—The Background
             & the Old Rules 23
        1.3. Quebec's MSB Legislation 26
        1.4. The 2014 Budget & Bill C-31 29
        1.5. Federal MSB Requirements in Brief 33
    2. Cryptocurrency, Money & the Currency Act 36
        2.1. Is Cryptocurrency Money? 36
        2.2. The Currency Act 44
    3. Cryptocurrency & Negotiable Instruments 48
        3.1. The Bills of Exchange Act in Brief 49
        3.2. Cryptorurrency's Place in the Bills of Exchange Act... 52
    4. Cryptocurrency in Commerce & Consumer Protection.... 56
    5. Cryptocurrency & Securities Law 66
        5.1. Institutional Background & Policy 66
        2.2. Is Bitcoin a Security? 69
        5.3. Bitcoin-Denominated Instruments as Securities 73
    6. Cryptocurrency & Taxation 76
    7. Conclusion 83

Germany 84
    Introduction 84
    1. Cryptocurrencies and Financial Institutions 87
        1.1. Cryptocurrency As a Unit of Account 87
        1.2. Domestic Relations 90
        1.3. Business Models That Qualify As Credit Institutions.... 91
        1.4. Business Models That Qualify As Financial
             Services Institutions 92

- 1.4.1. Arranging Dealings to Buy and Sell Cryptocurrencies 92
- 1.4.2. Operating a Multilateral Trading System 93
- 1.4.3. Trading on a Continuous Basis on Organized Markets and Unregulated Exchanges 93
- 1.4.4. Regulatory Exchange of Cryptocurrencies Against Fiat 95
- 1.5. Business Models That Do Not Qualify As Credit or Financial Services Institutions 95
2. Cryptocurrencies and Taxation 97
    - 2.1. Cryptocurrencies and VAT 97
        - 2.1.1. Definition 98
        - 2.1.2. Customer Payment in Cryptocurrency to a Business for the Provisions of Goods or Services 99
            - 2.1.2.1 Cryptocurrency As Private Money 99
            - 2.1.2.2 Cryptocurrency As an Ordinary Commodity 100
            - 2.1.2.3. Conclusion 101
        - 2.1.3. Mining the Block Reward 102
        - 2.1.4. Receiving the Mining Fee 102
        - 2.1.5. Trading with Cryptocurrencies (Exchanges) 103
    - 2.2. Cryptocurrencies and Income Tax 104
        - 2.2.1. Distinction between Income Arising from Private Activities and Economic Activities 105
        - 2.2.2. Private Activities 105
        - 2.2.3. Economic Activities 107
3. Cryptocurrencies and Criminal Law 107
    - 3.1. Creation and Use of Coins and Paper Money/ Paper Wallets 108
    - 3.2. Acting as a Finance or Financial Services Institution 109
    - 3.3. Mining Cryptocurrencies Using Botnets 110
    - 3.4. Theft of Cryptocurrencies 112
4. Cryptocurrencies and the Civil Law 114
    - 4.1. Definition 114
        - 4.1.1. Cryptocurrencies as Currencies 115
        - 4.1.2. Cryptocurrencies As a Thing or a Right 115
        - 4.1.3. Cryptocurrencies As Immaterial Goods 116
        - 4.1.4. Cryptocurrencies As Commodities 117
        - 4.1.5. Conclusion 118

  4.2. Contract Law 118
    4.2.1. Buying Cryptocurrencies................................ 118
    4.2.2. Buying an Item With Cryptocurrencies 119
    4.2.3. Other Contracts.. 121
  4.3. Legal Acts Sui Generis.. 121
  4.4. Revocation of the Contract 122
    4.4.1. The Delivered Items Have a Defect.............. 122
    4.4.2. Revocation of Consumer Contracts 124
    4.4.3. Delivery or Payment with
       Misappropriated Cryptocurrency................. 124
  4.5. Damages for Breach of Duty 125
  4.6. Tort Law 125
  4.7. Calculation of Damages 127
  4.8. Specific Performance of a Claim in
    Cryptocurrencies 128
 5. Anti-Money Laundering Law.. 129
  5.1. Money Laundering and Financing Terrorism
    as Crime 129
  5.2. Money Laundering Prevention 130
    5.2.1. Businesses That Are Obligated under
       the Money Laundering Act 130
    5.2.2. Obligations Without Incidents..................... 131
    5.2.3. Obligations With Incidents 131
    5.2.4. Obligations under the Banking Act.............. 133
 6. Conclusion... 133

The United Kingdom.. 140
 Executive Summary 140
 The interplay of intellectual property rights with Bitcoin 141
  Bitcoin's fundamental components 142
  Public/private keys 145
  Bitcoin identifiers 146
 What is the tax treatment of bitcoin in the UK?................... 147
  Introduction 147
  HMRC Briefing 2014... 148
  VAT and bitcoin 148
  Income tax and capital gains tax 149
  Corporation tax 149
  Position in other EU member states................................ 150
 What is the regulatory treatment of bitcoin in the UK?........ 152
  E-money... 153
  Payment services 154

The wider UK regulatory regime 162
Anti-Money Laundering.. 163
Consumer Rights Bill 166
The Legal and Regulatory Outlook for the UK 169
European Central Bank's October 2012 paper on
    virtual currencies 169
EBA's July 2014 Opinion on 'Virtual Currencies' 170
Bank of England's September 2014 Publications on
    Bitcoin 172
The Chancellor's August 2014 Speech on FinTech in
    the UK, the FCA's October 2014 remarks, and
    the UK Government's November 2014 Call for
    Evidence 175
Where now for the regulation of bitcoin in the UK? 176

The United States 178
  I. Introduction 178
  II. The Private Law of Bitcoin 179
    1. Direct Bitcoin Holdings and On-Block Chain
       Transactions 180
       1.1. Money and Currency.. 180
       1.2. Legal Attributes of Money... 182
            1.2.1. Payment of Money.. 182
            1.2.2. Title to Money 184
       1.3. Bitcoin as Money... 184
       1.4. The Private Law Characterization of Direct
            Bitcoin Holdings.. 185
       1.5. Bitcoin as Property 188
    2. Indirect Bitcoin Holdings and Off-Block Chain
       Transactions 190
       2.1. Financial Intermediaries 191
       2.2. Bitcoin Intermediaries.. 193
  III. The Public Law of Bitcoin.. 194
    1. Monetary Regime 195
       1.1. The Stamp Payments Act of 1862..................................... 195
       1.2. Anti-Counterfeiting Statutes 196
    2. AML Regime 196
       2.1 The Bank Secrecy Act 196
       2.2 Economic and Trade Sanctions/Office of
           Foreign Assets Control 201

3. Investment Regime 201
   1.1. Securities Exchange Commission 202
   1.2. Commodity Futures Trading Commission 205
4. Consumer Protection Regime 207
   4.1 Electronic Funds Transfer Act/Regulation E 207
   4.2 Section 5 of the FTC Act 209
5. Campaign Contributions 209
   5.1. Federal Election Commission 209
6. Internal Revenue Code 211
IV. Case Law 213

ACKNOWLEDGEMENTS

ooooooooooooooooooooooooooooooooooo

No book like this can get to press on the efforts of one person. A small but dedicated group has been mobilized and inspired to write, review, proofread, design, advise on, and assemble this volume. The thanks that are due all of these people extend well beyond mere words at the beginning of the book, but at least this is a start.

First, our authors deserve the lion's share of the gratitude: Paul Anning, Mark Brailsford, Lorna Brazell, Matthew Cleary, Jillian Friedman, Ryan Straus, Michael Taylor, and Christophe-Nikolaus von Unruh. Without them, this book would not exist. This is especially remarkable given that many of them are at the top of their respective fields with busy professional, academic, and personal lives and commitments.

Jerry Brito of Coin Center also deserves special thanks and mention for writing the superb introduction to this book.

The editors have been just as important. Brad Polizzano (tax attorney in New York City), Sophie Giguère (J.D. candidate at the University of Toronto), and Nicholas Torti (B.C.L.–LL.B. candidate at McGill University) have devoted many hours to this project. In particular, Jillian Friedman (cryptocurrency attorney in Montreal) acted as the senior editor on much of this book. I'm grateful for all of their efforts.

Many others have offered insightful thoughts, comments, and advice about very involved questions and issues concerning cryptocurrency and decentralized ledger technology more generally. They are all experts in different ways in this space. Those people include David Berger of the Digital Currency Council; Justin Blincoe and Ira Miller of Deginner; Tatiana Cutts of the Birmingham Law School; Ryan Lazanis and Helene Petoussis of Xen Accounting; Jonathan Levin, founder of Coinometrics; Michael Perklin of Bitcoinsultants; Gabriel Sukenik of Coinapult; Tim Swanson, author of The Anatomy of a Money-Like Informational Commodity and Great Chain of Numbers; Erik Voorhees of ShapeShift; and, Alex Waters of Coin.co.

Thanks also go to Tara Kelly of Tara Kelly Creative. She did a fantastic job designing the book, the website (www.thelawofbitcoin.

com), and the chapter headings. She also very ably advised us on typography. Francis Pouliot of the Bitcoin Embassy (Montreal) helped with marketing. Bitcoin PR Buzz handled public relations. Lisa Guylee is our media contact. I appreciate all of their contributions.

Finally, thanks to all of the people who shared our excitement about this project and have referred to the book and helped promote it.

As I have said before, I see this volume as part of the start of a conversation about the law of bitcoin, not the end. Let the debate begin.

Stuart Hoegner
February 2015

FOREWORD

JERRY BRITO

○○○○○○○○○○○○○○○○○○○○○○○○○○○○○○○○○○○

A common misconception about Bitcoin is that it is not regulated. The claim is frequently repeated in the media. Here is BBC News in August of 2014: "The so far unregulated digital currency has courted controversy because of its volatile value and its popularity among cybercriminals." USA Today in October: "The value in the decentralized and unregulated digital currency has plummeted since hitting a high of more than $1,130 in December 2013." And TIME Magazine in November: "A Texas man was charged with fraud in New York on Thursday, in what federal authorities claim is the first-ever Ponzi scheme involving the unregulated digital currency Bitcoin."

That last one is pretty telling. If the use of Bitcoin in certain circumstances wasn't regulated, for what was the Texas man arrested?

The truth is that a wide variety of laws and regulations have applied to the use of Bitcoin since its inception in 2009. The confusion seems to stem from the idea that as governments have not taken steps to regulate the currency specifically, it is therefore unregulated.

This could not be further from the truth, as the chapters in this book attest. The law of Bitcoin is one that is not only fast-emerging, but in many ways already exists. It is only a matter of looking at precedent and statutes and applying them to the novel circumstances that new technology makes possible. When that is not possible, it is an indication that we may need new laws.

Network vs. Actors

Part of the problem with saying that Bitcoin is unregulated is that it is not often clear what is meant by "Bitcoin." Do we mean the technology, the peer-to-peer network, or individual use of that network in commerce?

In some sense it may be accurate to say that the technology and the peer-to-peer network are unregulated. In fact, these may be beyond regulation. The technology is ultimately a protocol—a set of shared rules that can be expressed in writing—so that, in the U.S. at least, it is protected speech not subject to prior restraint under the First Amendment except in rare cases of compelling governmental interest. And the peer-to-peer network as a whole is practically impossible to regulate because it is decentralized—too many participants to police efficiently, and many outside of one's jurisdiction altogether.

In another, perhaps more pedantic sense, however, it may be more accurate to say that Bitcoin is *never* unregulated. After all, Bitcoin the protocol is ultimately a set of rules that regulate the decentralized digital currency (e.g., there will only ever be 21 million bitcoins), and the peer-to-peer network enforces these rules in its operation. Indeed, at its core Bitcoin is an attempt at regulation through cryptography rather than human institutions.

But typically, when one hears that "Bitcoin is unregulated," the implication is that governments have not yet acted to "regulate" the digital currency in some way. This is incorrect because particular activities of actors employing the Bitcoin network are subject to any number of existing regulations. Even when the technology is not specifically mentioned in a law or regulation, an activity or use of a new technology can be covered by existing laws or regulation. The chapters that follow survey the applicable laws of various countries and how they intersect with Bitcoin today.

Guidance vs. Regulation

Regulations tend to be written broadly so that they can accommodate changes in the future. When a new technology like Bitcoin comes along, there are often questions about how exactly to comply with the existing regulations, but not necessarily questions about if the regulations apply. To address these how-not-if questions, regulators will often issue guidance.

Law and Guidance

Guidance is not a new regulation, but a statement of how the existing regulation applies. The implication is that the regulation always applied to the new technology or activity, and that even without the guidance it would have applied. New regulations must first be proposed and regulators must consider comments from the public before promulgating a final rule. Guidance does not require due process because, technically, there is no new law being created; the existing applicable law is simply being explained.

For example, in the U.S., a business that accepts value from a customer and transmits it to a third party on behalf of that customer will be subject to federal money laundering and know-your-customer regulations, as well as state money transmission licensing requirements. The fact that Bitcoin is employed as the medium of exchange does not change the calculation. This was as true in January of 2009 when Bitcoin first launched as it is today.

In March of 2013, the Treasury Department's Financial Crimes Enforcement Network (FinCEN) issued guidance explaining which actors in the digital currency space were covered by existing regulations and how they should comply. FinCEN will tell you, however, that their guidance was not a new regulation, but a clarification of how their existing regulation already applied, and indeed applied from the inception of the Bitcoin network.

Similarly, the Internal Revenue Service issued guidance on the tax treatment of capital gains from bitcoin trading in March of 2014. This did not mean that capital gains before the guidance were not subject to tax, but rather it explained how the tax that was already owed should be calculated. As far as the IRS is concerned, its regulations and the tax law always applied to bitcoin traders with or without proffered guidance. Taxes on capital gains are due on trades as far back as January of 2009.

Often, however, a government agency will not issue guidance and will simply enforce the existing law or regulation. If it is successful, it demonstrates that the law or regulation has always applied. The case of Trendon Shavers, the Texas man noted in the quote above, illustrates this.

Shavers was engaged in a Ponzi scheme in which he sold shares in a fund and promised investors returns of up to 1 percent per day, or 7 percent per week. When the SEC brought suit against him, he argued that his fund offering did not qualify as a security under the law because "Bitcoin is not money, and is not part of anything regulated by the United States."

The judge in the case found that, to the contrary, "[i]t is clear that Bitcoin can be used as money." In a way, this now serves as guidance to all future actors who are considering issuing securities and taking investments in bitcoin. And, subject to review by higher courts, of course, the precedent also means that this was always the meaning of the existing law; not that new law was created.

So it's not right to say that Bitcoin is an unregulated digital currency given how many regulations apply to actors using the currency. Agency guidance in the U.S. underscores that fact. The same dynamic plays out in every other country. It cannot be overstated how important it is for entrepreneurs, legal professionals, and scholars in the Bitcoin space to understand the state of the law around the world.

Although there are important proceedings that will make new law, today much of the public policy work to be done in the Bitcoin space is not developing new regulations. Instead, it is figuring out how existing laws and regulations apply to activities that employ the Bitcoin network. The pages that follow are a guide to that endeavor.

WHAT IS BITCOIN?

STUART HOEGNER

○○○○○○○○○○○○○○○○○○○○○○○○○○○○○○○○○○○○

Lawyers are positioned imperfectly to define or set out the parameters of Bitcoin. Although not true of all counsel, we are often more concerned with narrow issues of law and not with financial technology's building blocks.

Yet define it we must, as any discussion of the law of a new technology must begin with a clear understanding of what that new technology comprises. This is especially true of a phenomenon as revolutionary[1] as the world's first truly decentralized digital-payments system.[2] Cryptocurrencies—of which bitcoin is but one—introduce much-needed competition into an industry that has become increasing insulated, heralding clear benefits for consumers and merchants.[3] Cryptocurrencies may even have the power to democratize finance in a way that is altogether without precedent.[4]

As we shall see, however, Bitcoin *qua* decentralized ledger is much more than merely cryptocurrency. It is also a major development in the way in which we register and transfer information and assets.[5] We are only just beginning to explore how the Bitcoin block chain (and other decentralized ledgers) can be used to register and store information, create and enforce smart contracts,[6] and produce digital autonomous

---

[1] Jerry Brito & Andrea Castillo, Bitcoin: A Primer for Policymakers 4 (2013), http://mercatus.org/sites/default/files/Brito_BitcoinPrimer_v1.3.pdf.
[2] *Id.* at 3.
[3] Jerry Brito & Eli Dourado, Comments to the New York Department of Financial Services on the Proposed Virtual Currency Regulation Framework 2–3 (2014), http://mercatus.org/sites/default/files/BritoDourado-NY-Virtual-Currency-comment-081414.pdf. *See also* Tatiana Cutts, HM Treasury Open Consultation, Digital Currencies: Call for Information ¶¶1.3–1.4 (2014) (unpublished submission) (on file with author).
[4] Brito & Dourado, *supra* note 3, at 3.
[5] Cutts, *supra* note 3, at ¶1.3.
[6] See, e.g., Leo Singer, Follow the money, CBA National Magazine, Fall 2014, at 14–18, *available at* http://www.nationalmagazine.ca/Articles/Fall-issue-2014/Follow-the-money.aspx.

organizations.⁷ But before we can begin to consider such issues, we must provide some definitions of the key concepts for the reader.

Placing our definitions on the table in this chapter allows us to set out clearly the parameters for the discussion that follows. We will focus here on cryptocurrency and not on the larger subject of virtual currency. Although "Bitcoin" is in the title, this book is not just about bitcoin. Rather, bitcoin will be used as a proxy for discussion of cryptocurrency more broadly.

In this chapter, we define and locate cryptocurrencies in the current tableau of virtual currencies. We then attempt to explain what Bitcoin is and describe its history. We finish with a brief review of the limitations of the chapters and and a description of the analysis that follows. This includes answering the questions: Why are we the authors of this book? What authority do we have in this space? And why did we focus on the United States, the United Kingdom, Germany, and Canada?

CRYPTOCURRENCIES & DECENTRALIZATION

Much has been written about the respective definitions of cryptocurrencies, digital currencies, and virtual currencies. Often, but by no means always, the same material is indicated by different labels. The U.S. Financial Crimes Enforcement Network's key interpretive guidance touching bitcoin and other currencies refers to "virtual currencies."⁸ The current (at the time of writing) study being undertaken by the Canadian Senate's Standing Committee on Banking, Trade and Commerce refers to digital currencies, but seems to be designed to cover much of the same subject matter. Given this, what labels are appropriate?

In this book, we generally adopt the taxonomy employed by the Financial Action Task Force (the "**FATF**"), an international body setting and promoting the implementation of standards to combat money laundering, terrorist financing, and other threats to the global financial system. According to the FATF, virtual currency is a digital representation of value that is traded digitally and has one or more of the following

---

7   *See, e.g.*, Vitalik Buterin, *DAOs, DACs, Das and More: An Incomplete Terminology Guide*, ETHEREUM BLOG (May 6, 2014), https://blog.ethereum.org/2014/05/06/daos-dacs-das-and-more-an-incomplete-terminology-guide/.

8   FINANCIAL CRIMES ENFORCEMENT NETWORK, APPLICATION OF FINCEN'S REGULATIONS TO PERSONS ADMINISTERING, EXCHANGING, OR USING VIRTUAL CURRENCIES (Mar. 18, 2013), *available at* http://fincen.gov/statutes_regs/guidance/pdf/FIN-2013-G001.pdf.

functions: a medium of exchange, a unit of account, and a store of value.[9] Virtual currency is not legal tender, is not issued or guaranteed by any jurisdiction, and fulfils its functions "only by agreement within the community of users of the virtual currency."[10] Virtual currency is distinct from fiat currency (i.e., the coins and banknotes of countries) and from e-money, which is simply a digital representation of fiat money.[11]

Digital currency is a digital representation of either virtual currency or e-money. Thus, digital currency is often used interchangeably with virtual currency.[12]

Virtual currency can, in turn, be subdivided into two groups: convertible and non-convertible. Convertible virtual currencies have equivalent values in fiat currencies and can be exchanged for fiat currencies (and vice versa). Examples cited by the FATF include bitcoin and Linden Dollars,[13] but would also include altcoins (i.e., alternative coins—cryptocurrencies other than bitcoin). A non-convertible, or closed, virtual currency is "intended to be specific to a particular virtual domain or world" and, under its terms of use, cannot be exchanged for fiat currency.[14] The FATF cites World of Warcraft Gold as an example of this type of currency,[15] but Alex Waters, CEO of Coin.co, points out that World of Warcraft Gold is often converted to fiat money on various websites through player auctions.[16] The FATF asserts that all non-convertible virtual currencies are centralized by definition: they are issued by a central authority that deems them to be non-convertible.

Convertible virtual currencies can be subdivided further into centralized and decentralized virtual currencies. Centralized virtual currencies have a single administering authority, i.e., a third party that controls the currency system or network. The administrator issues and redeems the currency, establishes the rules for its use, and maintains a central payment ledger.[17] An example is the now-defunct Liberty Reserve system, which purported to create a centralized, anonymous

---

[9] FINANCIAL ACTION TASK FORCE, VIRTUAL CURRENCIES: KEY DEFINITIONS AND POTENTIAL AML/CTF RISKS (June 2014) at 4, *available at* http://www.fatf-gafi.org/media/fatf/documents/reports/virtual-currency-key-definitions-and-potential-aml-cft-risks.pdf.
[10] *Id.*
[11] *Id.*
[12] *Id.*
[13] *Id.*
[14] *Id.*
[15] *Id.*
[16] E-mail from Alex Waters, CEO, Coin.co, to author (Feb. 2, 2015, 16:13 EST) (on file with author).
[17] FINANCIAL ACTION TASK FORCE, *supra* note 9, at 4.

digital currency to facilitate online transactions.[18] Decentralized virtual currencies are otherwise known as cryptocurrencies in the FATF's taxonomy. Cryptocurrencies "are distributed, open-source, math-based peer-to-peer virtual currencies that have no central administrating authority, and no central monitoring or oversight."[19] The paradigmatic example here is bitcoin.

This taxonomy is summarized in the following table:[20]

Taxonomy of Virtual Currencies

	Centralized	Decentralized
Convertible	Central administrator; centralized ledger; can be exchanged for fiat currency	No central administrator; decentralized ledger; can be exchanged for fiat currency
Non-Convertible	Central administrator; centralized ledger; cannot be exchanged for fiat currency, though black market may be present	Does not exist (but this may change in future)

This book concentrates on cryptocurrencies. Its focus is thus narrower than all virtual currencies but broader than just bitcoin. As the first cryptocurrency,[21] bitcoin seems to be pre-eminent. Popular knowledge of bitcoin, its share of the cryptocurrency market, and its key components—its convertibility, decentralization, and protection through cryptography—are features that appear in all cryptocurrencies. Accordingly, bitcoin will be our main proxy in this book for looking at cryptocurrencies in general. Most comments—indeed, most laws interpreted and cited in this book as they relate to bitcoin—are applicable equally to all cryptocurrencies. It is to the definition of bitcoin that we now turn.

---

[18] *See, e.g.*, United States v. Liberty Reserve, No. 13-CR-368, indictment (S.D.N.Y. May 28, 2013).
[19] FINANCIAL ACTION TASK FORCE, *supra* note 9, at 5.
[20] *Id.* at 8. This is similar, though not the same, as the taxonomy adopted by the European Central Bank in its 2012 overview of virtual currency. *See, e.g.*, EUROPEAN CENTRAL BANK, VIRTUAL CURRENCY SCHEMES 13–15 (2012), *available at* http://www.ecb.europa.eu/pub/pdf/other/virtualcurrencyschemes201210en.pdf.
[21] FINANCIAL ACTION TASK FORCE, *supra* note 9, at 5.

Bitcoin: The Ledger Analogy

Introduced as a concept in 2008 and manifested as a system in 2009,[22] Bitcoin was invented by the pseudonymous programmer (or group of programmers) known as Satoshi Nakamoto. According to the original white paper, the Bitcoin "system" is based on these key features:

1. it is *peer-to-peer* and *computationally impractical to reverse* (i.e., what many refer to as "irreversibility"), making centralized authorities irrelevant;[23]
2. it is *cryptographically secure*—transactions are publicly announced, with each owner transferring coins (or parts thereof) to the next owner by digitally signing a hash[24] of the previous transaction;[25] these transactions are put into consecutive blocks (the block chain), secured by cryptographic proofs ensuring that the data has not been tampered with;[26] and,
3. it uses *proof of work* among the nodes to discover new blocks to add to the chain.[27]

While the word "ledger" is nowhere used in Nakamoto's paper, the dominant paradigm for describing Bitcoin is the decentralized ledger.[28]

---

[22] Sergii Shcherbak, *How Should Bitcoin Be Regulated?*, 7 Eur. J. of Legal Stud. 45, 48 (2014).
[23] Satoshi Nakamoto, Bitcoin: A Peer-to-Peer Electronic Cash System 1 (2008), https://bitcoin.org/bitcoin.pdf.
[24] A hash function is a mathematical process that compresses data to produce shorter, fixed-size outputs. One can take an input of arbitrary length and compress it to one that is a fixed number, say, 160 bits. The output can appear random but retains the uniqueness of the original input data. *See, e.g.*, Shafi Goldwasser & Mihir Bellare, *Lecture Notes on Cryptography* 136 (2008), http://cseweb.ucsd.edu/~mihir/papers/gb.pdf.
[25] Nakamoto, *supra* note 23, at 2.
[26] Jonathan Levin, "*I Love the Blockchain, Just Not Bitcoin,*" CoinDesk (Nov. 16, 2014, 17:20 GMT), http://www.coindesk.com/love-blockchain-just-bitcoin/.
[27] Nakamoto, *supra* note 23, at 3. A proof of work is a piece of data that was difficult to produce so as to satisfy certain requirements. *See* Proof of Work, https://en.bitcoin.it/wiki/Proof_of_work (last visited Jan. 11, 2015).
[28] *See, e.g.*, Brito & Castillo, *supra* note 1, at 4; Josh Fairfield, *BitProperty*, 88 S. Cal. L. Rev. 1, 11–12 (forthcoming 2015); Richard Gendal Brown, *Cost? Trust? Something Else? What's the Killer App for Block Chain Technology?*, Thoughts on the Future of Finance (Jan. 15, 2015), http://gendal.me/2015/01/15/cost-trust-something-else-whats-the-killer-app-for-block-chain-technology/.

Traditionally, transactions outside of non-counterfeit banknotes or coins required intermediation, that is, some third party to confirm transmissions, unwind transactions (if necessary), and mediate disputes. For example, imagine a bank at which Declan and Elizabeth both have accounts. Assume Declan draws a cheque (a bill of exchange) in the amount of $100 on his account to Elizabeth and that all of the required bill formalities (unconditional promise, sum certain in money, payable to order, in writing and signed, etc.) are met. Elizabeth deposits it into her account at the same bank. The bank's assets do not change. From a basic accounting perspective, the bank merely debits (reduces) its liability to Declan and credits (increases) that owing to Elizabeth. This depicts a basic funds transfer.

Until the invention of bitcoin, this third party intermediary was invariably present in some form. If Declan wanted to send Elizabeth $100 over the Internet, he would have to rely on a third-party service, e.g., PayPal. When Declan sends $100 to Elizabeth using PayPal, PayPal deducts the amount from his account and adds it to her account.[29] PayPal is the curator of the common ledger determining who owes what.

Without this intermediation, online funds could be spent more than once. Imagine a simple digital payments system in which cash is just a computer file.[30] Here, Declan could send Elizabeth $100 by attaching the money file to a digital message. But sending the attachment would not necessarily remove it from Declan's computer.[31] If he retained a copy of the file, to continue the example, he would be able to send the *same* $100 to Isabella. This, manifestly, is not a sound basis for a payments system. Neither of Isabella or Elizabeth could rely on the fact that she was receiving convertible value—as opposed to a counterfeit, duplicate-spent amount—in any transaction. To make the system work, we need an intermediary to curate a central ledger, monitoring and verifying all transactions. That intermediary would have to be funded by the parties to the transaction.

So, until the advent of Bitcoin, this "double-spending" problem could only be solved by inserting an intermediary into transactions that oversaw a centralized ledger.[32] Bitcoin is truly innovative and

---

[29] Brito & Castillo, *supra* note 1, at 3.
[30] *Id.*
[31] *Id.*
[32] *Id.* at 3–4.

important because, for the first time, the double-spending problem can be solved without third-party intermediation.[33]

This is accomplished by distributing the necessary ledger among all of the users of the Bitcoin system through a peer-to-peer network:

> Every transaction that occurs in the bitcoin economy is registered in a public, distributed ledger, which is called the block chain. New transactions are checked against the block chain to ensure that the same bitcoins haven't been previously spent, thus eliminating the double-spending problem. The global peer-to-peer network, composed of thousands of users, takes the place of an intermediary[.][34]

Users can transact directly with each other without the need for a conventional third party.

Note here that financial transactions on the Bitcoin network are not denominated in fiat money, e.g., dollars, as they are on PayPal, but in bitcoins.[35] Therefore, perhaps confusingly, the word "bitcoin" refers to two things: (1) a decentralized, global payments network ("Bitcoin"); and (2) an international, decentralized, convertible, virtual currency, or cryptocurrency ("bitcoin"). Generally speaking, when one writes about upper-case "B" Bitcoin, one is referring to the former. When one refers to lower-case "b" bitcoin, it concerns the latter. This is how these terms—Bitcoin and bitcoin—will be used in this book. The value of bitcoin (the currency) in this global network is a function of what willing buyers will pay willing sellers in an open marketplace. The value is not based on gold or other precious metals, or the imprimatur of the state.[36] Bitcoin has value because it is useful and scarce.[37]

Transactions on the Bitcoin network are verified—and double-spending prevented[38]—through the use of public-key cryptography.[39] With this type of cryptography, each user is assigned a pair of keys:

---

[33] *Id.* at 4.
[34] *Id.*
[35] *Id.*
[36] *Id.*
[37] Erik Voorhees, *The Role of Bitcoin as Money*, ON LIFE AND LIBERTY (May 23, 2013), http://evoorhees.blogspot.ca/.
[38] Note that double-spending may not be completely prevented on the Bitcoin network. See Peter Todd, *Double-spending unconfirmed transactions is a lot easier than most people realize*, REDDIT, http://www.reddit.com/r/Bitcoin/comments/239bj1/doublespending_unconfirmed_transactions_is_a_lot/ (last visited Jan. 15, 2015).
[39] BRITO & CASTILLO, *supra* note 1, at 5.

"one private key that is kept secret like a password, and one public key that can be shared with the world."[40] When a user wishes to send bitcoins to another user (or, more properly, to separate units from one bitcoin address and attach those bitcoins to another address),[41] the sender creates a message, called a transaction, containing the recipient's public key.[42] The sender then 'signs' that message by employing her private key.[43] This digital signature, affixed through the private key, operates similarly to a handwritten signature in that it provides evidence that the owner of certain resources authorizes their transfer. However, unlike handwritten signatures, digital signatures are almost impossible to forge due to advanced cryptographic technology.[44] Clearly, in this environment, the security of the user's private key is paramount.

In this way, the network can verify the separation and re-association of the bitcoins. By looking at the 'sending' public key, anyone with Bitcoin software[45] can verify that the transaction was signed by the corresponding private key, that it is authentic, and that those funds are now associated with the recipient address.[46] The transaction is recorded and displayed in a new "block"—analogous to a new ledger page—of the block chain.[47] Cryptographic protocols ensure that participants on the Bitcoin network operate with an updated and verified record of all transactions that are valid within the network, which prevents double-spending and fraud.[48] The verification is driven by the protocol's restrictions on the outputs of the hashing function.[49] The hashing function in bitcoin works like the digital equivalent of a tamper-proof sticker on certain packaging that is perceptibly damaged if altered. When each update is written into the Bitcoin ledger, digital hashes protect it from being altered in the future. This ensures the

---

[40] *Id.*
[41] E-mail from Ryan Straus, Principal, Riddell Williams P.S., to author (Dec. 2, 2014, 16:02 EST) (on file with author).
[42] BRITO & CASTILLO, *supra* note 1, at 5.
[43] *Id.*
[44] E-mail from Michael Perklin, Principal, Bitcoinsultants, to author (Nov. 16, 2014, 9:16 EST) (on file with author).
[45] E-mail from Alex Waters to author, *supra* note 16.
[46] BRITO & CASTILLO, *supra* note 1, at 5.
[47] *Id.*
[48] E-mail from Alex Waters to author, *supra* note 16.
[49] E-mail from Jonathan Levin, Founder, Coinometrics, to author (Jan. 17, 2015, 17:21 EST) (on file with author).

accuracy and permanence of the information—whether financial or otherwise—on the block chain.[50]

The Bitcoin network itself depends on users that provide their computing power to audit and secure the network, i.e., to maintain, log, update, and reconcile transactions on the block chain (the ledger).[51] These users are what are often referred to as miners,[52] though they might also be described accurately as somewhat like bank tellers on the network, in that they continually receive customer transactions and update the ledger. Miners are rewarded for their work (computing power and related space, time, and cost) with newly created bitcoins (the currency).[53] Bitcoins are created or mined at a steady rate as thousands of dispersed computers solve complex mathematical problems that verify the transactions and information embedded in the block chain;[54] all participating miners cross-reference each other's work in real time to ensure integrity and consensus in both their own—and in their peers'—broadcasted updates.[55]

Bitcoins were initially produced at a rate of 50 bitcoins per new block (new blocks occur approximately every ten minutes). That rate halves approximately every four years (or exactly every 210,000 blocks), forming an asymptote curve over the lifespan of bitcoin 'minting.' The rate of production at the time of writing is 25 bitcoins per discovered block.[56] The Bitcoin protocol designates 21 million bitcoins as its 'cap.'[57] The 21 million limit, as such, is useful because it

---

[50] E-mail from Michael Perklin to author, *supra* note 44.
[51] BRITO & CASTILLO, *supra* note 1, at 5.
[52] *Id.*
[53] *Id.*
[54] *Id.* at 5–6.
[55] E-mail from Alex Waters to author, *supra* note 16.
[56] Shcherbak, *supra* note 22, at 49.
[57] According to Waters, the 'cap' on bitcoins at 21 million is no more a 'rule' than other Bitcoin rules. "It is possible that this total number of units may be changed and allowed to adapt to the needs of the network, albeit unlikely. The 21 million cap is actually representative of 2.1 quadrillion units of account (referred to now as satoshis). The denomination [of satoshis] has been shifted 8 decimal places for ease of use." E-mail from Alex Waters to author, *supra* note 16. The 21 million cap has also been described elsewhere as arbitrary. *See, e.g.*, BRITO & CASTILLO, *supra* note 1, at 7. However, Waters believes this to be unlikely: "My opinion is that this stems from a limit in 32-bit signed integer notation. In that context, a 21 million limit on the units shifted 8 decimal places would have utility in financial accounting and user experience for higher level software applications. 2.1 quadrillion is also significant in that it is within the same order of magnitude (single quadrillions) as if you were to convert the entire global money supply to cents, and count them as units of account." E-mail from Alex Waters to author, *supra* note 16.

provides a known supply and a known inflation schedule, unlike fiat money.[58] It is estimated that the last fraction of a bitcoin will be mined sometime near 2140.[59] Bitcoins are divisible to eight decimal places.[60] The smallest unit of account in bitcoin is the satoshi, somewhat like a penny, though comparatively much smaller.

The Bitcoin protocol is open-source, a critical feature, "which means that the review and modification of the protocol's code can be carried out by any developer."[61] Anyone can suggest changes to the core protocol by means of a Bitcoin Improvement Proposal, a design document that is the standard way of introducing features or information to Bitcoin.[62] Communications around these proposals takes place in open-involvement mailing lists and Internet Relay Chat channels. If, after debate and testing, a new feature is implemented, it will be included in the next version of the software. However, Bitcoin's primary security measure is majority consensus, meaning that protocol changes become effective only if they are adopted by a majority of users on the network.[63] Most major bitcoin businesses have developers that either follow or contribute to core development. Accordingly, the discussion about new features or changes reflects their views, among others.[64]

To summarize briefly, the ledger analogy essentially holds that the block chain is a ledger—or very much like a ledger—in which new transactions and data are continually embedded on the ledger pages (the blocks of the block chain) in a highly secure, transparent, and traceable way.

BITCOIN: MORE LIKE PLUMBING?

Some find the ledger analogy ambiguous[65] and prefer a 'plumbing-based' comparison. While the ledger may adequately explain the public- and private-key infrastructure used for the security of the

---

[58] Voorhees, *supra* note 37.
[59] *Id.*; Shcherbak, *supra* note 22, at 49; E-mail from Michael Perklin, Principal, Bitcoinsultants to author (Jan. 19, 2015, 12:41 EST) (on file with author).
[60] BRITO & CASTILLO, *supra* note 1, at 7.
[61] Shcherbak, *supra* note 22, at 49.
[62] Bitcoin Improvement Proposals, https://en.bitcoin.it/wiki/Bitcoin_Improvement_Proposals (last visted Jan. 26, 2015).
[63] *Id.*
[64] Telephone Interview with Jonathan Levin, Founder, Coinometrics (Jan. 26, 2015).
[65] E-mail from Jonathan Levin, Founder, Coinometrics, to author (Nov. 23, 2014, 18:54 EST) (on file with author).

Bitcoin network, Jonathan Levin, founder of Coinometrics, believes that bitcoin *qua* pipes in a plumbing network better illustrates where all bitcoins are currently held,[66] and our limitations in tracing bitcoin transactions.

Bitcoin, in this conception, should be considered a type of "monetary fluid" with a unit of account called "bitcoin." Each output of a transaction can be conceived of as a pipe with a particular capacity of bitcoin. Each transaction is a fitting that connects one or more existing pipes.[67] Any pipe (out of a transaction) can at most carry the same capacity of the sum of the pipes that led into the transaction.[68] In this paradigm, "Bitcoin is neither an account based payment system or a tokenized banking system. The protocol uses the history of all past transactions to generate a state of unspent bitcoins."[69] When we say that there are 13,726,625 bitcoins currently "in circulation" (as there are at the time of writing), what we really mean is that the Bitcoin protocol recognizes that there are 13,726,625 bitcoins "in unspent outputs that can be reassigned according to the rules of the payment system. The reassignment is irreversible and hence new transactions are additions to the growing complex system of pipes."[70]

The interesting issue in this paradigm is the lack of mapping between inputs and outputs:

> When warm water comes out of a tap, there is no separation between the hot and the cold. In bitcoin, if two transaction outputs are both inputs in the same transaction, *the protocol makes no attempts to map inputs to outputs*. Bitcoin retains the information that can reveal the *capacity* of the individual pipes that were feeding into the fitting [but no more]. In this way, bitcoin is not a token system but something far more fluid and complex.[71]

This 'disconnection' is illustrated using the following examples.

---

[66] E-mail from Jonathan Levin, Founder, Coinometrics, to author (Nov. 24, 2014, 17:12 EST) (on file with author).
[67] Jonathan Levin, *Bitcoin: New Plumbing for Financial Services*, CoinDesk (Nov. 29, 2014, 6:59 PM), http://www.coindesk.com/bitcoin-new-plumbing-financial-services/.
[68] *Id.*
[69] *Id.*
[70] *Id.*
[71] *Id.* This conception also reduces the amount of information that needs to be stored about transactions on the network.

The Law of Bitcoin

Figure 1

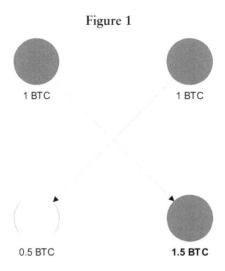

In Figure 1, each circle represents a transaction or an unspent output.[72] The grey nodes are transactions and the white node is an unspent amount. The number in each circle is the sum of the outputs of that transaction. Assume that this represents the purchase of a new smartphone with a cost of 1.5 BTC. Assume further that the two circles on the top are different transactions in the same bitcoin wallet. (A wallet is just a computer file that contains one or more private keys allowing the bitcoins in that wallet to be 'spent.') We can see from the figure that two bitcoins (1 BTC + 1 BTC) are separated from one address and re-associated with another in a transaction output (1.5 BTC) with 0.5 bitcoins as 'change,' or the 'unspent' amount from the transaction.

It is important to note that we do not entirely know which bitcoins go where. We can ask the question, "What is the minimum number of bitcoins that went from the source to the target?"[73] Or, to put it another way, if we assume that one bitcoin in our example is an output from one of the addresses, i.e., all of that address's bitcoins were "used up," for what remaining amount must we still account? Levin calls this the "minimum flow" of bitcoins. The minimum flow in Figure 1 is 0.5: we know that at least 0.5 bitcoins came from each of the top two nodes. We know that some of the monetary fluid from the top nodes came to the bottom right node, but only to the extent of 0.5 bitcoins.

---

[72] *Id.*
[73] *Id.*

Figure 2

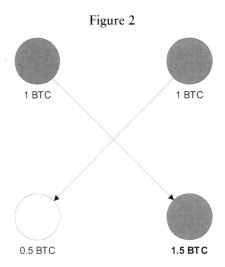

Now consider Figure 2. Assume that one of the funding transactions was with proceeds from fraud or theft. This illicit amount is in the top left grey node.[74] How many of the stolen bitcoins remain in the thief's possession? Bitcoin as a protocol does not have a technical answer to this question. Instead, as Levin notes, we would need to rely on applicable law to establish what portion of the 0.5 bitcoins remaining was actually stolen[75] or, for that matter, how many of the 1.5 bitcoins expended on the smartphone can be traced back to the victim of the theft.

We know where some of the bitcoins go in this rather contrived example because the minimum flow is a positive number. But that number can quickly be reduced to zero in a different example, or with even one additional transaction. Taking into account the multitude of transactions on the Bitcoin network, the minimum flow between any two points can easily be zero. Where it is zero, we have imperfect traceability. "Even though we can show the connections between all of the different transactions or pipes in bitcoin's history, we cannot say a lot about the flows of funds or monetary fluid."[76]

LIMITATIONS

---

[74] *Id.*
[75] *Id.*
[76] *Id.* This point is contentious. Some emphasize that bitcoins are highly traceable because of their association with previous addresses. *See, e.g.*, E-mail from Michael Perklin, Bitcoinsultants, to author, (Jan. 22, 2015, 12:46 EST) (on file with author).

Bitcoin is technology in its infancy. The study of its legal aspects is even younger. Lawyers, courts, regulators, and legislators are working to understand its meaning and implications in a dynamic environment where things seem to change daily. In this context, this book seems to have been published both, paradoxically, too soon and too late. In almost every country, the law has not has not had enough of a chance to catch up to technology, so it may be too soon, but so many developments are taking place now that this volume may be irrelevant at the point of publication (i.e., too late).

As we will demonstrate, there are significant private and public law issues regarding cryptocurrency, all of which we cannot hope to cover in a single edition. More research, more discussion, more analysis, and more debate about the law of bitcoin is welcome. This is a process to which this book will contribute.

Furthermore, anyone reading this book needs to keep in mind that the legal situation around cryptocurrency is fluid, that this book is not legal advice, that legal advice should only be obtained from one's own lawyer, and that one should always be open to updates and current views of the law.

Although things are changing quickly, and not everything in this book will be relevant for long, many of the ideas and concepts being put forward in this edition—some for the first time in one volume— will continue to apply to cryptocurrency, in the medium term at least. Writers cannot wait for this sector to "settle down" or become more static; if they do this, discussion of important issues may be delayed indefinitely.

As we alluded to above, "Bitcoin" is more than a form of virtual currency and a global payments network. It represents a revolution in how we record and authenticate information, transfer assets, and address corporate governance. These areas hold great promise for the future of Bitcoin and decentralized ledgers more generally. In this project, however, we focus primarily on the laws of cryptocurrency and not those of decentralized ledger technology.

What gives us the authority to write about cryptocurrency? Quite simply, many of the authors of this book have been researching, writing, and speaking about Bitcoin and other cryptocurrencies for some time: not just about current transactions or news items, but about what they perceive as some of the key legal implications associated with using this technology. Some of their thoughts have shaped and are continuing to shape critical discussions. They are designing and implementing some of the key consolidation and innovation taking place in the cryptocurrency space. We see ourselves as informed and authoritative—but not definitive or dispositive—voices in an emerging debate. We think it is only fitting that this debate is highly decentralized and references myriad disciplines and global actors.

For this first edition, we have deliberately chosen the U.S., the U.K., Germany, and Canada as subjects. This is not to take anything away from many other jurisdictions where legal issues are just as compelling and important. But we had to begin somewhere, and we wanted to start with jurisdictions that have at least started to grapple with some of the issues around cryptocurrency regulation and legal use and in which we felt that this group could meaningfully contribute. That is a tall order and it left us with the focus and material for four chapters. The United States has been active in providing administrative guidance and in actually prosecuting cases in which bitcoins were used. Canada has also been keenly discussing cryptocurrency and canvassing approaches, especially—though not exclusively—at the federal level. The United Kingdom has perhaps made the most overt attempt to at least advertise itself as a jurisdiction that wishes to foster financial innovation. Germany, as a civil law jurisdiction, offers a counterpoint to all of these and a possibly a window onto the approach of continental Europe to cryptocurrency. Subsequent editions of this volume may bring exposition of other jurisdictions. As legal interest and expertise in this nascent area grows, we are keen to discover and observe how lawyers and academics will grapple with the issues in this book and others. Time will tell where this exploration leads, but the discussion is bound to be fascinating.

Finally, we must address an issue raised by some actors in the cryptocurrency space. This is the argument that Bitcoin is disruptive technology, designed to shake up legacy financial institutions, and that trying to slot it into a legacy legal system is stultifying and, perhaps, even dangerous. This criticism has much force. In response, we believe simply that we must operate with existing institutions, procedures, and norms created to ensure certainty and finality for the consumers at the heart of financial systems. This is whether we like all of those institutions or not. We believe that consumers have a right to know—indeed, an obligation to know—their rights when they use this technology.

Conclusion

The limitations and challenges discussed here, while real, must not stand in the way of a thorough analysis of Bitcoin's legal framework. It is to this task that we now turn.

CANADA

STUART HOEGNER
JILLIAN FRIEDMAN

ooooooooooooooooooooooooooooooooooooo

Canada is an interesting market and regulatory environment for cryptocurrency, notably bitcoin. With one exception, the federal government and the provinces have incrementally tried to fit bitcoin into existing statutes and regulatory models, with some success. The exception is with respect to the Proceeds of Crime (Money Laundering) and Terrorist Financing Act[1] (the "**PCA**"), which has been amended to address what the federal government calls "virtual currencies." Bill C-31 (the 2014 budget implementation act, which was passed in the spring of 2014) was the vehicle for effecting those amendments.

Canada is a federal system with a division of powers between the federal and provincial governments and with two distinct, co-existing legal traditions: the civil law in Quebec and the common law in the remaining provinces. Under the Constitution Act, 1867,[2] certain powers are reserved to the national—or federal—government. For example, the regulation of trade and commerce (§ 91(2)), raising money by any mode or system of taxation (§ 91(3)), currency and coinage (§ 91(14)), issuance of paper money (§ 91(17)), and bills of exchange and promissory notes (§ 91(18)) are all *intra vires* Parliament. Other powers are reserved to the provinces, e.g., direct taxation within the provinces to raise revenues for provincial purposes (§ 92(2)), property and civil rights in the provinces (§ 92(13)), and the administration of justice in the provinces (§ 92(14)). In many spheres, the federal and provincial governments have concurrent jurisdiction or, in the parlance of Canadian constitutional law, subjects are said to have "double aspects."[3] Cryptocurrency touches all of these sundry heads of power and, accordingly, this chapter will look at federal

---

[1] S.C. 2000, c. 17 (Can.).
[2] 30 & 31 Vict., c. 3 (U.K.), *reprinted in* R.S.C. 1985, app. II, no. 5 (Can.).
[3] *See, e.g.*, Hodge v. The Queen, [1883] U.K.P.C. 59 (Can.) (holding that entertainment in taverns has a double aspect); R. v. Furtney, [1991] 3 S.C.R. 89 (Can.) (finding that gaming in Canada has a double aspect).

and provincial legislation and developments and both public and private law.

Some of the earliest comments from government agencies in Canada about cryptocurrency came from the Canada Revenue Agency (the "**CRA**"), Canada's national tax administrator. In a series of releases, the CRA has gradually subsumed more and more cryptocurrency transactions into the taxable chain of commerce. The provinces have also been active in other areas. Provincial regulators, for example, have been active in looking at bitcoin models that they believe are within the ambit of relevant securities legislation. This chapter will examine developments that affect these areas as well as issues that have not yet arisen but are bound to in the fullness of time (e.g., whether a bitcoin-denominated instrument can be a bill of exchange within the meaning of the Bills of Exchange Act[4]).

Canada's general approach to cryptocurrency is not unique. Its policy-makers are feeling their way through uncharted waters, and struggling to push truly novel and complex technical innovations into tested and familiar regulatory models. Bitcoin, as one example, fits comfortably into some existing legal paradigms and perhaps less so in others. Accordingly, the law as it relates to cryptocurrency can seem clear on certain issues and murky in others. In this context, it is worth noting that the Canadian Senate's—the upper house of Parliament's—Standing Committee on Banking, Trade and Commerce is currently engaged in a Study on the Use of Digital Currency. The breadth of materials and opinion being presented to the Banking Committee is noteworthy, and senators have been very engaged with the issues and in their questioning. The committee's proceedings and evidence are well worth reading as its work may impact future legislative and regulatory efforts. It is due to report out in 2015.

At several points in this chapter, the discussion will consider and use bitcoin as a proxy for cryptocurrency in general. This is for two reasons. First, bitcoin exhibits the key traits contained in all forms of cryptocurrency under consideration (i.e., decentralization and convertibility). Second, bitcoin is perhaps the leading and first true cryptocurrency and has been more in the public mind and imagination than other cryptocurrencies.

---

[4] R.S.C. 1985, c. B-4 (Can.).

1. ANTI-MONEY LAUNDERING & COUNTER-TERRORIST FINANCING RULES

The relevant anti-money laundering ("**AML**") and counter-terrorist financing ("**CTF**") rules in Canadian law are mainly found in three federal sources: the Criminal Code,[5] the PCA, and the Proceeds of Crime (Money Laundering) and Terrorist Financing Regulations[6] (the "**PCA Regulations**"). In this section, we will briefly review all of these sources and the provisions of Bill C-31 affecting the PCA and the PCA Regulations as regards cryptocurrencies. Certain bitcoin and other cryptocurrency business models—though by no means all of them—will fit within the definition of money services business ("**MSB**") in the PCA, either under the pre- or post-Bill C-31 versions. Accordingly, we assess the various requirements associated with being an MSB in Canada. We also briefly look at Quebec's approach to MSBs.

1.1. THE CRIMINAL CODE

Though much attention has been lavished by the bitcoin community on Canada's evolving approach to cryptocurrency under the PCA, the logical starting point in reviewing AML–CTF procedures is the Criminal Code. While the PCA and the PCA Regulations apply to business and transactions undertaken by identifiable parties (MSBs, banks, precious metals dealers, etc.), the AML–CTF provisions of the Criminal Code apply to *everyone*, subject to the proviso that the offence must be committed in Canada.[7]

Laundering proceeds of crime is defined in subsection 462.31(1) of the Criminal Code. That provision states that everyone commits an offence

> who uses, transfers the possession of, sends or delivers to any person or place, transports, transmits, alters, disposes of or otherwise deals with, in any manner and by any means, any property or any proceeds of any property with intent to conceal or convert that property or those proceeds, knowing or believing that all or a part of that

---

[5] R.S.C. 1985, c. C-46 (Can.).
[6] Proceeds of Crime (Money Laundering) and Terrorist Financing Regulations, SOR/2002-184 (Can.). Note that there are five regulations under the PCA. Here, we concern ourselves here primarily—though not exclusively—with the PCA Regulations, which we believe to be the most relevant to the current discussion.
[7] R.S.C. 1985, c. C-46, § 6(2) (Can.); R. v. Libman, [1985] 2 S.C.R. 178 (Can.).

property or of those proceeds was obtained or derived directly or indirectly as a result of

(a) the commission in Canada of a designated offence; or
(b) an act or omission anywhere that, if it had occurred in Canada, would have constituted a designated offence.

A designated offence is any offence that may be prosecuted as an indictable offence under the Criminal Code or any other act of Parliament (but not an indictable offence prescribed by regulation); or, conspiracy or attempt to commit, or being an accessory after the fact or counselling in relation to, such an offence.[8] Accordingly, four things are fundamentally required to make out a money laundering offence under subsection 462.31(1) of the Criminal Code: there must be 1) dealing in 2) property or proceeds 3) intending to conceal or convert them 4) while knowing or believing them to be from a designated offence.

At first blush, the provision may not appear to apply to many bitcoin users. It is not enough to simply deal in or transact with proceeds from a criminal activity; innocent Canadians may unknowingly have possession of bank notes (or bitcoins) that are proceeds from designated offences. There must be an intention to hide or launder the proceeds and there must be knowledge or belief of their illicit source. Many will presumably not have that intention, knowledge, or belief.

The ones who do and who have the illicit property will be caught up in the proceeds of crime section. While the term "proceeds" is undefined in the Criminal Code, "property" is defined very broadly. It appears to capture any item that could be recognized as an asset,

---

[8] Criminal Code, R.S.C. 1985, c. C-46, § 462.3(1) (Can.) (definition of "designated offence"). There are three types of offences under the Criminal Code: indictable offences, summary conviction offences, and 'hybrid' offences where the Crown may elect to proceed by way of indictment or summary conviction. The designated offence definition covers the first and third of these. Indictable offences are generally more serious offences.

whether tangible or intangible.⁹ The definition is also inclusive; it is not limited to the enumerated items in section 2 of the Criminal Code. Bitcoin and other cryptocurrencies would seem to be included here, whether the contraband property was originally converted to cryptocurrency from something else or vice versa.

However, anyone conducting exchange activities in the cryptocurrency space should be forewarned. Subsection 462.31 requires that the accused have, inter alia: 1) the intent to conceal or convert the property or proceeds; 2) knowing that all or part of that property or those proceeds were obtained by crime. These two components together form the mens rea of the money laundering offence.[10] While the mental state can be established with a finding of actual subjective belief, it can also be met by a finding of wilful blindness on the part of the accused.[11] There must be compelling indicia that the accused should reasonably have been aware of wrongdoing and that the property was tainted. In the formulation of the Supreme Court, wilful blindness can only be found where it can almost be said that the defendant actually knew: "He suspected the fact; he realized probability; but he refrained from obtaining the final confirmation because he wanted in the event to be able to deny knowledge."[12] Or, as a majority of the court put it ten years later: "A finding of wilful blindness involves an affirmative answer to the question: Did the accused shut his eyes because he knew or strongly suspected that

---

[9] It is acknowledged that there may well be an issue with recognizing bitcoin as an asset from an accounting perspective, but such a discussion is beyond this chapter's scope. Under International Financial Reporting Standards, recognition of an intangible asset requires that the item meet the definition of an intangible asset and the attendant recognition criteria. An intangible asset is "an identifiable non-monetary asset without physical substance." To be identifiable, it must be either separable or it must arise from contractual or other legal rights. We believe that bitcoins appear to meet this test. As for recognition, the item may only be recognized if it is probable that the expected future economic benefits that are attributable to the asset will flow to the entity and if the cost of the asset can be measured reliably. This latter point may present some difficulty in the context of variance among exchanges. Measurability at any moment in time may present practical issues for bitcoin. Still, we expect that both of these recognition criteria may generally be met for bitcoins. Note that IAS 38 (Intangible Assets) only applies to intangibles not captured by other standards (e.g., IAS 32 (Financial Instruments—Presentation)). See IAS 38—*Intangible Assets, available at* http://www.iasplus.com/en/standards/ias/ias38.

[10] R. v. Barna, [2014] O.J. No. 2373, ¶ 183 (Can. Ont. Sup. Ct.) (QL).

[11] *See, e.g., id.*, ¶ 186; R. v. Tejani, [1999] O.J. No. 3182, ¶ 38 (Can. Ont. C.A.) (QL); R. v. Battista, [2010] O.J. No. 4212 (Can. Ont. Sup. Ct.) (QL).

[12] R. v. Sansregret, [1985] 1 S.C.R. 570, 586 (McIntyre, J.) (Can.).

looking would fix him with knowledge?"[13] The accused essentially turns away because he wants to be able to claim that he didn't see.

In *Tejani*, the accused was a currency exchange dealer who was asked by a former drug dealer-turned-police-agent to exchange Canadian currency (supplied by the authorities) into U.S. currency. The appellant–accused had done business with the police agent before, exchanging up to C$250,000 every week over the course of several months. The accused never asked the dealer his name, line of business, about the source of his money, or required any forms to be completed. Over five months, approximately C$4 million had been exchanged.

In the police sting, the appellant was handed C$100,000 in Bank of Canada notes. The police agent told the accused that he was late because his friends had been "busted on the road for drugs," and that the agent had, consequently, lost C$300,000.[14] The appellant asked the agent to fill out a form indicating his name, birth date, social security number, and the source of the funds. The agent argued with the accused about the form, indicating that "he did not want to get his fingerprints on it and that he did not want to create a paper trail because he did not want to get busted."[15] The appellant took the funds, gave the police agent a receipt, and told the agent he could pick up the U.S. funds that afternoon. The accused was subsequently arrested and charged with money laundering.

The Ontario Court of Appeal upheld the conviction, concluding that the trial judge's conclusion that the accused was wilfully blind to the illicit nature of the funds was reasonable.

Similarly, this seems an easy result to get to where there is a bitcoin-to-fiat (or vice versa) exchange where one or more principals or employees know that the exchange is dealing in illicit proceeds from a designated offence. The more nuanced case is where there is an exchange or a bitcoin ATM-like machine with no affirmative requirements to register as an MSB or other prescribed procedures. Does a failure to make any inquiry about customers or limit transactions in an exchange or ATM setting constitute wilful blindness in Canada? It will always depend on the particular facts. What is said by a customer—if anything—and the volume and size of transactions may all be relevant. (Note that *Tejani* involved substantial amounts of money.) However, anyone undertaking exchange-type activities is shrewd to not shut her eyes to objective warning signs or to have no procedures to collect and analyze relevant

---

13 R. v. Jorgensen, [1995] 4 S.C.R. 55, ¶ 103 (Sopinka, J.) (Can.).
14 *Tejani*, O.J. No. 3182 at ¶ 12 (Laskin, J.).
15 *Id.*

customer and transaction data. Accordingly, the well-advised person exchanging bitcoin-to-fiat and fiat-to-bitcoin will have standards in place to, at a minimum, make inquiries about who its customers are and to limit the size and number of transactions over a particular period of time (at least, not without further due diligence procedures being performed). In fact, anyone dealing in value in the stream of commerce will want to be alert to the risks of dealing in offence-related proceeds. These considerations are separate and apart from any requirements imposed by the PCA and the PCA Regulations, to which we now turn.

1.2. The Proceeds of Crime (Money Laundering) and Terrorist Financing Act—The Background & the Old Rules

First, some background on the Financial Transactions and Reports Analysis Centre of Canada ("**FinTRAC**") is necessary. FinTRAC is an independent agency of the Canadian government that reports to the federal Minister of Finance. It is Canada's financial intelligence unit for purposes of the Financial Action Task Force's 40 Recommendations.[16] FinTRAC's mandate is to facilitate the detection, deterrence, and prevention of money laundering and terrorist financing activities. It carries out this mandate through, inter alia, the receipt and analysis of financial transaction reports from reporting entities, ensuring reporting entity compliance with the PCA and the PCA Regulations, undertaking research relevant to AML–CTF initiatives, and maintaining a registry of MSBs in Canada.[17]

FinTRAC was established and is empowered under the PCA.[18] The PCA's objects are to implement specific measures to deter and detect money laundering and terrorist financing; to facilitate the investigation and prosecution of money laundering and terrorist financing offences; to respond to organized crime threats by providing law enforcement with the information it needs to deprive criminals of their illicit proceeds; to assist in fulfilling Canada's international AML–CTF

---

[16] Financial Action Task Force: International Standards on Combating Money Laundering and the Financing of Terrorism and Proliferation—The FATF Recommendations (2012), *available at* http://www.fatf-gafi.org/media/fatf/documents/recommendations/pdfs/FATF_Recommendations.pdf; Financial Transactions and Reports Analysis Centre of Canada: Who We Are, *available at* http://www.fintrac.gc.ca/fintrac-canafe/1-eng.asp.

[17] Financial Transactions and Reports Analysis Centre of Canada: Who We Are, *supra* note 16.

[18] PCA, S.C. 2000, c. 17, §§ 40, 41 (Can.).

obligations; and, to protect Canada's financial system and prevent its use by those seeking to launder funds or finance terrorism.[19]

Much of FinTRAC's information comes from reports filed by reporting entities. If you are a casino, life insurer, accountant, securities dealer, or dealer in precious metals in Canada, then you, among others, will need to report up to FinTRAC in certain cases, register with FinTRAC, keep prescribed records, and obtain certain information about your customers.

The PCA-related discussions about cryptocurrencies, both pre-and post-introduction of Bill C-31, were confined almost exclusively to the definition and operational requirements of MSBs. This makes sense as the MSB appeared to be the most logical place that bitcoin exchanges, for example, could be subsumed under federal legislation.

Prior to Bill C-31's passage, an MSB was a person or entity engaged in one or more of three discrete lines of business: foreign exchange dealing; remitting or transmitting funds by any means or through any person, entity, or electronic funds transfer network; or, issuing or redeeming money orders, travellers' cheques, or other similar negotiable instruments (but not including cheques payable to a named person or entity).[20] "Funds," in turn, were defined in the PCA Regulations as "cash, currency or securities, or negotiable instruments or other financial instruments, in any form, that indicate a person's or an entity's title or interest in them."[21]

Under these rules, FinTRAC took the view that bitcoins (and other cryptocurrencies) were not "funds" within the ambit of the PCA and the PCA Regulations. The agency essentially viewed bitcoins as goods. Accordingly, a cryptocurrency-only transaction would be a barter transaction. A purchase or sale of bitcoins was simply a purchase or sale of goods. As they were goods and not funds, they were also not foreign exchange within the meaning of the PCA. Therefore, bitcoins could not be subject to the foreign exchange dealing or funds transmission rules. That left the remaining MSB categories of issuing or redeeming money orders or other similar negotiable instruments. As we shall see below, bitcoin is not likely money and an instrument denominated in bitcoin is unlikely to be susceptible to negotiation. Consequently, FinTRAC viewed many bitcoin exchange business activities as not falling within any of the three branches of the MSB

---

[19] *Id.* § 3.
[20] *Id.* § 5(h).
[21] PCA Regulations, SOR/2002-184, § 1(1) (Can.) (definition of "funds").

definition in the PCA.²² FinTRAC also viewed the sale of pre-paid bitcoin cards at retail locations as not falling within activities covered by the MSB definition.²³

In an interview with the FinTRAC spokesperson in May 2013, we reviewed the following scenarios and fact patterns under the old (pre-Bill C-31) PCA and PCA Regulations:

1. *Exchanges among participants*—Assume that individuals A and B are customers on a bitcoin exchange, and that A, B, and the exchange are all persons resident in Canada. A sells bitcoins to B and B pays A in Canadian dollars. Assume no remittance or transfer of funds to or by the exchange; the transaction is strictly peer-to-peer between A and B, with the exchange acting only as a facility for linking up or matching customers. In respect of these transactions only, the exchange could not register as an MSB with FinTRAC under the old regime as bitcoins were perceived as goods. No more was happening than A was selling goods to B.

2. *Exchange as counterparty*—Now assume that A, instead of selling bitcoins directly to B, sells to the exchange itself, i.e., the exchange purchases bitcoins from its own fiat reserves and holds bitcoins on and for its own account. Here again, pre-C-31, FinTRAC did not see this as foreign exchange dealing, remitting or transferring "funds," or issuing or redeeming negotiable instruments. This is still an exchange of goods (bitcoins) for money (fiat). Therefore, registration as an MSB was not required.

3. *Bitcoins as mere intermediary*—If the 'bitcoin part' of the transaction is solely as an intermediary step between two fiat currencies, then the exchange would be a foreign exchange

---

22 This was communicated by FinTRAC to multiple individuals and businesses in Canada. *See, e.g.*, E-mail from Sophie Marie Desjardins, Communications Officer, FinTRAC, to Confidential Party (May 23, 2013, 14:48:00 EDT) (on file with authors); E-mail from Caitlin Singh, Senior Compliance Officer, Regional Operations & Compliance, FinTRAC, to Confidential Party (Jul. 10, 2013, 13:57:07 EDT) (on file with authors); *FinTRAC (Canada) declares Bitcoin processor not Money Service Business*, available at https://quickbt.com/ca/pdf/20130822_FinTRAC_declares_non_msb.pdf; Bitcoin Exchange—Not Covered, FinTRAC Policy Interpretations—MSB Registration (Oct. 22, 2013), *available at* http://www.fintrac.gc.ca/publications/FINS/2-eng.asp?s=8.

23 Prepaid Bitcoin Card—Covered or not?, FinTRAC Policy Interpretations, MSB Registration (Jan. 21, 2014), *available at* http://www.fintrac.gc.ca/publications/FINS/2-eng.asp?s=8.

dealer and subject to the MSB rules. For example, assume that A transmits Canadian dollars to the exchange. The exchange converts those dollars to bitcoins (either from its own reserves or with another counterparty) and then converts them back to U.K. pounds for receipt by B, an individual in the U.K. This uses the bitcoin 'goods' merely as an intermediary step when the true business of the exchange is dealing in foreign exchange, i.e., taking one fiat currency and delivering another.

Again, the law in Canada has changed—though the changes have not taken effect at the time of writing—and the old, pre-C-31 position is being provided both because it is still current and to give a sense of where AML–CTF policy has been under FinTRAC, the PCA, and the PCA Regulations. We shall turn to the 2014 legislative and regulatory changes, but first we offer some comments on Quebec's approach to MSBs.

1.3. Quebec's MSB Legislation

This chapter would be incomplete without briefly mentioning provincial MSB legislation. Currently, Quebec is the only province in Canada with a law that specifically targets MSBs in a way that overlaps with the PCA. This is done under the auspices of Quebec's Money-Services Businesses Act[24] (the "**QMA**") and regulations thereto. Note that a Quebec MSB that must comply with the QMA will also have to answer to FinTRAC and the federal rules if it meets the federal definition of an MSB.

Any person operating an MSB in Quebec for remuneration, which includes charging fees, must hold a licence to do so. Under the QMA, five categories of services qualify as an MSB: currency exchange; funds transfer; issue or redemption of traveller's cheques, money orders, and bank drafts; cheque cashing; and the operation of an ATM, including the "leasing of a commercial space intended as a location for an automated teller machine if the lessor is responsible for keeping the machine supplied with cash."[25] Persons operating an MSB as defined by the QMA but who are governed by other specific laws as regards those MSB activities—e.g., banks and insurers—are not subject to the QMA's provisions.[26]

---

[24] S.Q. 2010, c. 40 (Can.).
[25] *Id.* § 1.
[26] *Id.* § 2.

The QMA is administered and enforced by the Autorité des Marchés Financiers (the "**AMF**"), Quebec's financial services and markets regulator. In February 2015, the AMF made its first public comment about regulating cryptocurrency exchanges and bitcoin ATMs under the QMA. While the obligations of bitcoin ATMs are now clearer in Quebec, it remains unsettled whether non-ATM businesses undertaking or facilitating exchanges between cryptocurrency and fiat—and possibly those that exchange cryptocurrency to cryptocurrency—for or on behalf of their customers may qualify as offering funds transfer services provincially. If captured by the QMA, persons operating such non-ATM businesses may need to hold a funds transfer MSB licence and comply with the QMA regulations.

The Quebec government's policy statement setting out how the AMF interprets and applies the provisions of the QMA states that a currency exchange "consists in exchanging, based on an exchange rate, a currency or a unit of currency for another. An exchange may consist of the sale or purchase, or both the sale and purchase, of a currency."[27] "Currency" is not defined in the QMA or in the policy statement. Quebec does not make a distinction between currency exchanges that operate in brick and mortar establishments and businesses offering their services only online. The jurisdictional scope of the law generally includes any MSB operating in or offering services in Quebec.

As will be seen below, we take the general view that bitcoin is neither a currency nor money for legal purposes. The most recent statements from the AMF indicate that bitcoin related exchange businesses do not require licenses under the currency exchange licence category. Whether that will be the case in Quebec for purposes of other Quebec laws is unclear. However, if cryptocurrency exchange services are considered to be funds transmitters, which recent developments at the time of writing suggest to be the case, then a cryptocurrency exchange operating in Quebec will require a licence from the AMF and will have to comply with certain requirements. The application process begins with appointing a respondent that is domiciled in Quebec or that has a place of business or work in Quebec; and, is a director, officer or partner of the MSB. The licence application must be filed by the appointed respondent.[28] The applicant must provide information about the directors, officers, and other employees of the MSB so that

---

[27] Autorité des Marches Financiers, *Policy Statement to the Money-Services Businesses Act* (Feb. 5, 2014), at § 1, *available at* http://www.lautorite.qc.ca/files/pdf/consultations/entreprises-services-monetaires/2011juin10-esm-ig-cons-en.pdf.

[28] QMA § 5.

the provincial police can undertake a background check. The police issue a security clearance report in respect of those MSB personnel that exercise their functions in Quebec.[29]

The AMF can refuse to grant a license to an MSB on a number of grounds, including if it is "not of good moral character,"[30] has made an assignment of property or is insolvent or bankrupt,[31] has had its right to operate revoked by a Canadian or foreign money services regulator in the last ten years,[32] or has been convicted of certain Criminal Code offences in the previous ten years.[33]

A licence-holding MSB, as well as its executives and partners, among others, must, as continuing requirements, be of "good moral character" and show the integrity needed to carry on their activities.[34] MSBs must keep certain records as set out in the QMA and as prescribed by regulation. The necessary records must be readily available for inspection by the AMF.[35] While all customers of an MSB, other than customers of ATMs, must be identified before a money service can be provided to them, only customers conducting transactions exceeding the limits set out in the regulations (currently C$3,000) must have their identity verified.[36] The regulations set out specific rules for identifying and verifying the identity of customers of MSBs that provide services on the Internet.[37]

Interestingly, the QMA specifically identifies and categorizes ATMs. In February 2015, the AMF amended the Policy Statement to the Money-Services Businesses Act and issued a press release stating that "businesses operating a virtual currency automated teller machine or a platform for trading virtual currency must obtain a licence" issued by the AMF.[38] The only licence category to have been amended to include "virtual currency" is the ATM licence category. The activity requiring an ATM MSB licence is the "making available to the public

---

[29] *Id.* § 8.
[30] *Id.* § 11(1).
[31] *Id.* § 11(2).
[32] *Id.* § 11(3).
[33] *Id.* § 11(4).
[34] *Id.* § 23.
[35] *Id.* § 29.
[36] Money-Services Businesses Act Regulations, M.O. E-12.000001-2012-02, §§ 1, 8 (Can.).
[37] *Id.* §§ 7, 10.
[38] Autorité des Marches Financiers, *Virtual currency ATMs and trading platforms must be authorized*, Feb. 12, 2015, available at http://www.lautorite.qc.ca/en/press-releases-2015-autre.html_2015_virtual-currency-atms-and-trading-platforms-must-be-authorized12-02-2015-09-4.html.

a means of purchasing, with cash, virtual money from an automated distributor, without the intervention of a natural person."[39] It would appear that, for the time being, over-the-counter buying and selling of bitcoin by an individual would still be exempt from any QMA licensing requirements. Ultimately, the nature of the business model will dictate whether non-ATM buying and selling of bitcoin, including over-the-counter models, will require a funds transmitter licence. As these provisions are new at the time of writing, little is known about how these changes will be implemented. The general provisions on ATMs themselves are recent, having come into force in January 2013. They require businesses operating one or more ATMs to register with the AMF. Since most bitcoin ATM models have the ATM acting as an automated exchange, it is conceivable that eventually the AMF might require a bitcoin ATM operator to obtain both a Quebec funds transmitter licence and a licence to operate the ATM. If a bitcoin ATM is considered to be providing both funds transmitter and ATM services, then the business behind that ATM would need to file an application with the AMF in respect of all money services it intends to offer.[40] For the moment, unmanned bitcoin ATMs operating in Quebec are only required to obtain an ATM licence, not a funds transmitter licence.

While the Quebec licensing requirements for bitcoin exchanges remain open questions, we see possibly greater clarity as regards software developers and bitcoin ATM manufacturers. Though they may be essential to the operation of the exchange or ATM business, in general, peripheral or support services for the operation of money services are not money services, per se, within the meaning of the QMA.[41] Examples of support activities include information exchange services and software services used to operate the business. Based on these types of exclusions, we may also come to see that hardware services are considered peripheral activities consistent with the policy statement.

1.4. The 2014 Budget & Bill C-31

In a widely expected move in the first half of 2014, the Canadian government increased the scope of its legislative oversight over

---

[39] Autorité des Marches Financiers, *Policy Statement to the Money-Services Businesses Act, supra* note 27, § 5.
[40] S.Q. 2010, c. 40, § 4 (Can.).
[41] Autorité des Marches Financiers, *Policy Statement to the Money-Services Businesses Act, supra* note 27, Part I.

cryptocurrencies, including bitcoin. This changed the PCA materially. Further changes to the PCA Regulations and other regulations under the PCA are coming. Those regulatory changes are unavailable at the time of writing; we expect publication no earlier than 2015. However, we now know that certain businesses transacting in bitcoins and other cryptocurrencies will be clearly within the ambit of the PCA and, therefore, FinTRAC's area of responsibility.

On February 11th, 2014, Canada's finance minister, the late Jim Flaherty, presented the federal government's annual budget plan to Parliament. In *The Road to Balance: Creating Jobs and Opportunities*, the government included a short but important section about what it called "virtual currencies," including bitcoin. Virtual currency, according to the budget, is an emerging risk that threatens "Canada's international leadership in the fight against money laundering and terrorist financing."[42] Accordingly, the government proposed to introduce legislative amendments and regulations to address virtual currencies, specifically including bitcoin, and to enhance FinTRAC's ability to disclose threats to Canada's security to its federal partners. To implement and support these initiatives, the government proposed to provide FinTRAC with up to C$10.5 million over five years; up to C$2.2 million per year on an ongoing basis; and, a further amount of up to C$12 million on a cash basis over five years to improve analytics.[43]

Specific changes contemplated by the government came in the form of Bill C-31, the federal budget implementation act.[44] Bill C-31 effectively expanded the definition of MSB in paragraph 5(h) of the PCA to include persons engaged in the business of "dealing in virtual currencies," as defined in the PCA Regulations.[45] A person or entity "dealing in virtual currencies" is subject to the MSB rules whether it has a place of business in Canada (paragraph 5(h) of the PCA) or it does not have a place of business in Canada but provides the service to Canadian customers and the service is "directed at" Canadian

---

[42] THE ROAD TO BALANCE: CREATING JOBS AND OPPORTUNITIES—2014 BUDGET PLAN, 133 (2014), *available at* http://www.budget.gc.ca/2014/docs/plan/pdf/budget2014-eng.pdf.
[43] *Id.* at 134.
[44] Economic Action Plan 2014 Act, No. 1, S.C. 2014, c. 20 (Can.), *available at* http://www.parl.gc.ca/content/hoc/Bills/412/Government/C-31/C-31_4/C-31_4.PDF.
[45] *Id.* § 256(2).

customers (paragraph 5(h.1)).[46] New section 5.1 clarifies that Part I of the PCA (containing the record keeping, identity verification, reporting, and registration requirements—see further below in this section) does not apply to persons or entities referred to in paragraph 5(h.1) in respect of any services they provide to persons or entities outside of Canada.[47]

The definition of "money services business" for purposes of the PCA Regulations has not yet been changed, but is supposed to be as part of new regulations to be promulgated. Currently, subsection 1(1) of the PCA Regulations provides that an MSB means a person or entity referred to in paragraph 5(h) of the PCA. That will be expanded to include both paragraphs 5(h) and 5(h.1) of the PCA.

Therefore, those who are engaged in the business of dealing in virtual currencies will be covered under the MSB definition in the PCA. This appears to be the main area of focus for the government. What "dealing in virtual currencies" means will be left up to regulations to be drafted and finalized by the Department of Finance. However, the government has provided some guideposts about what it intends to cover. In remarks before the Senate's Standing Committee on Banking, Trade and Commerce, David Murchison, the Director of the Department of Finance's Financial Sector Division, made the following statement about what "dealing in virtual currencies" will mean: "We would aim, in these regulations, to cover virtual currency exchanges, but not individuals or businesses. We think that this approach will allow for financial innovation, which we see to be one of the interesting markers behind this. Again, there will be an opportunity for public consultation on both these initiatives."[48] This may seem somewhat ambiguous—exchange businesses may, after all, be conducted by individuals or businesses—but FinTRAC subsequently clarified somewhat that the new PCA Regulations "will aim to cover entities

---

[46] *Id.* Under Bill C-31, the extension to those with a place of business in Canada and those without but who are providing directing those services to Canadian customers now also applies to other types of MSBs, i.e., foreign exchange dealers, funds transmitters, and issuers and redeemers of travellers' cheques and money orders. *Id.*

[47] *Id.* § 257.

[48] *Study on the Use of Digital Currency Before the Standing Senate Committee on Banking, Trade and Commerce*, Issue 6, 41st Parl., 2nd Sess. (2014) (statement of David Murchison, Director, Financial Sector Division, Department of Finance Canada) (Can.), *available at* http://www.parl.gc.ca/content/sen/committee/412/BANC/06EV-51275-E.HTM.

such as virtual currency exchanges, not individuals or businesses that use virtual currencies for buying and selling goods and services."[49]

Therefore, several things seem reasonably clear at the time of writing. One is that we do not yet know exactly what dealing in virtual currencies means, either in terms of "virtual currencies" or "dealing." It appears to, at a minimum, include those in the business of facilitating exchanges from cryptocurrency to fiat money and vice versa. Whether it will include exchanges from one cryptocurrency to another is not clear, however. It is also unclear whether those operating bitcoin ATM machines, which have been installed in several locations in Canada, will qualify as "dealers." It would not be surprising if bitcoin ATM businesses were covered by these rules given the exchange-like characteristics of ATM services. The new rules may be narrowly tailored to cover only those actually exchanging funds, or they may also apply to intermediaries between a customer and an actual exchange. Other questions concern escrow services denominated purely in bitcoin, arbitrageurs among bitcoin exchanges, and bitcoin miners. Whether any, some, or all of these will be virtual currency exchanges or akin to them is unknown. As to virtual currencies themselves, we know from prior pronouncements and remarks that they will likely include cryptocurrencies, and will certainly include bitcoin.

Second, the government is apparently not targeting individuals or businesses that are simply using cryptocurrencies for buying and selling goods and services outside of an exchange business. Accordingly, a person using bitcoins for expenses or receiving bitcoins as income, without more, should not be considered to be dealing in virtual currencies. Third, the Department of Finance intends to undertake a public consultation process with respect to the new regulations, which has not yet begun at the time of writing. Through that process, the public, including the cryptocurrency community, should have input into the scope and content of new regulations. Fourth, and in a related point, Finance Canada appears to value the financial innovation and related aspects of cryptocurrency, which is a positive sign for those businesses in the space looking to develop new products and markets.

Fifth and finally, Bill C-31 received royal assent on June 19, 2014. However, the text of the bill states that its changes as regards MSBs will come into force at a later date; FinTRAC has confirmed that these changes will only come into effect once the new regulations are also

---

[49] *FINTRAC Advisory regarding Money Services Businesses dealing in virtual currency, available at* http://www.fintrac.gc.ca/new-neuf/avs/2014-07-30-eng.asp.

drafted and in force.⁵⁰ Accordingly, the new (Bill C-31) regime is not, at the time of writing, applicable to those dealing in virtual currency. The current rules are the 'old' rules covered above.

1.5. Federal MSB Requirements in Brief

What is the upshot of Bill C-31 and the regulatory changes? Whether under the old or the new rules, what are the consequences of being a federal MSB in Canada? We shall summarize the registration, compliance, and other requirements of the PCA and the PCA Regulations here, but this is only a brief overview. The reader should turn to the legislation, the PCA Regulations, and the other regulations promulgated under the PCA for further detail.

Every MSB must register with FinTRAC in prescribed form and manner, providing information about, inter alia, its business, branches, agents, owners, and banking.⁵¹ Thereafter, MSBs must establish and implement, in accordance with the PCA Regulations, a program intended to ensure compliance with Parts 1 (record-keeping, verifying identity, reporting suspicious transactions, and registration) and 1.1 (protecting Canada's financial system) of the PCA.⁵² The program must include policies and procedures to assess the risk of a money laundering or a terrorist financing offence in the course of the MSB's activities⁵³ and, where that risk is high, the MSB must take special measures to address it.⁵⁴ The PCA Regulations require every MSB to, among other things, appoint a person responsible for implementing its compliance program;⁵⁵ to develop and implement written compliance policies and procedures and keep them up to date;⁵⁶ to assess and document the AML–CTF risks of the MSB's business;⁵⁷ to develop and maintain a written ongoing compliance training program for employees and agents;⁵⁸ and, to

---

⁵⁰ *Id.*
⁵¹ PCA, S.C. 2000, c. 17, § 11.1 (Can.); Proceeds of Crime (Money Laundering) and Terrorist Financing Registration Regulations SOR/2007-121 (Can.). Note that new § 11.1 of the PCA refers both to paragraph 5(h) MSBs and to paragraph 5(h.1) MSBs. Economic Action Plan 2014 Act, No. 1, S.C. 2014, c. 20, § 261 (Can.).
⁵² PCA § 9.6(1).
⁵³ *Id.* § 9.6(2).
⁵⁴ *Id.* § 9.6(3) act; Proceeds of Crime (Money Laundering) and Terrorist Financing Regulations, SOR/2002-184, § 71.1 (Can.).
⁵⁵ PCA Regulations § 71(1)(a).
⁵⁶ *Id.* § 71(1)(b).
⁵⁷ *Id.* § 71(1)(c).
⁵⁸ *Id.* § 71(1)(d).

institute and document a review of the MSB's policies and procedures, risk assessment, and training program every two years.[59]

Once registered and with the required personnel and programs in place, MSBs must then collect and analyze information about identity. MSBs are required to ascertain the identity of every person conducting any of the following transactions:

1. issuing or redeeming money orders, travellers' cheques, or other similar negotiable instruments in an amount of C$3,000 or greater;[60]
2. remitting or transmitting C$1,000 or more by any means through any person or entity;[61] or,
3. a foreign currency exchange transaction of C$3,000 or more.[62]

We expect that the new regulations will expressly set out similar ranges and thresholds for virtual currency transactions, e.g., identity will need to be ascertained where the tender of either fiat or virtual currency is equal to or greater than certain thresholds.

Ascertaining identity requires reference, where an individual is present, to her birth certificate, driver's licence, provincial health card, passport, or other similar document.[63] Where the person is not physically present, the PCA Regulations set out extensive remote identification methods.[64] Section 63 of the PCA Regulations provides for some exceptions to identification, e.g., when one recognizes a customer in respect of whom one has already ascertained identity.[65] Where a corporation is the transacting party, there are requirements for ascertaining the corporation's and its principals' identities.[66]

MSBs are also required to report such items as large cash transactions to FinTRAC, i.e., the receipt from a client of an amount in cash of C$10,000 or more in the course of a single transaction, unless the cash is received from a financial entity or public body; or the transmission to outside of Canada or receipt from outside of Canada, at a client's request, of C$10,000 or more in a single

---

[59] *Id.* § 71(1)(e).
[60] *Id.* § 59(1)(a).
[61] *Id.* § 59(1)(b).
[62] *Id.* § 59(1)(c).
[63] *Id.* § 64(1)(a).
[64] *Id.* § 64(1)(b).
[65] *Id.* § 63(1).
[66] *Id.* §§ 59(2), 65(1).

transaction.[67] Certain prescribed information in the schedules to the PCA Regulations must be provided to FinTRAC in the course of reporting, as set out in section 28 of the PCA Regulations. With some exceptions, MSBs must report suspicious transactions when required to do so by the Criminal Code and sanctions regulations.[68]

Finally, we turn to record-keeping requirements under the PCA and the PCA Regulations. The requirement to keep prescribed records is in section 6 of the PCA. The main provision in the PCA Regulations governing record-keeping for MSBs is section 30, which currently refers to paragraph 5(h) of the PCA. As with other parts of the PCA Regulations discussed above, we expect that either this item will be changed in the new PCA Regulations to refer to both paragraphs 5(h) and 5(h.1) of the PCA, or other regulatory changes will make this expanded scope effective. The PCA Regulations generally require that MSBs keep, among other things: a record of every client credit file it creates in the normal course of business;[69] records of all internal memoranda received or created in the normal course of business and that concerns services provided to clients;[70] and, detailed reporting records where it receives C$3,000 for issuance of a specified negotiable instrument,[71] where C$3,000 or more in money orders are cashed with it,[72] and where the MSB transmits or remits C$1,000 or greater.[73] Here again, we expect the new PCA Regulations to expand section 30 (or to create an equivalent new section) that explicitly covers dealing in virtual currency.

While Bill C-31 has received royal assent, we continue to be subject to the old pre-Bill C-31 rules until such time as new regulations are in force. Accordingly, understanding both the old PCA and PCA Regulations and the legislative and anticipated regulatory changes are important. Some knowledge of the MSB rules—codified in the PCA, the PCA Regulations, and in the QMA—is also critical. The Criminal Code and its discrete proceeds of crime regime should be borne in mind when looking at this area.

---

[67] *Id.* § 28(1). "Cash" is defined as current coins under the Currency Act and banknotes issued by the Bank of Canada pursuant to the Bank of Canada Act that are intended for circulation, as well as current coins and bank notes of other countries. *Id.* § 1(2) (definition of "cash"). "Financial entity" includes a bank under the Bank Act and a corporation to which the Trust and Loan Companies Act applies. *Id.* (definition of "financial entity").
[68] PCA, S.C. 2000, c. 17, § 7.1(1) (Can.).
[69] PCA Regulations, SOR/2002-184, § 30(a).
[70] *Id.* § 30(a.1).
[71] *Id.* § 30(c).
[72] *Id.* § 30(d).
[73] *Id.* § 30(e).

2. Cryptocurrency, Money & the Currency Act

The statutory basis for Canadian currency is found in a short piece of legislation called the Currency Act.[74] Among other things, the Currency Act establishes Canada's monetary unit (the dollar) and tells us the dollar's denominations (dollars and cents).[75] It also defines legal tender[76] and sets out that references in public accounts and legal proceedings to "money or monetary value" are to be in Canadian currency.[77] It is this law that gives the Canadian dollar its power; it has been observed that the value of Bank of Canada (Canada's central bank) bank notes derives solely from their quality of being legal tender under the Currency Act.[78]

Three main questions are posed for cryptocurrency by the Currency Act. First, what is the relationship between cryptocurrency and the legal tender provisions of the Currency Act, if any? Second, can a judgment from or order of a Canadian court be issued in cryptocurrency? Third, can a contract between two willing parties in Canada be struck in cryptocurrency? All of these queries will be addressed in this part of the chapter, and most of them turn on the issue of what exactly is "money" in Canadian law.

2.1. Is Cryptocurrency Money?

What "money" is, and whether bitcoin and other cryptocurrencies constitute "money," is critical to our discussion. Indeed, in the words of F.A. Mann,

> money is a fundamental notion not only in the economic life of mankind but also of all departments of law. In fact, a great deal of a lawyer's daily work centres about the term 'money' itself and the many transactions or institutions based on that term, such as debt, damages, value, payment, price, capital, interest, pecuniary legacy.[79]

Or, as Mann's subsequent editor put it, quoting Ecclesiastes, "money answers everything."[80]

---

[74] R.S.C. 1985, c. C-52 (Can.).
[75] Id. § 3.
[76] Id. § 8.
[77] Id. § 12.
[78] Guy David, *Money in Canadian Law*, 65 Can. Bar Rev. 192, 199 (1986).
[79] Francis A. Mann, The Legal Aspect of Money 3 (1938).
[80] Mann on the Legal Aspect of Money 5 (Charles Proctor, ed., 7th ed. 2012).

And yet, for such a basic and important concept, there is a paucity of Canadian cases that squarely address the issue. Certainly whether bitcoins are—or any cryptocurrency is—money is a matter of first impression in Canada, but jurisprudence addressing even the underlying definition of money is in short supply. The characterization of money was far from settled in Canadian law almost thirty years ago,[81] and the position seems largely unchanged now.

We know that "money" in the Currency Act means something beyond a "legal tender." This is because a tender of payment of money is a legal tender if it is made in current coins or in notes issued pursuant to the Bank of Canada Act.[82] Money, as a result, is broader than a legal tender; money *includes* a legal tender if it meets certain conditions. Accordingly, money is not only "legal tender" money.[83]

But, if broader, then what is money? Is bitcoin money in Canadian law? The answer is most likely no, at least at the time of writing.[84]

Several approaches to the question are possible. Mann, in his original tract, says that anything has to be four things to be money:

1. it has to be a chattel personal, i.e., property that is not real property;
2. it must be issued under the authority of law, i.e., by fiat (this is the state theory of money);[85]
3. it has to be denominated with reference to a distinct unit of account; and,
4. it must be meant to serve as a universal medium of exchange.[86]

By contrast, Herman Oliphant sets up a somewhat broader definition, as follows: "[A]nything which for a substantial period of time and throughout any important commercial community is, by general consent, used and treated in common payments as cash in

---

[81] David, *supra* note 78, at 207; *cf.* William E. Britton, Handbook of the Law of Bills and Notes 122 (1943).
[82] Currency Act § 8(1).
[83] *See* Reference Re Alberta Statutes, [1938] S.C.R. 100, 116 (Can.); David, *supra* note 78, at 213.
[84] Consistent with the approach taken by David, *supra* note 78, at 205 n.73, in this chapter, we disregard cases dealing with the interpretation of "money" in wills. Those cases are primarily concerned with ascertaining the testator's intention and not with properly addressing and defining the legal concept of money.
[85] Note that Proctor disputes that state issuance is critical, calling the state theory of money "rather dated and…difficult to accept in its original form." Mann on the Legal Aspect of Money, *supra* note 80, at 29.
[86] Mann, *supra* note 79, at 7–19; *see also* David, *supra* note 78, at 204.

the ordinary course and transaction of business is money."[87] Even for Oliphant, however, there are "instruments payable in property" that "in no sense" approximate money.[88] He cites the example of "good merchantable whiskey" and calls these instruments generally acceptable "only in communities but one step removed from a barter economy."[89] Note that the CRA's view of bitcoin as a commodity and not a currency[90] comports with Oliphant's view of items that are "in no sense" money.

A cogent conception of the topic by Alfred Mitchell Innes is that money is simply transferable credit, supported by accounting.[91] Yet another view is that of Guy David, which may broadly comport with Innes's outline. David's favoured, normative approach is to equate money with any medium, tangible or intangible, specifically adopted as a means of effecting payments.[92]

Using Mann's approach, bitcoin is clearly not money because it is not state-issued. Bitcoin may fulfil all of the other elements of this definition. It might be an intangible chattel personal, it is denominated with reference to a distinct unit of account (a bitcoin, subdivisible into satoshis), and it is meant to serve as a universal medium of exchange. Oliphant's conception of money offers potentially more room for cryptocurrency, but bitcoin founders in several elements of this definition, as well. It appears not to have been used for a substantial period of time or throughout any important community or by general consent. However, this just substitutes definition for analysis. No-one knows how long a

---

[87] Herman Oliphant, *The Theory of Money in the Law of Commercial Instruments*, 29 Yale L.J. 606, 618 (1920).
[88] *Id.* at 608.
[89] *Id.*
[90] *Study on the Use of Digital Currency Before the Standing Senate Committee on Banking, Trade and Commerce*, Issue 13, 41st Parl., 2nd Sess. (2014) (statement of Eliza Erskine, Director, Income Tax Rulings Directorate, Canada Revenue Agency) (Can.), *available at* http://www.parl.gc.ca/content/sen/committee/412/BANC/13EV-51506-E.HTM.
[91] A. Mitchell Innes, *What is Money?*, 30 Banking L.J. 377, 392–397 (1913); A. Mitchell Innes, *The Credit Theory of Money*, 31 Banking L.J. 151, 152 (1914). *See also*: David Graeber, Debt: The First 5,000 Years 37–41 (2011); Felix Martin, Money: The Unauthorized Biography—From Coinage to Cryptocurrencies 14 (Vintage Books 2015) (2013); Tatiana Cutts, Are There Really Property Rights in Money? 14–16 (Nov. 26, 2014) (unpublished manuscript) (on file with author); Tatiana Cutts, HM Treasury Open Consultation, Digital Currencies: Call for Information ¶ 2.1 (2014) (unpublished submission) (on file with author).
[92] David, *supra* note 78, at 209.

substantial period of time has to be, what comprises an important community—or, indeed, how "throughout" the community, once defined, adoption needs to be extended, or felt—or how "general" the consent must be. Certainly the case law offers few answers. Given the academic and judicial commentary and opinion, however, we believe it is highly unlikely that bitcoin—launched in 2009 and with a C$3.5 billion market capitalization at the time of writing—would be considered anything other than a niche product in Canada, and certainly not legal money.

The only definitions that would appear to accommodate bitcoin are Mitchell Innes's and David's. As to Mitchell Innes, bitcoin seems to be transferable credit supported by a system of accounting. It is also an intangible medium specifically adopted as a means, inter alia, of effecting payments (David's test). In fact, most people know bitcoin as a currency or a payment platform (i.e., Bitcoin) or both. Mitchell Innes's definition is clear, salutary, and seems to comport with historical evidence about how people engaged in commerce. From an economic perspective, bitcoin may well be money. However, remember that the exercise being undertaken here is not whether an economist sees bitcoin as money, whether the legal definition of money in other jurisdictions accommodates bitcoin, or whether "money" should normatively include bitcoin as a matter of law in Canada. It is whether Canadian law sees bitcoin as money. While Mitchell Innes's definition is cogent and convincing, we believe that the case law in Canada will not currently support such a broad characterization of money.

What do the cases say? There are not many of them. *Moss v. Hancock* is said to contain a classical legal definition of money:[93]

> [T]hat which passes freely from hand to hand throughout the community in final discharge of debts and full payment for commodities, being accepted equally without reference to the character of or credit of the person who offers it and without the intention of the person who receives it to consume it or apply it to any other use than in turn to tender it to others in discharge of debts or payment for commodities.[94]

---

[93] *Id.* at 203.
[94] [1899] 2 Q.B. 111, 116 (U.K.). *Miller v. Race* stands for the proposition that bank notes transferred for good consideration and without collusion pass free and clear of prior claims and equities.

Quaere whether bitcoin currently passes from hand to hand "throughout the community." This language seems to suggest a universality that bitcoin may lack, not for want of ingenuity or design but for want of adoption. More problematic is the fact that this definition presupposes that money accepted in commerce is taken free and clear of prior claims ("being accepted equally without reference to the character of or credit of the person who offers it"), consistent with the rule for bank notes in *Miller v. Race*.[95] This is circular: bitcoin as money would need to be received free of prior claims, and the lack of prior claims means that it is money. But as we shall see in below, this just leads to the question of whether bitcoin is received free and clear of prior claims, like bank notes, promissory notes, and bills of exchange. Our answer is that it likely is not so received in Canada, so the *Moss v. Hancock* definition will not suit us. (A similar Catch-22 is at play in Mitchell Innes's definition. Money is transferable credit. For credit to be transferable, it must be negotiable, but to be negotiable in Canada under the Bills of Exchange Act, a bill or note must be "in money.")

The leading case in Canada on the definition of money is the *Alberta Reference*.[96] In that case, the Supreme Court considered the creation of "Alberta Credit" in the province of Alberta. Alberta Credit was the unused capacity of the industries and people of Alberta to produce wanted goods and services.[97] The value in "money" of Alberta Credit was to be ascertained by the Provincial Credit Commission and then used for government purposes to provide government services, consumer discounts, and to advance credit to those in "agriculture or manufacturing or industry."[98]

Through this scheme, the Alberta government attempted to deal with the Great Depression by redressing the then-existing distribution of wealth, which it considered to be "inadequate, unjust and not suited to the welfare, prosperity and happiness of the people of Alberta."[99]

---

[95] (1758), 1 Burr. 452, 97 Eng. Rep. 398 (K.B.) (U.K.).
[96] [1938] S.C.R. 100 (Can.).
[97] *Id.* at 107.
[98] *Id.* at 107, 110–11 (Duff, C.J., concurring).
[99] *Id.* at 108.

The "present monetary system" was also said to be "obsolete and a hindrance to the efficient production and distribution of goods."[100]

The Court could barely hide its contempt for the government's policies and, either in spite of this or because of it, in a series of concurring decisions held the entire scheme to be *ultra vires* the provincial legislature's powers. On the issue of money, the Chief Justice wrote:

> But money as commonly understood is not necessarily legal tender. Any medium which by practice fulfils the function of money and which everybody will accept in payment of a debt is money in the ordinary sense of the words even although it may not be legal tender; and this statute envisages a form of credit which will ultimately, in Alberta, acquire such a degree of confidence as to be generally acceptable, in the sense that bank credit is now acceptable; and will serve as a substitute therefor.[101]

Accordingly, the Chief Justice's comments stand for at least two propositions relating to bitcoin. First, as we have already seen, money includes more than just a legal tender. Second, money means something that is universally accepted ("which everybody will accept").

The role of the state theory of money appears to be more ambiguous. On the one hand, the Chief Justice makes a direct comparison to bank credit, which suggests that money need not be state issued. There is also no express statement that money must be state issued. However, the holding is confined to the particular facts of the case, which contemplates state-issued Alberta Credit. The only form of money relevant on these facts was state-issued. The objective of the provincial government was to make Alberta Credit as acceptable as and a substitute for bank credit. Though it is a close question, on

---

[100] *Id.* at 109. Radical economic change was not the sole objective. The ominously-named "An Act to ensure the Publication of Accurate News and Information," referred to as the Press Bill, was also part of the *Alberta Reference*. The Press Bill required any proprietor, editor, publisher, or manager of any newspaper published in Alberta to print in that newspaper any statement from the government "which has for its object the correction or amplification of any statement relating to any policy or activity of the government." The Press Bill also required every newspaper to, on demand, reveal to the government all sources of any statements in that newspaper. On violation of the Press Bill, the Alberta government proposed to allow itself the power to prohibit publication of any newspaper. *Id.* at 142–43 (Cannon, J., concurring). All members of the panel held the Press Bill to be beyond the province's powers.

[101] *Id.* at 116 (Duff, C.J., concurring).

balance, issuance under fiat may well be one of the Chief Justice's requirements in the *Alberta Reference*, though it is open to future courts to take a different view of the matter.

The other key decision to consider is *Bank of Canada v. Bank of Montreal*.[102] This was a fascinating fact pattern with a rare 4-4 split on an even-numbered court. In 1959, the Bank of Montreal arranged with the post office to have Bank of Canada bank notes delivered to a Bank of Montreal branch in northern Ontario. While in transit, the package of bank notes was destroyed by a fire on a bus operated by one of the defendants. A test question on a single five dollar note (of a kind exactly like the five dollar notes destroyed in the fire) made its way to the Supreme Court.

The question was whether the bank note was a promissory note within the meaning of the federal Bills of Exchange Act. If it was, the holder (the Bank of Montreal) was entitled to claim a duplicate promissory note under then-section 156 (now section 155) of the Bills of Exchange Act from the Bank of Canada or, alternatively, it was entitled to damages equal to the full face value of the destroyed notes. If it was not, then the Bank of Canada was not responsible for any damages.

Justice Jean Beetz, writing for himself and three others on the panel, held that the bank note was a promissory note. He emphasized that the note contained the language of a promissory note ("Bank of Canada will pay to the bearer on demand"), which appeared on the note pursuant to applicable federal legislation.[103] Justice Beetz acknowledged that the note was not convertible into anything: that, upon presentment, the bearer would receive a different five dollar bank note, if anything. He acknowledged that the bank note was also money. However, with respect to bills of exchange, form prevails over substance. A note in the form set out by the Bills of Exchange Act was a note subject to the remedies and protections under that legislation.[104] (Note that modern Canadian bank notes are clearly not promissory notes under the Bills of Exchange Act.[105]) Justice Beetz dismissed the Bank of Canada's appeal from the Ontario Court of Appeal.

---

[102] [1978] 1 S.C.R. 1148 (Can.).
[103] *Id.* at 1165, 1170 (plurality opinion).
[104] *Id.* at 1169.
[105] *See id.* at 1170; Bradley Crawford, 2 Crawford and Falconbridge Banking and Bills of Exchange 1158 (1986); David, *supra* note 78, at 198–99.

Chief Justice Bora Laskin led the remaining four judges in what was effectively a dissent. (As there were insufficient numbers to allow the appeal, the appeal was dismissed pursuant to Justice Beetz's opinion.) Chief Justice Laskin pointed out that bank notes were not convertible and called it a "charade" to say that they were.[106] Nothing would be paid to the bearer on demand. The Chief Justice preferred substance over form: "To say that a bank note of the kind involved here imports similar legal consequences, that a non-convertible bank note is paid off by the giving of a bank note of similar face value is to go around in a circle: legal tender is exchanged for legal tender."[107]

However, on the subject of money, the judges were, in our view, in agreement. The Chief Justice viewed the bank notes as money. In fact, his whole decision was based on what he perceived to be the absurdity of saying that "an unconditional promise to pay a sum certain in money is itself money."[108] Justice Beetz did not disagree that a bank note was money; he just disagreed that something that was money could not also be a promise to pay within the meaning of the Bills of Exchange Act.[109]

Finally, consider Bradley Crawford, a leading authority on bills of exchange in Canada. He suggests that some forms of transferable value—he cites demand bank balances and cheques as examples—are money in a popular sense, and even in some technical legal and economic senses. But, says Crawford, "according to the prevailing academic opinion, they are not money in the general legal sense, since they are not legal tender and are not 'passed in currency,'" i.e., universally acceptable as payment.[110]

Accordingly, the weight of authority in Canada, such as it is, appears to demonstrate that value, to be money, must be universally accepted, or (possibly) state-issued, or both. The *Alberta Reference*, which is still the leading authority on the characterization of money,

---

[106] *Bank of Canada*, [1978] 1 S.C.R. 1148 at 1153 (Laskin, C.J., dissenting).
[107] *Id.* at 1156.
[108] *Id.* at 1154.
[109] *Id.* at 1168. *Contra* David, *supra* note 78, at 208. David suggests that "[t]he legalistic approach of Beetz J. would tend to limit the scope of the concept of money, whereas the more liberal approach of Laskin C.J.C. would have the opposite effect." *Id.* We disagree. We see the issue as narrower and do not see that the Chief Justice's approach to what is "legal money" is necessarily broader than Justice Beetz's. In fact, we suggest that it may be Justice Beetz's conception that is less "limiting," inasmuch as the holding of the case is that a bank note can be both money *and* a bill of exchange.
[110] CRAWFORD, *supra* note 105, at 1159.

can be interpreted such that money must be both. (The outliers are David and Mitchell Innes, who are making arguments that, while salutary and important, are not binding authority in Canada.) But even if we were to adopt the liberal view that one or the other—fiat or universal acceptance—suffices, bitcoin cannot measure up to this definition of money at present. It is not issued by governmental edict nor is it universally accepted; in fact, only a narrow—though growing—fraction of consumers and merchants accept, use, and transact in bitcoin.

Again, however, many of the elements of this discussion have not yet been defined: general acceptance for a substantial period, the degree of acceptance required, etc. This is clearly a problem. A full-fledged inquiry into what every element of the sundry definitions could mean is well beyond the scope of this chapter, but should be developed in the context of cryptocurrency. Further study and research is welcome. In the meantime, Canadian law appears to be loath to accept demand bank balances denominated in Canadian dollars as money. In this context, we cannot accept that the Canadian courts are ready as a general proposition to recognize a niche currency like bitcoin as money. We do not believe that "money" or like expressions (e.g., "monetary value") in the Currency Act or the Bills of Exchange Act include bitcoin at the time of writing.

2.2. The Currency Act

It now becomes a matter of applying this knowledge to the questions raised by the Currency Act. Recall that the first query was as to the relationship between cryptocurrency and the legal tender provisions. There has been some interest in this question in the media.[111] We already know from the previous section that bitcoins are not legal tender pursuant to the Currency Act; bitcoins are not current coin and they are not notes issued by the Bank of Canada. Accordingly, it is perhaps unsurprising that the government would confirm what was in the Currency Act and known for years.

Accordingly, there is no particular relationship between bitcoin and these sections. Bitcoin as a currency is simply not included in the Currency Act, so a tender of bitcoins is not a legal tender. The legal tender provisions do not restrict any private party from accepting,

---

[111] *See, e.g.,* David George-Cosh, *Canada Says Bitcoin Isn't Legal Tender*, CoinDesk (Jan. 17, 2014, 18:10 GMT), http://www.coindesk.com/bitcoin-not-legal-tender-canada-government-official/.

sending, or transacting in bitcoins. Parties agreeing to provide and pay for goods and services in bitcoins are still largely free to do so irrespective of the legal tender section of the Currency Act.

The second question is more captivating: whether a judgment of a Canadian court may be issued in cryptocurrency. Section 12 of the Currency Act provides as follows:

> All public accounts established or maintained in Canada shall be in the currency of Canada, and any reference to money or monetary value in any indictment or other legal proceedings shall be stated in the currency of Canada.

Canadian courts have consistently confirmed that money judgments must be expressed in Canadian currency.[112] One decision has suggested that all references to "money or monetary value" in any action are included in "other legal proceedings" and must be in Canadian currency.[113] Others have held that the Currency Act provision does not include statements of claim[114] or offers to settle.[115] An interesting issue arises as to the date of the conversion to Canadian currency. Canadian courts have traditionally felt themselves bound to use the breach date rule in contracts (i.e., conversion as at the date of the breach of the contract),[116] but have lately been less constrained and appear ready to choose the judgment date or another date where appropriate.[117] Some provincial legislation sets out requirements for the conversion date[118] but expressly allows the courts the discretion to choose a date for conversion that the court considers equitable.[119]

---

[112] *See, e.g.*, Batavia Times Publ'g Co. v. Davis (1978), 20 O.R. 2d 437 (Can. Ont. H.C.J.); Carsley Silk Co. Ltd. v. Koechlin Baumgartner & Cie (1971), 23 D.L.R. 3d 255 (Can. Que. C.A.); Kellogg Brown & Root Inc. v. Aerotech Herman Nelson Inc., [2004] 11 W.W.R. 23 (Can. Man. C.A.); Alpine Canada v. Non-Marine Underwriters, Lloyd's, London (1999), 245 A.R. 252 (Can. Alb. Q.B.); Zucchetti Rubinetteria S.p.A. v. Natphil Inc., [2011] O.J. No. 2813 (QL) (Can. Ont. Super. Ct. J.) (QL).

[113] Levine v. Pacific Int'l Sec. Inc. (1997), 46 B.C.L.R. 3d 110 (Can. B.C. Sup. Ct.).

[114] *Kellogg Brown & Root*, [2004] 11 W.W.R. 23.

[115] Champion Int'l Corp. v. Sabina (The), [2003] F.C.J. No. 64 (Can. T.D.) (QL), *aff'd* [2003], F.C.J. No. 1479 (Can. C.A.) (QL).

[116] *See, e.g.*, Gatineau Power Co. v. Crown Life Ins. Co., [1945] S.C.R. 655 (Can.).

[117] *See, e.g., Batavia Times*, (1978), 20 O.R. 2d 437; *Kellogg Brown & Root*, [2004] 11 W.W.R. 23.

[118] *See, e.g.*, Foreign Money Claims Act, R.S.B.C. 1996, c. 155, §1(2) (Can.); Courts of Justice Act, R.S.O. 1990, c. C.43, § 121(1) (Can.).

[119] Courts of Justice Act § 121(3).

No consideration has yet been given to how bitcoin will fit within section 12 of the Currency Act. We believe that "money or monetary value"[120] does not include bitcoin. Accordingly, there should be no restriction on stating bitcoin amounts in, for example, any pleadings or offers to settle. Bitcoins are not money, so they need not be expressed or converted into Canadian dollars. Claims, counterclaims, cross-claims, and set-offs for amounts pleaded in bitcoin should be acceptable.

As to judgments in the common law provinces, we believe that three broad approaches are possible. First, the courts may take claims for bitcoin amounts arising from contract as amounts to be converted to Canadian dollars using a conversion date rule pursuant to the developed case law or provincial statute. This would easily accommodate bitcoin in the current structure of enforcing "foreign-denominated" judgments in Canadian currency. However, this is also essentially an admission that bitcoin is "money or monetary value," and we are not sure that the courts are ready to move that far or for the implications of such a finding. Still, it would be open to a court to simply take a bitcoin amount—arrived at through a trial or on summary judgment, for example—and express it in Canadian dollars with or without due consideration of the issues raised by section 12 of the Currency Act.

The second approach would be more consistent with bitcoin not representing money, as such. This is a commodity approach that was developed by David in his article.[121] An order to deliver bitcoin as a commodity would not offend section 12 of the Currency Act. However, this comes with its own problems. *Quaere* whether such an order would amount to specific performance, i.e., delivery of a particular quantity of bitcoin. Specific performance has long been regarded as a secondary remedy in common law Canada; the primary remedy is money damages. Specific performance is only available when money compensation is inadequate,[122] which presumably will not happen often in the case of a dispute involving bitcoin as a currency. A claimant may have difficulty obtaining judgment where the court perceives it as specific enforcement. Note that the same may not be true in Quebec, where the civil law governs contracts, or, more properly, the law of obligations. In Quebec, the general rule is that a creditor

---

[120] We are aware of no particular controlling authority in Canada on the meaning of "monetary value."
[121] David, *supra* note 78, at 219.
[122] STEPHEN M. WADDAMS, THE LAW OF CONTRACTS 494 (4th ed. Can. Law Book 1999).

The Law of Bitcoin

under a contract may demand specific performance of an obligation.[123] Accordingly, a specific enforcement remedy when it comes to bitcoin may be more tenable in Quebec than in the rest of Canada.

The third approach is a hybrid of the first two, and we believe represents the most likely outcome in common law Canada, and the most doctrinally sound one. We expect that a court will not characterize bitcoins as money or monetary value. However, the common law court will generally not order specific performance. Accordingly, in order to satisfy a party's claim in any given case, we believe the court is likely to take the value of bitcoin that would have been awarded but for the bar on specific performance and express that as a measure of money damages in Canadian dollars. This hybrid approach may well adopt the conversion date rules outlined in the first approach.

We believe our final question of the section, *viz.*, can a contract between two willing parties be struck in cryptocurrency, is quickly disposed of given the preceding discussion. The Currency Act states:

> Every contract, sale, payment, bill, note, instrument and security for money and every transaction, dealing, matter and thing relating to money or involving the payment of or the liability to pay money shall be made, executed, entered into, done or carried out in the currency of Canada, unless it is made, executed, entered into done or carried out in
>
> (a) the currency of a country other than Canada; or
> (b) a unit of account that is defined in terms of the currencies of two or more countries.[124]

This provision appears to offer more room than section 12, but this broader space may be illusory in the case of bitcoin. Other currencies are allowed but they must be currencies of a country or countries, i.e., they must be state-issued, or there must be a unit of account defined in terms of the currencies of two or more countries. Bitcoin does not qualify as money or the currency of any country. As to paragraph 13(1)(b), we do not believe that bitcoin is "defined" in terms of the currencies of two or more countries. (Although, if it were so defined, then one of two things follows: either bitcoin is money and can play the role of money in this section of the Currency Act or bitcoin is still not money but can still generally denominate contracts

---

[123] Civil Code of Quebec, S.Q. 1991, c. 64, §§ 1590, 1601 (Can.).
[124] Currency Act, R.S.C. 1985, c. C-52, § 13(1) (Can.).

and other items. Note that this section, interpreted either of those two ways, would purport to allow a bill of exchange or promissory note to be denominated in bitcoin.)

Here again, we believe this should not bar the drafting and denominating of agreements and related documents in bitcoins because bitcoins are not money. Amounts in these agreements and other instruments need not be expressed in Canadian currency or the currency of any other country or countries. The issue may ultimately come back to the previous question: what to do about judgments and enforcement? Our view is that contracts and other items denominated in bitcoins coming before the Canadian common law courts will most likely give rise to judgments and orders denominated in money, i.e., in Canadian currency, because specific enforcement of bitcoin judgments will be perceived to be generally unavailable. As a means of anticipating this, it may be advisable for parties to fix Canadian currency amounts in their agreements, or to anticipate conversion and allow for that in their transactions. This may provide for more certainty in any litigation that develops among contracting parties given the open questions about what courts might do with bitcoin.

We have now assessed the concept of money in Canada and determined that bitcoin is not likely money as a matter of law. That has allowed us to address several provisions of the Currency Act as they potentially relate to cryptocurrency. We now turn to the Bills of Exchange Act and whether cryptocurrency-denominated instruments can fit into that legislation.

3. Cryptocurrency & Negotiable Instruments

The Bills of Exchange Act is the primary federal law governing commercial paper and negotiable instruments in Canada. It codifies many of the customs and usages of the law merchant on the subject and will not be unfamiliar to anyone with some knowledge of the United Kingdom Bills of Exchange Act and Article 3 of the U.S. Uniform Commercial Code. Much of the law of negotiable instruments has also been codified in the international Convention Providing for a Uniform Law for Bills of Exchange and Promissory Notes.[125] The law of negotiable instruments has its origins in the practises of merchants who would use bills of exchange as instruments of credit and make

---

[125] Convention Providing a Uniform Law for Bills of Exchange and Promissory Notes, Jun. 7, 1930, 143 L.N.T.S. 257.

them negotiable by endorsement, thereby facilitating trade.[126] This started as custom in the law merchant and is now part of the common law[127] and the Bills of Exchange Act. In fact, the common law of England, including the law merchant, continues to apply to all bills, notes, and cheques in Canada save and except where those provisions are inconsistent with the express provisions of the Bills of Exchange Act.[128]

While the rules of negotiable instruments may seem complicated and arcane, the central propositions are simple: If an instrument is issued in a special form (i.e., it is negotiable) and it is transferred in a particular way (i.e., it is negotiated) to a person who takes the instrument in good faith, for value, without notice, and before it was overdue—in other words, to a holder in due course—then the person will be able to enforce the instrument subject only to so-called real defences.

The key questions in this section are these: How does cryptocurrency fit within this framework, or does it at all? Can a bitcoin-denominated instrument be a bill or note within the meaning of the Bills of Exchange Act? Can such instruments therefore obtain the legal protections afforded to holders in due course? If not, what does this mean for cryptocurrency, if anything?

3.1. THE BILLS OF EXCHANGE ACT IN BRIEF

To answer these questions, we must understand more about the Bills of Exchange Act and its requirements.[129] To begin with, it applies to bills of exchange (including cheques) and promissory notes. A bill of exchange (or, simply, a "bill") is an unconditional order in writing from one person (the drawer) to another, signed by the person giving it, requiring the addressee party (the drawee) to pay, on demand or at a fixed or determinable future date, a sum certain in money to or to the order of a specified person or bearer (the payee).[130] The paradigmatic example of a bill of exchange in modern times is the cheque. A bill

---

[126] LAZAR SARNA & LEORA ASTER, ANNOTATED BILLS OF EXCHANGE ACT 1 (Lexis Nexis 1989).
[127] CRAWFORD, *supra* note 105, at 1171.
[128] Bills of Exchange Act, R.S.C. 1985, c. B-4, § 9 (Can.).
[129] This will not be a comprehensive overview of bills of exchange and promissory notes in Canada. For further background reading, see CRAWFORD, *supra* note 105, and JOHN D. FALCONBRIDGE, THE LAW OF NEGOTIABLE INSTRUMENTS IN CANADA (7th ed. Ryerson Press 1946).
[130] Bills of Exchange Act, § 16(1).

is therefore a tripartite instrument. By contrast, a promissory note (a "note") is an unconditional promise in writing made by one person (the maker) to another person, signed by the maker, to pay on demand or at a fixed or determinable future time, a sum certain in money to, or to the order of, a specified person or to bearer (the payee).[131] Accordingly, a note has only two parties, not three. Subject to Part IV of the Bills of Exchange Act, the provisions of the Bills of Exchange Act relating to bills also apply, *mutatis mutandis*, to notes.[132] In particular, the negotiability and holder in due course rules apply to both bills and notes.

Two things are worth noting at this stage. First, any instrument that does not comply with the requirements will not receive the special rights or protections available under the Bills of Exchange Act.[133] Accordingly, it is critical to comply with the legislation's formalities. Or, as Justice Beetz put it in *Bank of Canada*, with respect to negotiable instruments, form prevails over substance.[134] Second, as the scheme of the Bills of Exchange Act is to promote the currency or negotiability of instruments,[135] the principal requirement of a bill is certainty;[136] it must be clear to parties transacting in the bill what its key terms are.

Negotiability means transferability such that the transferee becomes the instrument holder, i.e., she receives the instrument consistent with the Bills of Exchange Act's formalities.[137] An instrument payable to bearer is negotiated by delivery.[138] A bill payable to order is negotiated by the holder's endorsement.[139] A bill may be non-negotiable, cutting off future transferees and holder in due course status, if, for example, there are words in it prohibiting transfer.[140]

---

[131] *Id.* § 176(1).
[132] *Id.* § 186(1).
[133] *Id.* § 16(2).
[134] [1978] 1 S.C.R. 1148, 1169 (Can.).
[135] MacLeod Sav. & Credit Union Ltd. v. Perrett, [1981] 1 S.C.R. 78, 86 (Can.).
[136] *Id.*; Emil J. Hayek, *Recent Developments in Canadian Law: Bills of Exchange*, 17 OTTAWA L. REV. 589, 593 (1985).
[137] Bills of Exchange Act § 59(1).
[138] *Id.* § 59(2).
[139] *Id.* § 59(3).
[140] *Id.* § 20(1). Though it will not be addressed here in any detail, some do not view negotiability as having a bearing on marketability in efficient markets: "In reality, there is little evidence to support the conventional wisdom that negotiability is essential to marketability ... Security of title is provided not by the legal doctrine of negotiability, but by reliance on the trust- and credit-worthiness of financial intermediaries, backed up by governmental regulatory and insurance schemes." James S. Rogers, *Negotiability, Property, and Identity*, 12 CARDOZO L. REV. 471, 479 (1990).

"Holder" is defined in section 2 of the Bills of Exchange Act as "the payee or endorsee of a bill or note who is in possession of it, or the bearer thereof." A person may be the holder as the original bearer or payee or may acquire the status of holder through negotiation.[141] The holder may or may not be a holder in due course, depending on the circumstances in which she acquired the instrument.[142]

A holder in due course is a special kind of holder that has taken a bill or note, complete and regular on its face, under two broad sets of conditions: she became the holder before it was overdue and without notice of previous dishonour, if that occurred;[143] and, she took the bill in good faith and for value, and at the moment of negotiation she had no notice of any defect in title of the person negotiating it.[144] A holder in due course is a "privileged person" that may acquire a better title to the instrument than the person negotiating it to the holder in due course.[145] Among other things, a holder in due course holds the bill free from any defect of title of any prior party and free from "mere personal defences."[146] It is often said that a holder in due course holds the instrument free from all except real defences.[147]

A personal defence is one that is personal to one of the original contracting parties, in the sense that it relates to something that she has done or has omitted to do, e.g., defendant delivers a note to plaintiff but plaintiff also owes defendant money and, therefore, defendant has a claim for set off. By contrast, defects of title relate to the instrument itself and are therefore good defences even against a remote party, though not against a holder in due course. Examples of defects of title are most types of fraud: B draws a bill on A payable to the order of B, and obtains A's acceptance by falsely representing to A that he has delivered certain goods that A has agreed to buy, or by fraudulently delivering worthless goods in breach of his contract with A.[148] Both

---

[141] FALCONBRIDGE, *supra* note 129, at 107.
[142] *Id.*
[143] Bills of Exchange Act § 55(1)(a).
[144] *Id.* § 55(1)(b).
[145] FALCONBRIDGE, *supra* note 129, at 107.
[146] Bills of Exchange Act § 73(b).
[147] FALCONBRIDGE, *supra* note 129, at 117–19.
[148] *Id.* at 122. Note that fraud in the factum ('real fraud' or *non est factum*) is a real defence, e.g., A non-negligently signs a note that B fraudulently represents is a credit application. A's signature is null and she has a real defence. Generally, however, most fraud is 'personal' fraud that merely renders title to the instrument defective. *Id.* at 121; *see also* CRAWFORD, *supra* note 105, at 1531–32.

defects of title and personal defences are, confusingly, species of what are called personal defences, as distinct from real defences.[149]

Real defences are based upon the nullity of the property or the instrument itself. If the signature is void, it is not rendered valid by the fact that the instrument is transferred to any holder, even a holder in due course.[150] The instrument is void ab initio. Examples of real defences are want of legal capacity[151] and forgery.[152]

3.2. Cryptocurrency's Place in the Bills of Exchange Act

Accordingly, bills and notes may—if the requisites are met—be afforded protections that are exceptions to the rule of *nemo dat quod non habet* ("no-one gives what he does not have"). Generally, one cannot transfer a property with superior ownership rights than the transferor (the *nemo dat* rule). For an example of the *nemo dat* rule being codified into law in Canada, consider Article 1713 of the Civil Code of Quebec (the sale of property by a person other than the owner or a person authorized to sell it may be declared null). But *nemo dat* does not apply to properly negotiated bills and notes or to bank notes (cash) transferred in good faith and for value received.[153]

What does this mean for cryptocurrency? We believe that neither bitcoin *qua* currency nor instruments denominated purely in bitcoin without, at a minimum, reference to an exchange rate, can be bills or notes within the meaning of the Bills of Exchange Act. We believe that these are limitations on how bitcoin can be integrated within the traditional realms of trade and finance.

It seems easy enough to conclude that bitcoin itself, as a currency, is not a negotiable instrument generally or a bill or note within the meaning of the Bills of Exchange Act. A bitcoin, or a fraction thereof, is a digital unit that represents value and that is, in turn, represented by code. The code does not encrypt a promise to pay; it is the payment itself. It is not an order to pay (conditional or otherwise), it is not in writing, and it is not addressed to order or bearer. We do not get to the questions of negotiation or subsequent holders' rights; the original property—the bitcoin itself—is *not negotiable* as a threshold matter.

---

[149] FALCONBRIDGE, *supra* note 129, at 117.
[150] *Id.* at 118.
[151] Bills of Exchange Act § 47; FALCONBRIDGE, *supra* note 129, at 134.
[152] Bills of Exchange Act § 48.
[153] Miller v. Race, (1758), 1 Burr. 452, 97 Eng. Rep. 398 (K.B.) (U.K.).

The question then becomes whether an instrument denominated in bitcoin can be a bill or note. Recall the definition of bill from the above discussion: an unconditional order in writing, signed by the drawer, requiring the drawee to pay, on demand or at a fixed or determinable future date, a sum certain in money to order or bearer. The key components of this definition for bitcoin are whether it can be a sum certain in money.

As to a sum certain, the obligation to pay must be ascertainable on the face of the instrument. The general rule in Canada is that there must be certainty that is intrinsic to the bill itself, i.e., the sum must be stated on the face of the instrument or ascertainable from materials within the instrument.[154] This is not an absolute rule, however, and extrinsic circumstances may be referenced in the bill,[155] e.g., if it is impossible to implement a provision of the Bills of Exchange Act without having recourse to extrinsic evidence.[156] Much of the case law relating to "sum certain" concerns whether an instrument to pay the total proceeds of the sale of certain described goods is sufficiently certain, or whether such things as provisions for "costs" or "attorneys' fees" on confession of judgment are sufficiently certain to make an instrument negotiable.[157]

A sum certain is not necessarily undermined by volatility. Section 162 of the Bills of Exchange Act provides that a bill drawn outside of Canada but payable in Canada will, absent an express stipulation in the instrument, be calculated according to the exchange rate for sight drafts at the place of payment, i.e., to Canadian dollars at the time of satisfaction.[158] Any instability in the original currency does not render the sum uncertain, so the volatility of bitcoin or any other cryptocurrency should not interfere with the certainty of the amount of the obligation.

The problem, as in the case of the Currency Act, is with the instrument being denominated "in money" or, more accurately in the case of cryptocurrency, in something that is likely not money as a matter of law. Our discussion in the previous section demonstrates that legal money in Canada appears to comprise a medium of exchange that is either state-issued or universally accepted, or possibly both. John Falconbridge is more restrictive. He posits that a bill within the

---

[154] MacLeod Sav. & Credit Union Ltd. v. Perrett, [1981] 1 S.C.R. 78, 86 (Can.).
[155] *Id.* at 87.
[156] *Id.* at 86.
[157] CRAWFORD, *supra* note 105, at 1236–37.
[158] *Id.* at 1291–92; FALCONBRIDGE, *supra* note 129, at 27.

meaning of the Bills of Exchange Act must be payable in something that is legal tender in Canada.[159] We know that bitcoin and, indeed, any cryptocurrency, is none of these things. In our view, there is no indication from the published decisions that Canadian courts are currently ready to accept that a cryptocurrency is legal money for purposes of denominating a note or bill under the Bills of Exchange Act.

We view several possible workarounds as ineffective. What if an instrument drawn outside of Canada were to be denominated in bitcoin and then converted to Canadian dollars on payment in Canada? This would seem to satisfy section 162 of the Bills of Exchange Act; that provision does not refer to foreign currency. However, the money problem does not go away. The examples in the literature seem to exclusively contemplate foreign currency issued by a country.[160] This is a matter of first impression, but it appears that our courts would be unlikely to consider bitcoin on all fours with French francs or U.S. dollars, at least not without a foreign state adopting bitcoin as its own currency. Such a bill would also not address inland bills, i.e., bills that are drawn and payable within Canada or drawn within Canada on a person resident in Canada.[161]

Another approach is to denominate the instrument in a tokenized amount that is linked to a fiat currency, e.g., in Tethers[162] or, possibly, in BitUSD. Another example would be a digital asset whose value mirrors a state-issued currency unit for unit. But here again, Tether (or any token thus far) is not part of the state theory of money and is not universally accepted, so it would seem not to be money. Such a token might appear to be closer to a currency because it is tethered to it, but it is not the currency itself, so we expect that Tether, for example, would not make a bill or note negotiable.

Finally, the amount in the instrument could be fixed to Canadian dollars in the instrument itself. If the exchange rate is intrinsic to the instrument, this may work if the parties are *ad idem* on the exchange rate used, provided that the reference to Canadian dollars fulfils the role of money. But this would essentially be a Canadian dollar-denominated instrument, not a bitcoin-denominated instrument, which defeats the intention of the parties to transact in cryptocurrency. If an exchange rate were extrinsic to the instrument, then the same

---

[159] FALCONBRIDGE, *supra* note 129, at 27.
[160] *Id.; see also* CRAWFORD, *supra* note 105, at 1291–92.
[161] *See* Bills of Exchange Act, R.S.C. 1985, c. B-4, § 24(1) (Can.). All bills that are not inland bills are foreign bills. *Id.* § 24(2).
[162] *See* TETHER, www.tether.to (last visited Dec. 5, 214).

problem of "money" is present, i.e., cryptocurrency does not appear to be money. No workaround is immediately apparent to us, though we caution that these are matters that are only starting to be researched and questioned.

What this means for bitcoin is straightforward and striking, in our view: transactions in bitcoins may not extinguish prior claims. They might not be received with the same degree of certainty that prior claims on them are at an end or, at least, are narrowly circumscribed to real defences. These instruments, accordingly, appear to be subject to *nemo dat*. With bitcoin-denominated bills and notes, there apparently cannot be a negotiation or a holder in due course; a bitcoin-denominated instrument cannot be a bill or note in the first place, so the dispositive matter seems to be its lack of negotiability. This could exclude cryptocurrency from an important role and space in the financial sector. This background could also explain at least a part of the premium attributable to newly mined bitcoins. "Virgin" bitcoins have commanded a premium for some time in certain marketplaces.[163] This limitation of bitcoin in the existing legal structure and economy might explain why: there are no prior claims on the asset with which to contend.

Certain responses to these conclusions made by cryptocurrency enthusiasts are valid. There is privity of contract and a personal right of action as between contracting parties, irrespective of the position of a subsequent holder. Even without holder in due course status, the validity and enforceability of a properly drafted contractual instrument denominated in bitcoin should endure. There are examples of subsequent holders being protected from deficient rights. In Quebec, a holder of an instrument payable in bitcoin may still generally sue as the holder of a valid contractual instrument possessing it as an assignee.[164] However, in the case of assignment, a debtor may set up against the assignee any payment made to the assignor before the assignment as well as any other cause of extinction of the obligation.[165] As another example, in Quebec, if bitcoins (as movable property) are sold in the ordinary course of business to an unsuspecting purchaser, and if a prior party has rights to those bitcoins, the true owner must reimburse the innocent purchaser to the extent of the price that the

---

[163] Jon Matonis, *Bitcoins Affected by New York's BitLicense May Trade at Discount*, COINDESK (Jul. 30, 2014 13:47 GMT), http://www.coindesk.com/bitcoins-affected-new-yorks-bitlicense-may-trade-discount/.
[164] Civil Code of Quebec, S.Q. 1991, c. 64, §§ 1637, 1639 (Can.).
[165] *Id.* § 1643.

purchaser paid.[166] Also, under the Civil Code of Quebec, in a contract of sale the seller must generally warrant to the buyer that the property is free of all rights except those that she has declared at the time of the sale.[167] In the context of the Quebec Consumer Protection Act (the "QCPA"), a merchant transferring ownership of goods to a consumer through contract must either free those goods from all charges and encumbrances in favour of any third party, or declare their existence at the time of the sale.[168] In any sale of bitcoins in Quebec, for example, either or both of these statutes may place warranty or disclosure obligations on the bitcoin seller. Furthermore, consumers are vested with a high degree of autonomy and responsibility in the bitcoin world; perhaps the guilty party in *Miller v. Race*—the original possessor of the bank note that negotiated it to the plaintiff after stealing it from the mail—does not loom as large in the cryptocurrency space.

We do not believe that this is a complete response to the issues. Purchasers should understand the full suite of legal rights in the instrument or property that they are buying and in which they are transacting. If nothing else, these matters will start to come before the courts, so we must understand them and their implications. For now, we limit ourselves to relatively narrow items. Cryptocurrency-denominated instruments do not appear to qualify as negotiable instruments under federal legislation. We should not be taken as saying that this is a failure of any cryptocurrency, or that bitcoin, as an example, is bound to fail, in Canada or elsewhere. Although it may result in some market exclusions, cryptocurrencies may yet generate their own solutions and grow to become more powerful tools in international finance and trade.

4. Cryptocurrency in Commerce & Consumer Protection

Consumers transacting in cryptocurrencies in Canada may currently take advantage of many of the protections afforded to them under (mostly) provincial law. Some have suggested that bitcoin offers consumers no protection. This is false. The relevant question for policy makers is not so much whether consumers need some protection and recourse in bitcoin transactions—from none—but whether they need more protection and recourse than they already have.

---

[166] *Id.* § 1714.
[167] *Id.* § 1723.
[168] Consumer Protection Act, C.Q.L.R. 1978, c. P-40.1, § 36 (Can.).

In Ontario, consumers' rights are set out in the province's Consumer Protection Act, 2002[169] (the "**OCPA**"), among other statutes.[170] The OCPA sets out consumer and merchant rights and obligations generally and with reference to certain specific types of consumer agreements. The OCPA applies to all consumer transactions if the consumer or the merchant is in Ontario when the transaction takes place.[171] Importantly, the OCPA is a floor for consumers, not a ceiling. Nothing in the legislation limits—or is to be interpreted as limiting—any right or remedy that a consumer may have at common law (e.g., as a remedy under a contract) or through the application of another statute.[172]

The OCPA is applicable to a wide variety of consumer interactions and parties to a consumer transaction[173] may not contract out of key provisions of the OCPA. Any term or acknowledgement, whether part of the consumer agreement or not, that negates or varies any deemed condition or warranty under the OCPA is void.[174] Any ambiguity allowing for more than one reasonable interpretation of a consumer agreement provided to the consumer or of any information that must be disclosed under the OCPA is to be interpreted to the benefit of the consumer.[175]

To take just one example, Ontario law has specific provisions that apply to Internet agreements. These provisions generally apply where the customer's total payment obligation under the agreement of purchase exceeds C$50.00.[176] "Payment" is defined in section 1 of the OCPA; it means "consideration of any kind, including an initiation fee." This broad language certainly includes bitcoin and other convertible cryptocurrencies, whether defined as barter or otherwise. Accordingly, where there is a payment obligation in bitcoin greater

---

[169] S.O. 2002, c. 30 (Can.).

[170] The rights of consumers are also protected under such legislation as the Collection Agencies Act, R.S.O. 1990, c. C.14 (Can.) and the Payday Loans Act, 2008, S.O. 2008, c. 9 (Can.), but the focus here will be on the OCPA as it covers many common consumer transactions. Ontario's Sale of Goods Act, R.S.O. 1990, c. S.1 (Can.) will be discussed below.

[171] OCPA § 2(1).

[172] *Id.* § 6.

[173] Consumer transaction means any instance of conducting business or other dealings with a consumer, including a consumer agreement. *Id.* § 1 (definition of "consumer transaction"). A consumer agreement means "an agreement between a supplier and a consumer in which the supplier agrees to supply goods or services for payment." *Id.* § 1 (definition of "consumer agreement").

[174] *Id.* § 9(3). The same provision voids any term that tries to negate any implied condition or warranty under the Sale of Goods Act.

[175] *Id.* § 11.

[176] *Id.* § 37; Ontario Reg. 17/05 (Consumer Protection Act, 2002) (Can.).

than C$50.00 in an Internet agreement, the full panoply of OCPA protections would seem to be available to the consumer.

Before a consumer enters into an Internet agreement, the supplier must disclose the following to the consumer pursuant to subsection 38(1) of the OCPA and the regulations thereto:

1. the name of the supplier and, if different, the name under which the supplier carries on business;
2. the telephone number of the supplier, the address of the premises from which the supplier conducts business, and information respecting other ways, if any, in which the supplier can be contacted by the consumer, such as the fax number and electronic mail address of the supplier;
3. a fair and accurate description of the goods and services proposed to be supplied to the consumer, including the technical requirements, if any, related to the use of the goods or services;
4. an itemized list of the prices at which the goods are proposed to be supplied to the consumer, including taxes and shipping charges;
5. a description of each additional charge that applies or may apply, such as customs duties or brokerage fees, and the amount of the charge if the supplier can reasonably determine it;
6. the total amount that the supplier knows is payable by the consumer under the agreement, including amounts that are required to be disclosed under paragraph 5, above;
7. the terms and methods of payment;
8. as applicable, the date or dates on which delivery, commencement of performance, ongoing performance and completion of performance will occur;
9. for goods and services that are to be delivered,
    i) the place to which they will be delivered, and
    ii) if the supplier holds out a specific manner of delivery and intends to charge the consumer for delivery, the manner in which the goods and services will be delivered, including the name of the carrier, if any, and including the method of transportation to be used;
10. for services to be performed, the place where they are to be performed, the person for whom they are to be performed, the supplier's method of performance and, if the supplier holds out that a specific person will perform any of the services, that person's name;

11. the rights, if any, that the supplier agrees the consumer will have in addition to the rights under the OCPA and the obligations, if any, by which the supplier agrees to be bound in addition to the obligations under the OCPA, in relation to cancellations, returns, exchanges, and refunds;
12. the currency in which amounts are expressed, if it is not Canadian currency;[177] and,
13. any other restrictions, limitations and conditions that would be imposed by the supplier.[178]

A supplier must provide the consumer with an express opportunity to accept or decline the agreement and to correct errors before the consumer enters into it.[179] Any disclosures required of the supplier (including those pursuant to subsection 38(1) of the OCPA, noted above) must be clear, comprehensible, and prominent[180] and disclosure must be available in a manner that ensures that the consumer has accessed the information[181] and that the consumer is able to retain and print the information.[182]

The supplier must deliver a written copy of the Internet agreement to the consumer within fifteen days of the formation of the agreement.[183] The copy of the Internet agreement must include all of the information enumerated in subsection 38(1) of the OCPA noted above, the name of the consumer, and the date upon which the agreement was entered into.[184] The supplier is considered to have delivered a written copy of the agreement if a copy is sent by electronic mail, by fax, or by regular mail.[185]

---

[177] Note that "currency" does not likely include bitcoin or other cryptocurrencies. See section 2.1, above. Merchants are well-advised to express the equivalent amount of bitcoin prices in fiat currencies.
[178] OCPA § 38(1); Ontario Reg. § 32.
[179] OCPA § 38(2).
[180] Id. § 5(1).
[181] Id. § 38(3)(a).
[182] Id. § 38(3)(b).
[183] Id. § 39(1); Ontario Reg. 17/05 § 33(1).
[184] OCPA § 39(2); Ontario Reg. 17/05 § 33(2).
[185] OCPA § 39(3); Ontario Reg. 17/05 § 33(3). For example, meeting the terms of paragraph 33(3)(1) of the regulations qualifies for the deemed supply of the agreement in subsection 39(3) of the OCPA: "Transmitting it in a manner that ensures that the consumer is able to retain, print and access it for future reference, such as sending it by e-mail to an e-mail address that the consumer has given the supplier for providing information related to the agreement."

A consumer may cancel an Internet agreement within seven days of entering into it if the supplier does not: disclose the information required in subsection 38(1) of the OCPA, (see above);[186] or, provide the consumer with an express opportunity to accept or decline the agreement or to correct errors immediately before entering into it.[187] A consumer may cancel an Internet agreement within thirty days of entering into the agreement if the supplier is non-compliant with any requirement under section 39, i.e., not delivering a copy of the agreement with the prescribed information within fifteen days of the agreement being entered into, or not delivering a copy of the agreement by one of the methods outlined in the OCPA Regulations.[188]

Furthermore, where an Internet agreement deals with the sale and delivery of goods, the implied conditions and warranties set out under the Sale of Goods Act generally apply, with certain exceptions, to the Internet agreement.[189] The implied conditions of sale under the Sale of Goods Act are: the seller has the right to sell the goods;[190] the goods sold will correspond with their description;[191] the goods are fit for their purpose, where the purpose is made known;[192] and, the goods are of merchantable quality.[193] In addition, two implied warranties apply unless the contract demonstrates a different intention: the buyer will have and enjoy quiet possession of the goods;[194] and, the goods are free from undeclared or undisclosed encumbrances.[195]

Part IX of the OCPA contains procedures for legal enforcement of consumer remedies under the legislation, including private rights of action and the right to request charge-backs from credit card issuers.

Quebec consumers are protected through the mutually reinforcing provisions of the Civil Code of Quebec and the QCPA. The Civil Code is the legislative backbone for consumer protection law in Quebec. Article 1384 of the Civil Code references consumer contracts and sets

---

[186] OCPA § 40(1)(a).
[187] Id. § 40(1)(b).
[188] Id. § 40(2).
[189] Id. § 9(2).
[190] Sale of Goods Act, R.S.O. 1990, c. S.1, § 13(a) (Can.).
[191] Id. § 14.
[192] Id. § 15(1).
[193] Id. § 15(2).
[194] Id. § 13(b).
[195] Id. § 13(c).

out that their scope is delimited by the QCPA.[196] Thus, some of the provisions of the Civil Code are particularly relevant for consumer transactions and merit review. A sale of a good to a consumer where the merchant accepts bitcoin would likely be subject to the section on sale in the Civil Code. Even if payment in bitcoins would not be treated as payment in money, the provisions on sale in the Civil Code apply to contracts for exchange, *mutatis mutandis*.[197] This means, among other things, that the seller is bound to deliver the goods purchased[198] and warrant as to their quality[199] and, where there has been a default by the seller, the prejudiced buyer is entitled to cancel the sale and have his bitcoin payment(s) refunded.[200]

The QCPA has broad application to every contract for goods and services entered into between a consumer and merchant in the course of business.[201] The QCPA applies to all consumer contracts concluded—or presumed to be concluded—in Quebec and that are governed by Quebec law as determined by the provisions on private international law in the Civil Code.[202] We believe that the QCPA also applies to contracts where bitcoin is tendered as payment, not just money or legal tender. (The QCPA does not stipulate that consideration for goods and services must be in legal tender or money.) Similar to the OCPA in Ontario, the QCPA also contains an express provision that any ambiguity or doubt in a contract must be resolved in the consumer's favour.[203]

Like the OCPA, the QCPA contains provisions out of which the parties may not contract. A merchant cannot limit the consequences associated with his own actions or those of his representatives, so, for example, a professional merchant cannot limit his liability, even if the

---

[196] Sylvie A. Bourassa, Consumer Protection Act and Regulation Respecting its Application vii (Yvon Blais 2014). See generally Civil Code of Quebec, S.Q. 1991, c. 64, §§ 1371–1456 (general provisions on obligations), §§ 1708–1805 (chapters on sale), §§ 2098–2129 (contracts of enterprise or for services in book five (Obligations)) (Can.).
[197] Civil Code of Quebec § 1798.
[198] Id. § 1716.
[199] Id. § 1716, 1726.
[200] Id. §§ 1604–1606, 1736.
[201] QCPA, C.Q.L.R. 1978, c. P-40.1, § 2 (Can.).
[202] Gérald Goldstein, *La protection du consommateur: nouvelles perspectives de droit international privé dans le Code civil du Québec*, in Barreau du Québec—Développements récents en droit de la consommation 1994 143 (Yvon Blais 1994); Nicole L'Heureux & Marc Lacoursière, Droit de la consommation 16 (6th ed. Yvon Blais 2011).
[203] QCPA § 17.

consumer agrees, for harm suffered by the consumer because of the merchant's fault.[204] Also like the OCPA, legal warranties are imposed on a sale of goods or contracts of service, whether they are express or not. One example is the warranty related to title referenced above. In addition, goods must be fit for the purposes for which those goods are ordinarily used,[205] must conform to their description in the contract of sale,[206] and must be durable in normal use for a reasonable time.[207] As in Ontario, the Quebec protections are a minimum, not a maximum; the law does not prevent the merchant or manufacturer from offering a more advantageous warranty to the consumer.[208]

With respect to advertising, merchants must also respect stringent rules. False or misleading representations to consumers by merchants, manufacturers, and advertisers are prohibited.[209] Any statements or advertisements made by a merchant or manufacturer are binding on the party making them.[210] Accordingly, a bitcoin ATM or exchange is prohibited, for example, from claiming to charge a 5% fee on a transaction but actually charging a 10% fee. Furthermore, the merchant would be left with the 5% fee, as advertised.

Quebec merchants have general duties to inform consumers, which can be important when addressing a novel technology and often misunderstood digital asset such as bitcoin. Where there is a lack of instructions given that are necessary for the protection of the consumer against risk or danger of which the consumer would otherwise be unaware, the consumer is entitled to take legal action directly against the merchant or the manufacturer.[211] This is particularly relevant in the bitcoin space. Suppose that many bitcoin users are unfamiliar with basic precautions that need to be taken to achieve a minimum level of security for their private key(s). In this context, a seller of bitcoins in the ordinary course of business (for example, an owner or operator of a bitcoin ATM) may have disclosure obligations to consumers with which it transacts. The merchant cannot defend itself by relying on the fact that it was unaware of the lack of instructions given. Making sure that customers are aware of the risks associated with wallet security and bitcoin price volatility, and are properly instructed on

---

[204] *Id.* § 10.
[205] *Id.* § 37.
[206] *Id.* § 40.
[207] *Id.* § 38.
[208] *Id.* § 35.
[209] *Id.* § 219.
[210] *Id.* § 41.
[211] *Id.* § 53.

using the ATM, are all potential obligations that are in play. Note that the same obligations apply to online sellers. Here again, fees charged for services—such as, potentially, access to an ATM, or fees on an exchange service—cannot be false or misleading and must be precisely indicated to the consumer.[212]

Under Quebec law, merchants also have obligations in consumer contracts entered into online. A distance contract is deemed to be entered into at the address of the consumer.[213] Accordingly, any contract transacted online with a consumer domiciled in Quebec is subject to Quebec law. The QCPA provides that, for distance contracts, which includes Internet commerce, a merchant may not collect or offer to collect a partial or full payment from the consumer before performing his principal obligations unless the consumer can request a chargeback of the payment under the QCPA or a regulation.[214] Whether or not chargebacks are possible, the merchant must refund all sums paid by the consumer within fifteen days of the cancellation of the contract.[215] If the consumer paid with a credit card, then the consumer has sixty days following the merchant's default in tendering a refund to request a chargeback from the card issuers. The QCPA provides for how the consumer must go about requesting a chargeback.[216] It appears at this time that the Quebec statute only provides for chargebacks where credit cards are used. Interestingly, this may mean that if a merchant wishes to sell products online to Quebec consumers and receive bitcoins as payment, the merchant will need to fulfill his end of the bargain before the consumer is required to pay. Note that the OCPA also has a provision for requesting refunds by means of a chargeback when credit cards are used.[217]

These are examples of some baseline protections that are available to consumers as a matter of law, whether they pay for goods and services in bitcoin, other cryptocurrencies, or with some other payment medium. However, the more effective protections for consumers may come from the Bitcoin protocol itself.

---

[212] *Id.* § 12. Note that the Supreme Court of Canada recently confirmed that the duty to disclose fees to consumers pursuant to provincial law applies to banks and credit card companies charging fees for currency conversion: Bank of Montreal v. Marcotte, 2014 SCC 55 (Can.); Amex Bank of Canada v. Adams, 2014 SCC 56 (Can.).
[213] QCPA § 54.2.
[214] *Id.* § 54.3.
[215] *Id.* § 54.13.
[216] *Id.* §§ 54.14–54.15.
[217] OCPA, S.O. 2002, c. 30, § 99 (Can.).

Consider an example of payment for goods ordered online using bitcoin. If A orders goods from B over the Internet and pays with bitcoin, A uses her private key to sign a message containing instructions to forward the requisite amount of bitcoins to B in consideration for the goods. But what if B does not send the goods once bitcoins are received through her public key? The irreversibility of bitcoin transactions—in our example, without B's private key—is attractive to merchant B, but does not particularly assist A, our consumer.

One solution is the use of multi-signature bitcoin addresses.[218] These require multiple permissions (signatures) to transmit funds from a bitcoin wallet. In our example, say that A and B each provide their public keys to an escrow service. The escrow agent then uses its own key to generate a unique bitcoin address to which A can send payment. Transfer of payment from that address requires two out of three of A, B, and the escrow agent. Once goods are shipped, B can be confident that A cannot unilaterally take back the bitcoin from escrow, which protects B. B also cannot unilaterally take the bitcoin from escrow, which protects A. Once A receives the goods, A and B can both jointly release funds from escrow or the escrow agent can arbitrate any dispute.

Any solution involving escrow and counterparties would need to recognize fees and costs incurred through their use. One of the great characteristics of Bitcoin is its low transaction costs. Care should be taken to properly and transparently account for any erosion of this benefit through intermediary agents and services.

It is clear that certain of the consumer protections in place when using a credit card, for example, are not present in a bitcoin environment. A consumer using a credit card, whether online or in a bricks and mortar setting, can generally contact the card issuer immediately in case of merchant fraud and simply reverse the transaction. This centralization is anathema to bitcoin, although multi-signature escrow services, discussed above, are possible and can benefit both consumers and merchants. On this point, we can make at least four short observations. First, the weight of protection afforded by credit cards may have simply shifted from merchant to consumer. That might be a good thing from the perspective of the

---

[218] *See, e.g.*, Vitalik Buterin, *Multisig: The Future of Bitcoin,* BITCOIN MAGAZINE, Mar. 12, 2014, http://bitcoinmagazine.com/11108/multisig-future-bitcoin/; John Villasenor, *Could 'Multisig' Help Bring Consumer Protection to Bitcoin Transactions?*, FORBES, Mar. 28, 2014, *available at* http://www.forbes.com/sites/johnvillasenor/2014/03/28/could-multisig-help-bring-consumer-protection-to-bitcoin-transactions/.

consumer, but not the merchant. (It should be noted that credit card issuers can act as arbitrators in disputes, so should not necessarily be perceived as favouring consumers over merchants.) Second, in the words of one commentator, the bitcoin industry is still nascent,[219] quite unlike the credit card industry, and it may not be reasonable to draw direct comparisons between the two. The bitcoin sector may simply require more time to build its own solutions on a legislative baseline. Third, bitcoin transactions introduce further consumer choice into the marketplace. Credit card companies charge fees for their services, and those fees are important. They pay for things like insurance. Consumers may be able to choose between a good or service to be paid for in bitcoin, at lower cost, and without insurance, and the same commodity paid for by means of credit card at higher cost and with insurance protections.[220] Finally, the flipside of credit card protection is the fact that one is putting one's credit card number out into the marketplace, which can increase identity theft and fraud. One's private key in a bitcoin wallet is, or is supposed to be, highly private. In this sense, use of credit cards can actually decrease consumer protection, especially as regards protecting privacy and preventing identity theft, when compared to bitcoin.[221]

Finally, in 2014 the Financial Consumer Agency of Canada (the FCAC) issued a fact sheet on cryptocurrencies.[222] The FCAC is an agency of the federal government that, inter alia, supervises federally regulated financial institutions, with a particular focus on consumer protection. The fact sheet confirmed that cryptocurrency is not legal tender and claimed that there is no regulatory oversight of them in

---

[219] *Beyond Silk Road: Potential Risks, Threats, and Promises of Virtual Currencies: Hearing before the S. Comm. on Homeland Security & Governmental Affairs*, 113th Cong. (2013) (statement of Jerry Brito, Senior Research Fellow, The Mercatus Center, George Mason University), *available at* http://www.hsgac.senate.gov/hearings/beyond-silk-road-potential-risks-threats-and-promises-of-virtual-currencies.

[220] *Id.*

[221] *Study on the Use of Digital Currency Before the Standing Senate Committee on Banking, Trade and Commerce*, Issue 13, 41st Parl., 2nd Sess. (2014) (statement of Tim Byun, Chief Compliance Officer, Bitpay) (Can.), *available at* http://www.parl.gc.ca/content/sen/committee/412/BANC/13EV-51527-E.HTM; *Beyond Silk Road: Potential Risks, Threats, and Promises of Virtual Currencies: Hearing before the S. Comm. on Homeland Security & Governmental Affairs*, 113th Cong. (2013) (statement of Jeremy Allaire, Chief Executive Officer, Circle Internet Financial, Inc.), *available at* http://www.hsgac.senate.gov/hearings/beyond-silk-road-potential-risks-threats-and-promises-of-virtual-currencies.

[222] Financial Consumer Agency of Canada, *Virtual currencie*s (Apr. 1, 2014), *available at* http://www.fcac-acfc.gc.ca/Eng/forConsumers/topics/paymentOptions/Pages/Virtualc-Monnaies.aspx.

Canada. Canadian financial institutions, it went on, such as banks or credit unions, "are not involved" in virtual currency transactions or oversight, though it is unclear exactly what this means.[223] The communication warns that virtual currencies are not covered by deposit insurance and provide limited recourse if, for example, one does not receive the goods one purchased with them—but see the multi-signature discussion, above—or if the exchange holding one's funds fails. The fact sheet does offer useful guidance about how to protect oneself in the bitcoin space, including waiting for multiple confirmations on the block chain and keeping one's bitcoin wallet in cold (offline) storage.[224]

Whether consumers need or want more protection in the stream of commerce is open to debate. However, an informed discussion should acknowledge the remedies that consumers already have available to them as a matter of law and how the Bitcoin technology itself might be used to augment their protection.

5. Cryptocurrency & Securities Law

In this section, we will review the general outline of the securities framework in Canada, both in terms of constitutional authority and the provinces' protection of the public interest through sundry registration and disclosure requirements. We will also examine bitcoin itself through the prism of "security" in different provincial securities laws. While we find it hard to conclude that bitcoins can be securities in and of themselves in most settings, it seems clear that bitcoins can be used to denominate securities and can be otherwise aggregated and deployed as securities by different parties (e.g., issuers and dealers).

5.1. Institutional Background & Policy

In Canada, the provinces are the primary authorities regulating the securities markets. Securities laws are clearly *intra vires* the provinces pursuant to their power to regulate property and civil rights in the provinces.[225] To some extent, securities law is an area of concurrent jurisdiction as between Parliament and the provincial

---

[223] *Id.*
[224] *Id.*
[225] Reference re: Securities Act, [2011] 3 S.C.R. 837 (Can.); Multiple Access Ltd. v. McCutcheon, [1982] 2 S.C.R. 161 (Can.).

governments,[226] so the federal government also has a role to play in regulating securities markets. For example, the Canada Business Corporations Act[227] regulates federally incorporated companies and the Criminal Code prohibits misrepresentation and fraud. While certain aspects of securities legislation are similar across the various provinces, issuers of securities regularly must still deal with up to thirteen different regulators in Canada.[228] In addition to hosting Canada's largest capital market, Ontario also has one of the most stringent and sophisticated securities regulatory regimes in the country. While securities laws in other provinces are similar to Ontario's, care should always be taken with Quebec as it has different procedural and substantive requirements.[229] Canada also has important self-regulatory organizations, such as the Investment Industry Regulatory Organization of Canada.[230]

The purpose of securities legislation in Canada is the protection of the public by means of "full, true and plain disclosure of all material facts relating to securities being issued."[231] Securities laws are founded on the need to protect investors from fraudulent and unfair practices and the desire to create fair and efficient capital markets in which the investing public has confidence.[232] Each province has a legislative and regulatory structure charged with protecting the public through enforcing the provincial securities laws. In Ontario, for example, the Securities Act has two broad purposes: protecting investors from unfair, improper, or fraudulent practices; and, fostering fair and efficient capital markets and confidence in the capital markets.[233]

Very generally, securities laws and regulators in Canada meet these objectives through registration and disclosure requirements, including prospectus requirements. Provincial laws typically provide that any person trading in securities in Canada as principal or agent (a "dealer") or advising Canadian residents on the buying or selling of securities (an "adviser") must be registered with the securities

---

[226] *Multiple Access* [1982] 2 S.C.R. 161 (Can.).
[227] R.S.C. 1985, c. C-44 (Can.).
[228] INTERNATIONAL SECURITIES LAW HANDBOOK 116 (Marcus Best & Jean-Luc Soulier eds., Wolters Kluwer, 3d ed. 2010).
[229] *Id.* at 116.
[230] *Id.* at 113.
[231] Pac. Coast Coin Exch. of Canada Limited. v. Ontario Sec Comm'n, [1978] 2 S.C.R. 112, 126 (Can.) (quoting Re Ontario Sec. Comm'n & Brigadoon Scotch Distribs. (Canada) Ltd., [1970] 3 O.R. 714, 717 (Can.)).
[232] VAUGHN MACLELLAN, HALSBURY'S LAWS OF CANADA—SECURITIES, §HSC-2 (LexisNexis 2013).
[233] Ontario Securities Act, R.S.O. 1990, c. S.5, §1.1 (Can.).

authorities. Many provinces also require registration of any person purchasing securities as principal or agent for purposes of resale (called "underwriters").[234] For example, various categories of dealers that are firms—investment dealers, mutual fund dealers, exempt market dealers, etc.—are generally required to be registered pursuant to National Instrument 31-103.[235] In the Ontario Securities Act, each of the terms dealer, underwriter, and adviser is defined and subject to registration requirements pursuant to section 25 of the legislation, unless an exemption applies (e.g., as to dealers and underwriters, an exemption based on trading in debt securities issued by the federal or a provincial government[236]). Investment fund managers must also generally be registered.[237] Quebec contains similarly broad registration[238] and prospectus requirements.[239] As to disclosure, in Ontario, trading in a security on one's own account or as an agent, when that trading would qualify as an issuance of a new security, for example, requires a prospectus.[240]

Cryptocurrency, and specifically bitcoin, must be measured against this framework in at least two respects. First, does cryptocurrency itself constitute a security subject to the general registration regime and disclosure rules? We believe the answer to this question is no. Second, can cryptocurrency be used as the unit of account underlying some part of the securities transaction, whether it be consideration for issuance or the enterprise of the issuer? This question can likely be answered in the affirmative, and this kind of investment product packaging has been the source of queries, reviews, and actions taken to date by sundry securities regulators in Canada.

---

[234] INTERNATIONAL SECURITIES LAW HANDBOOK, *supra* note 228, at 116.
[235] National Instrument 31-103, *Registration Requirements, Exemptions and Ongoing Registrant Obligations* (NI 31-103 July 2009), § 7.1.
[236] Ontario Securities Act § 35(1).
[237] *Id.* § 25(4).
[238] Quebec Securities Act, C.Q.L.R. 2013, c. V-1.1, § 148 (Can.).
[239] *Id.* § 11.
[240] Ontario Securities Act § 53(1). Note that exempt market dealers may be exempt from the prospectus requirements when acting as underwriters in respect of a distribution of securities. *Id.* § 26(4). Certain nuances of the applications to and exemptions from the registration and prospectus requirements are beyond the scope of this chapter, and it should be remembered that we are dealing here in general securities rules.

2.2. Is Bitcoin a Security?

We turn first to the question: is bitcoin a security in and of itself? Much turns on the answer. If the answer is yes, save an applicable exemption, bitcoin dealers in Ontario, whether acting as principals or agents, must be registered, for example, under subsection 25(1) of the Ontario Securities Act. Advisers on purchasing or selling bitcoins would also need to be registered under subsection 25(3), again barring an exemption.

To address this issue, the starting point is the definition of "security." In the Ontario legislation, security includes a document constituting evidence of title to or an interest in the capital, assets, property, profits, earnings, or royalties of any person or company;[241] an investment contract;[242] and, "any document, instrument or writing commonly known as a security."[243] The Quebec Securities Act is similarly broad, providing that the statute's provisions apply to, inter alia, an investment contract[244] as well as "any security recognized as such in the trade, more particularly, a share, bond, capital stock of an entity constituted as a legal person, or a subscription right or warrant."[245] Note that the definition of security in both Quebec and Ontario is broad and clearly inclusive. The types of securities listed are merely examples in a non-exhaustive list. In the formulation of the Supreme Court, quoting Professor Louis Loss, the various categories are not mutually exclusive and are meant to be "catchalls."[246] The Ontario Securities Act is to be "construed broadly, and it must be read in the context of the economic realities to which it is addressed."[247] In addition, and in an approach very different than the one our courts take to negotiable instruments, substance triumphs over form.[248]

Even in the context of such a purposive approach, we believe that bitcoins are not evidence of title to or an interest in the capital or other economic value of any person or company. Bitcoins as currency are not issued by any person or company but through the running of open source software that rewards computers with bitcoins for contributing

---

[241] *Id.* § 1(1)(b) (definition of "security").
[242] *Id.* § 1(1)(n) (definition of "security").
[243] *Id.* § 1(1)(a) (definition of "security").
[244] Quebec Securities Act § 1(7).
[245] *Id.* § 1(1).
[246] Pac. Coast Coin Exch. of Canada Limited. v. Ontario Sec Comm'n, [1978] 2 S.C.R. 112, 127 (Can.).
[247] *Id.*
[248] *Id.*

computing power to supporting and securing the network, a crucial task needed to enable and verify transactions. As was pointed out in an early law review article about bitcoin by Reuben Grinberg, bitcoin itself is not a stock because it lacks important characteristics of shares of capital stock, e.g., the right to receive dividends contingent on profits and voting rights in proportion to the number of shares owned.[249] Furthermore, we expect that bitcoins are neither "commonly known as a security" nor "recognized as such in the trade" of securities. These are matters of first impression and discussions about bitcoin's taxonomy—whether it is a security per se or better classified as a commodity or some other form of asset—are still in their infancy. It can hardly be said that bitcoin is commonly known as a security or that it is recognized as such in any trade, let alone the securities trade.

The term "investment contract," however, is ripe for further discussion under both the Quebec and Ontario statutes. It is possible to see how one may contemplate the purchase, ownership, and sale of bitcoins as a form of investment contract. As Grinberg puts it, "[i]f a bitcoin is a security, it will be because it falls within the vague and broad phrase 'investment contract.'"[250] The term "investment contract" in the Ontario Securities Act was considered in *Pacific Coin*. (*Pacific Coin* has also been applied in securities decisions by the Quebec courts.[251]) In *Pacific Coin*, the Supreme Court looked to both the common enterprise test set out in *SEC v. W.J. Howey Co.*[252] and the risk capital test applied in *State v. Hawaii Market Center, Inc.*,[253] both U.S. decisions. The common enterprise test, as modified and applied in *Pacific Coin*, asks if there is an investment of money in a common enterprise, with the expectation of profits from the undeniably significant efforts of those other than the investors, including "essential managerial efforts."[254] By contrast, the risk capital test states that an investment contract is created whenever:

---

[249] Reuben Grinberg, *Bitcoin: An Innovative Alternative Digital Currency*, 4 Hastings Sci. & Tech. L.J. 159, 195 (2012).
[250] *Id.* at 196.
[251] *See, e.g.*, Québec (Commission des valeurs mobilières) c. Infotique Tyra Inc., [1994] J.Q. No. 651 (Can. Que. C.A.) (QL).
[252] 328 U.S. 293 (1946).
[253] 485 P. 2d 105 (Haw. 1971). The United States can provide valuable guidance to interpreting securities statutes in Canada owing to the use of similar terms (e.g., "investment contract") and the same policy considerations in securities law in both countries. *Pacific Coin*, [1978] 2 S.C.R. at 126.
[254] *Id.* at 128–29.

1. an offeree furnishes initial value to an offeror;
2. a portion of the initial value is subjected to the risks of the enterprise;
3. the contribution of value is based on an inducement giving rise to a reasonable understanding that a valuable benefit will accrue to the offeree over and above the initial investment; and,
4. the offeree does not exercise practical and actual control over the enterprise's managerial decisions.[255]

The definition in the Quebec Securities Act is broadly similar to the risk capital test: "An investment contract is a contract whereby a person, having been led to expect profits, undertakes to participate in the risk of a venture by a contribution of capital or loan, without having the required knowledge to carry on the venture or without obtaining the right to participate directly in decisions concerning the carrying on of the venture."[256] We shall look briefly at each of these definitions.

As to the common enterprise test and certain elements of the Quebec definition, several prongs could sway us towards characterizing bitcoin as a security. While miners can devote hardware, time, and energy to mining bitcoins, many do use money to buy bitcoins on exchanges or elsewhere.[257] Thus, they are contributing capital or investing money. It is also at least possible that many bitcoin purchasers and holders expect to profit from their holdings.[258] They may also meet the Quebec investment contract requirement in that the purchaser of bitcoin is participating in a risk, i.e., that the value of the digital asset will decline. This is not unlikely given bitcoin's volatility. Grinberg calls the "efforts of others" question a close one: on one hand, bitcoin holders may be seen as relying for profit on the activities of developers and businesses in the bitcoin economy. On the other hand, bitcoins are valuable because they are scarce and useful. They do not rely on developers or any other identifiable group for their value.[259] Furthermore, one might characterize a holder, by virtue of her status as a holder, as free to participate in building the bitcoin ecosystem.

It is on the question of common enterprise that bitcoin likely fails to be an investment contract and, therefore, a security. One may

---

[255] Pac. Coast Coin Exch. of Canada Limited. v. Ontario Sec Comm'n, [1975] O.J. No. 2281, ¶ 11 (Can. Ont. C.A.) (QL), aff'd, *Pacific Coin*, [1978] 2 S.C.R. 112.
[256] Quebec Securities Act, C.Q.L.R. 2013, c. V-1.1, § 1 (Can.).
[257] Grinberg, *supra* note 249, at 196–97.
[258] *Id.* at 198.
[259] *Id.* at 198–99.

argue that there is "horizontal commonality" among bitcoiners,[260] i.e., that their contributions are pooled and the success of each 'investor' depends on the success of the overall venture.[261] In *Pacific Coin*, the Supreme Court suggested some common interest as between the investor and the promoter; the enterprise is "common" when it benefits both.[262] However, this definition seems to founder on its uniformity requirement; it is by no means clear that every bitcoin owner's—or even most bitcoin owners'—success or failure is tied to the success or failure of bitcoin as a whole. As Grinberg points out, the individuals choosing to support bitcoin are independent of one another and there is fundamentally no money-making business that seeks to raise money through 'investment' in bitcoin itself.[263] Accordingly, there appears to be no uniformity of purpose or action, and thus no common enterprise.

Bitcoin itself does not appear to be an investment contract under the risk capital test or Quebec tests, either. First, the references to "enterprise" and "venture" in those conceptions may be telling, as they appear to suggest some organized or coherent undertaking, which bitcoin seems to lack. Second, from where does the necessary inducement come? Remember that a "common enterprise" may be one undertaken for the benefit of investors and of the promoter that solicits capital. Furthermore, can such an inducement give rise to a reasonable understanding that a valuable benefit will accrue? Certainly there are bitcoin enthusiasts attempting to induce people to hold and use bitcoin. Is there proximate cause between those inducements and new adopters? We believe the answer is no. The relationships between a limited class of enthusiasts and adopters and between holding bitcoin and profit seem too tenuous. As to Quebec, the Court of Appeal appears to see an investment contract as necessarily including significant centralization and efforts on behalf of management to do various things for the venture.[264] The lack of human organization and leadership and of common enterprise, and Bitcoin's essential qualities as software and a network, make it challenging to fit it into the investment contract paradigm under any of these tests.

---

[260] *Id.* at 197.
[261] For competing interpretations of "common enterprise" in the United States, see, for example, James D. Gordon III, *Defining a Common Enterprise in Investment Contracts*, 72 Ohio St. L.J. 59, 66–70 (2011).
[262] *Pacific Coin*, [1978] 2 S.C.R. 112, 129.
[263] Grinberg, *supra* note 249, at 197.
[264] *Infotique Tyra*, [1994] J.Q. No. 651, ¶ 53.

5.3. Bitcoin-Denominated Instruments as Securities

If bitcoin itself appears not to be a security, it also appears that bitcoin can be an instrumentality through which a security is created. Such a security would doubtless be subject to the Canadian securities regime where there is sufficient nexus to Canada. Consider an issuer that wishes to make shares of its capital stock available to the retail public in exchange for bitcoin consideration or investment. Or consider an entity that operates a website advertising various investment funds, whether denominated in bitcoin or accepting bitcoin for issuances or on a secondary market. Another example might include an investment fund whose assets include bitcoins and other cryptocurrencies being bought and sold based on market expertise. In an excellent forthcoming law review paper, Jerry Brito, Houman Shadab, and Andrea Castillo set out several instances of securities products in the bitcoin space, including the Winkelvoss Capital exchange traded fund.[265] While Canadian securities regulators have not set out general rules addressing these scenarios, the breadth of the definition of security combined with the objective of public protection suggests that these examples would be transactions in securities; with a coherent organization behind it, there seems to be little of the ambiguity involved in the prior investment contract discussion as it relates to bitcoin alone.

In fact, several securities regulators have already been active in this space. In January 2014, the Ontario Securities Commission (the "OSC") selected a corporation with offices in Ontario for an issue oriented review of the corporation's continuous disclosure record pursuant to section 20.1 of the Ontario Securities Act. The corporation had conducted a public roadshow and issued press releases about a number of initiatives involving cryptocurrency. One such venture had a proposed settlement of a private placement to be received exclusively in bitcoins. Another proposed two new corporations to be created to invest in bitcoin and in early stage bitcoin and other cryptocurrency companies.

The review by the OSC touched on many areas of modern securities law: marketing of the private placement, disclosure of risks during the roadshow, whether certain disclosures amounted to material changes, accounting under International Financial Reporting Standards, and the corporate structure of the business. Following what the corporation called "discussions" with the OSC, it abruptly

---

[265] Jerry Brito et al., *Bitcoin Financial Regulation: Securities, Derivatives, Prediction Markets, and Gambling*, 15 Colum. Sci. & Tech. L. Rev. 29 (forthcoming 2015).

abandoned its plans. Clearly the corporation had built a business model wherein investments in bitcoins—and through the receipt of bitcoins—were being assembled as a security for the investing public. Equally clearly, the OSC was aware of it, was well-acquainted with the securities implications of bitcoins, and was willing to act.

In February 2014 in Quebec, the AMF issued an alert about bitcoins. The authority cautioned Quebeckers about the risk of fraud and a lack of compulsory deposit insurance in the bitcoin space. It added that it would monitor the introduction of cryptocurrency in Quebec and would take action in case of any violation of the provincial Securities Act, the Derivatives Act, or the QMA.[266] Two months later, the OSC issued its own general bulletin. In that document, the OSC stated that virtual currency is not subject to "traditional financial regulation. This may change as regulators consider and make new rules to oversee its use and activities related to it."[267] The OSC also expressed the "certainty" that all such currencies should be approached with extra caution.[268]

The prairie province of Saskatchewan is also worth mentioning in this context. On May 1, 2014, the provincial Financial and Consumer Affairs Authority (the "**FCAA**") issued a temporary cease-trade order against Dominion Bitcoin Mining Company Ltd.[269] This order was extended on May 22, 2014. The temporary order alleged that Dominion Bitcoin was trading in securities without being registered and was soliciting investors in furtherance of distributions without a prospectus. Dominion Bitcoin argued that it was not soliciting or "signing up" investors and that it was only selling mining services, resulting in bitcoins.[270] The FCAA stated that it does not "regulate bitcoin or the mining of bitcoin. Whether a person pays for a share in Canadian dollars, bitcoins, or other property—Saskatchewan securities laws apply to the sale of shares. To keep Saskatchewan investors safe,

---

[266] Autorité des marches financiers, *Alert—Bitcoin virtual currency*, Feb. 5, 2014, *available at* http://www.lautorite.qc.ca/en/press-releases-2014-autre.html_2014_alert-bitcoin.html.

[267] Ontario Securities Commission, Office of the Investor, *The real risks of virtual currency*, Apr. 2014, *available at* http://www.osc.gov.on.ca/documents/en/Investors/inv_news_20140404_real-risks-virtual-currency.pdf.

[268] *Id.*

[269] *Temporary Cease Trade Order Issued Against Dominion Bitcoin Mining Company*, May 6, 2014, *available at* http://www.saskatchewan.ca/government/news-and-media/2014/may/06/cease-trade-order.

[270] Jeff Gray, *Regina bitcoin startup denies wrongdoing*, The Globe & Mail, May 8, 2014, *available at* http://www.theglobeandmail.com/report-on-business/industry-news/the-law-page/regina-bitcoin-startup-denies-securities-allegations/article18570615/.

we need to make sure that anyone selling or publicizing the sale of shares in the province complies with the rules."[271] Subsequently, the FCAA confirmed to the media that the cease trade order on Dominion Bitcoin had expired.[272] Dominion Bitcoin's president was also quoted as saying that the FCAA has "absolutely no idea what bitcoin is."[273] In a press release on Dominion Bitcoin's website (www.dominionbitcoin.com) at the time of writing, the corporation's chairman stated that Dominion Bitcoin feels "fully vindicated as the FCAA has not made a finding of wrong doing. We believe that the authorities are now more informed as to the nature of Bitcoins."[274]

An interesting issue arises with respect to decentralized autonomous organizations ("**DAOs**") in the context of securities law.[275] These are virtual code sets that can accomplish the objectives of an entity (e.g., the registration of domain names, performing escrow services) through the use of automation. The use of DAOs to raise funds, spend them, and make distributions through participation of its stakeholders (by means of shares, units, or some other means of representing ownership) is a highly anticipated use of this technology and has already been subject to experimentation. Clearly there are initial jurisdictional questions that may arise here, but an issuance of ownership units and their trade in a secondary market may engage provincial securities rules in Canada, at least to the extent that any relevant participants (e.g., investors or principals of issuers) are in Canada. Threshold questions of property, asset, venture, and enterprise are engaged. The issue of DAO technology and its intersection with securities law should be followed closely as it has the potential to become an area of interest to regulators.

---

[271] *Cease Trade Order Extended Against Dominion Bitcoin Mining Company*, May 22, 2014, *available at* https://www.saskatchewan.ca/government/news-and-media/2014/may/22/cease-trade-order.

[272] *Bitcoin mining company 'fully vindicated' after expiry of cease trade order*, CBC News, Sept. 12, 2014, *available at* http://www.cbc.ca/news/canada/saskatoon/bitcoin-mining-company-fully-vindicated-after-expiry-of-cease-trade-order-1.2765131.

[273] *Id.*

[274] Note that the chairman of Dominion Bitcoin went further some months ago: "Not only that, but if the company did start soliciting investors, Mr. [Jason] Dearborn argued, investments made in bitcoins would not be even subject to securities rules. 'We would take investment directly in bitcoins, as well, which we don't think falls under the purview of the securities commission.'" Gray, *supra* note 270. To the extent that this suggests that investments made using bitcoins cannot give rise to the application of Canadian securities laws (for example, because bitcoin is not money), we disagree.

[275] These are similar to, although not necessarily the same as, decentralized autonomous corporations, digital autonomous companies, and other permutations.

We have reviewed the general securities regulation framework in Canada. We have seen that it seems difficult for the current definition of "security" to accommodate bitcoin being held directly by the public. It also seems to be clear that bitcoin can be a medium or instrumentality through which a security can be created. The various securities regulators in Canada certainly take that view. It is worth making one final note, at the risk of stating the obvious: a cryptocurrency business undertaking multiple business lines may clearly have to answer to multiple regulators. Should a business have a component dealing in fiat-to-cryptocurrency exchange, it may be an MSB for purposes of the PCA; a bitcoin fund or share trading platform that is a separate business line could also be subject to securities oversight. Both of these business lines might have consumer protection concerns. While the regulatory landscape may be fragmented, it behooves business owners and entrepreneurs to be comprehensive in how they take in that landscape.

6. Cryptocurrency & Taxation

Cryptocurrency transactions related to productive sources of income are captured by the Income Tax Act[276] and other Canadian tax legislation. The CRA has generally characterized bitcoin as a commodity[277] and has made ad hoc comments on different bitcoin transactions where they perceive that existing approaches (e.g., commodities and barter) apply. This leaves at least some questions about the taxation of cryptocurrency in Canada unanswered.

We begin with the two main charging provisions in the Income Tax Act. The first requires that persons resident in Canada pay an annual tax on their worldwide income.[278] The second requires non-residents that are not taxable under subsection 2(1) to pay tax on three categories of income: income from an office or employment in Canada;[279] income from a business that was carried on in Canada;[280] and, income from the disposal of a taxable Canadian property.[281]

In fleshing out the details of those rather short provisions, Parliament has taken a broad approach to characterizing things like

---

[276] R.S.C. 1985, c. 1 (Can.).
[277] *Study on the Use of Digital Currency Before the Standing Senate Committee on Banking, Trade and Commerce, supra* note 90.
[278] Income Tax Act, R.S.C. 1985, c. 1, § 2(1).
[279] *Id.* § 2(3)(a).
[280] *Id.* § 2(3)(b).
[281] *Id.* § 2(3)(c).

"income." For example, the Income Tax Act sets out that a resident's income from employment in a year "is the salary, wages and other remuneration, including gratuities, received by the taxpayer in the year."[282] As regards fringe benefits alone, generally "the value of board, lodging and other benefits of any kind whatever received or enjoyed by the taxpayer in the year in respect of, in the course of, or by virtue of" the office or employment is to be included in income.[283] The courts have generally interpreted the employment inclusions into income broadly[284] and the CRA has spent considerable time and ink trying to extend this coverage by way of examples.[285] Computation of business income is another example. A taxpayer's income from business or property is the taxpayer's "profit,"[286] with an extensive list of broad income inclusions rounding out that term.[287]

In other words, the approach by successive governments to income inclusions has been expansive. The Income Tax Act captures a great deal of economic activity. Even before the CRA first used the word "bitcoin" in a public release in 2013, the economic value associated with bitcoin in a source transaction was bound to be includable in a taxpayer's income in some fashion. If one's salary—or one's fees or other sales—were paid and received in bitcoin, they would clearly be includable in income. Similarly, deductions for legitimate expenses paid for using bitcoin would ultimately reduce one's taxable income in the ordinary course.

In April 2013, a CRA representative sent an e-mail to the Canadian Broadcasting Corporation outlining the federal government's views on the taxation of bitcoin.[288] This was consistent with the CRA's subsequent fact sheet on digital currency—its first official pronouncement—released in November 2013.[289] In the fact sheet, digital currency was described as "virtual money that can be used to buy and sell goods or services on the Internet" and specifically

---

[282] *Id.* § 5(1).
[283] *Id.* § 6(1)(a).
[284] *See, e.g.*, The Queen v. Savage, [1983] 2 S.C.R. 428 (Can.).
[285] *See, e.g.*, Employees' Fringe Benefits, Interpretation Bulletin IT-470R (Can.).
[286] Income Tax Act, R.S.C. 1985, c. 1, § 9(1).
[287] *See, e.g., id.* § 12(1).
[288] *Bitcoins aren't tax exempt, Revenue Canada says*, CBC NEWS, Apr. 26, 2013, *available at* http://www.cbc.ca/news/business/bitcoins-aren-t-tax-exempt-revenue-canada-says-1.1395075.
[289] Can. Revenue Agency, *What you should know about digital currency*, Nov. 5, 2013, *available at* http://www.cra-arc.gc.ca/nwsrm/fctshts/2013/m11/fs131105-eng.html?utm_source=mediaroom&utm_medium=eml.

cited bitcoins as an example.²⁹⁰ (The use of "money" is curious in the context of our previous discussion and the CRA's stated view that bitcoin is a commodity.) It stated that bitcoins are not controlled by any state or central bank and can be traded "anonymously."²⁹¹

In the fact sheet, the CRA suggested two bases for taxing bitcoin transactions: one based in the concept of barter dealings, the other treating bitcoin as within the scope of securities transactions. The former cited the example of paying for a movie with bitcoin; the value of the movie purchased would be includable in the seller's income. This makes conceptual sense. If one sells one's goods or services in the marketplace for bitcoin, that is generally revenue for accounting and tax purposes, provided one is in the business, for example, of selling those goods or services.²⁹²

As to securities, the CRA suggested that people who were buying and selling bitcoins to speculate or as a store of value in themselves were buying and selling digital currency "like a commodity."²⁹³ Any "resulting gains or losses could be taxable income or capital for the taxpayer."²⁹⁴ (Interestingly, losses were mentioned but their deductibility was omitted; presumably a taxpayer losing value on bitcoins purchased on account of capital would be eligible for a capital loss.) So-called income gains are fully includable in income in Canada. Capital gains are effectively only one-half taxable, so the characterization matters. The CRA pointed to its long-standing

---

²⁹⁰ *Id.*
²⁹¹ *Id.*
²⁹² This is an important conceptual point, but one that can be overlooked. Income in Canada, to be taxable, must be from a productive "source." *See* Income Tax Act, R.S.C. 1985, c. 1, § 3(a); Benjamin Alarie, *Exploring the Source Concept of Income: The Taxation of Poker Winnings in Canada* (Working Paper, Jun. 13, 2011), 5–6, 10–12, *available at* http://papers.ssrn.com/sol3/papers.cfm?abstract_id=1809270. The CRA states in its fact sheet that "[w]here digital currency is used to pay for goods or services, the rules for barter transactions apply. A barter transaction occurs when any two persons agree to exchange goods or services and carry out that exchange without using legal currency." This insinuates that any time barter passes back and forth, a taxable transaction takes place, which is false. If A helps B move house and B buys A dinner in return, that is not a taxable transaction, unless perhaps A is in the business of moving people's personal property, i.e., unless A receives the dinner as a business source of income.
²⁹³ *What you should know about digital currency, supra* note 289.
²⁹⁴ *Id.*

administrative position on capital versus income transactions to help determine which rule applies.[295]

The CRA went further in an internal memorandum dated December 23, 2013.[296] In that memorandum, the government recapitulated its views about securities and barter involving bitcoin. However, the CRA also suggested that the Goods and Services Tax ("**GST**") or Harmonized Sales Tax ("**HST**") would apply to the transaction if it were a taxable supply within the meaning of the Excise Tax Act.[297] The GST–HST is a form of value-added tax levied by the federal government.[298] Accordingly, where a taxable supply of professional services, for example, is rendered, whether charged or paid for in bitcoins or otherwise, GST–HST will be exigible on that transaction. Furthermore, the CRA clarified in the memorandum that bitcoins can be the subject of gifts to qualified registered charities and that "it is the fair market value of the Bitcoins themselves at the time the Bitcoins are transferred that must be used in determining the eligible amount of the gift for tax purposes."[299]

The CRA's comments in a 2014 technical interpretation[300] are also apposite. In this interpretation, the Income Tax Rulings Directorate confirmed the substance of earlier comments about the applicability of the barter and securities rules. For the first time, the CRA also engaged with the question of how bitcoin mining is to be taxed. Technical interpretations are redacted and not all of the underlying facts are clear. However, citing *Stewart v. Canada*,[301] the department agreed that

---

[295] Transactions in Securities, Interpretation Bulletin IT-479R (Can.). Though regarded as a commodity by the CRA, it may be challenging to determine whether someone is holding bitcoins on account of income or capital. That is because bitcoins have many of the hallmarks of money in an economic sense, though we believe they are not legal money. Still, it may be no more difficult than determining whether Canadian dollars held in a business or personally are held on account of income or capital.

[296] C.R.A. Intern. Mem. 2013-051470117 (Dec. 23, 2013) (Can.).

[297] R.S.C. 1985, c. E-15 (Can.).

[298] Where the value-added tax is levied separate and apart from a provincial sales tax, if any (e.g., in Quebec), it is called GST. Where the tax is levied in a 'harmonized' way with a provincial sales tax (e.g., in Ontario), it is called HST.

[299] C.R.A. Intern. Mem. 2013-051470117, *supra* note 296.

[300] C.R.A. Technical Interpretation 2014-0525191E5 (Mar. 28, 2014) (Can.).

[301] [2002] 2 S.C.R. 645 (Can.) (discussing whether a taxpayer has a source of income for purposes of section 9 of the Income Tax Act).

the addressee appeared to be "operating a bitcoin mining business."[302] The bitcoins produced through mining, presumably through both bitcoin issuance and through transaction fees, then become inventory in the hands of the miner, requiring a valuation at the end of the taxation year. Several methods of valuing inventory were then set out in the interpretation by the CRA.

Importantly, the technical interpretation also touches on the tax consequences when bitcoin inventory of a business is lost or stolen. Such losses are normally deductible, but only if, in the CRA's view, "such losses are an inherent risk of carrying on the business and the loss is reasonably incidental to the normal income-earning activities of the business."[303] In the context of bitcoin, where inadequate security precautions are taken to preserve bitcoin amounts, loss through simple inadvertence and exposure to theft may not be enough to qualify for deductibility. Finally, the CRA made brief comments about virtual currencies being acquired as gifts. The CRA noted that true gifts (e.g., not in the course of employment) are not taxable in the hands of recipients but distinguished these gifts from fringe benefits and other receipts received in the course of an office or employment, which are generally taxable (and often deductible to employers).

We can make two observations about what the CRA has said about bitcoin thus far. First, interpretation bulletins,[304] technical interpretations, and other administrative materials issued by the CRA do not have the force of law. They can be revoked or amended at any time. None of the pronouncements by the CRA thus far is an advance tax ruling giving a taxpayer certainty about any particular contemplated transaction.[305] Having said that, the courts in Canada have yet to deal with bitcoin taxation matters, and tax litigation in this sphere may not arise for some time. Accordingly, the administrative materials put into the public realm by the CRA are important in setting out preliminary guideposts about how cryptocurrency will be taxed. As those materials do not have the force of law binding the government to its current views, they also allow the CRA to pivot

---

[302] C.R.A. Technical Interpretation 2014-0525191E5, *supra* note 300. *See generally* Robert Graham, *Bitcoin mining taxation*, CBA NATIONAL TAXATION SECTION NEWSLETTER, Mar. 2014, *available at* http://www.cba.org/cba/sections_taxation/news2014/bitcoin.aspx.

[303] *Id.*

[304] *See, e.g.*, Can. Revenue Agency, *Notice—Bulletins do not have the force of law*, *available at* http://www.cra-arc.gc.ca/formspubs/pbs/tntc-eng.html.

[305] *See generally* Advance Income Tax Rulings, Information Circular IC70-6R5 ¶6 (Can.).

quickly to respond to what it perceives as new tax issues. That is both a potential threat to stability and an opportunity to map out potentially better approaches.

Second, the CRA has at least made an attempt to address several aspects of the taxation of cryptocurrency transactions: barter, securities, mining, GST–HST issues, theft, some gift issues, and charitable donations. This is ad hoc guidance, but guidance all the same. With the volume of altcoins in circulation and the potential for new ones, the CRA clearly has no appetite to set up a test for whether or not any particular unit of account qualifies as a "digital currency" meriting a particular approach under the Act. If bitcoins would meet the threshold definition, would Ripple, Litecoin, or Dogecoin? Certainly a taxonomy is possible here, likely with decentralization and convertibility as the two determinants, which is what the Financial Action Task Force has said about organizing virtual currencies.[306] But the novelty of the subject-matter means that the CRA considers itself on safer ground to just slot cryptocurrencies into current templates as they come across different fact patterns, consistent with its overall characterization of bitcoin as a commodity, not a currency.

It may also be that the CRA is hesitant to locate cryptocurrency in a bigger tableau because cryptocurrency is itself so multi-faceted. Bitcoin's (the currency's) legal characterizations are driven by its usage; it appears that it can be packaged as a security, as barter, as a financial instrument, and as mining inventory, among other things. Taxation touches all of these areas. If this is the source of the CRA's caution and incrementalism, then it is salutary.

An ad hoc illustration comes with its own form of uncertainty, however. We know very little about how other bitcoin transactions—outside of the CRA's carefully selected examples—will be taxed. We shall have to wait and see. For example, are bitcoin-to-fiat (and vice versa) transactions on Canadian exchanges subject to GST–HST when undertaken by Canadian residents? At the time of writing, the CRA has issued no guidance on this point. Supplies of "financial services" within the meaning of the Excise Tax Act are generally either exempt supplies[307] or zero-rated[308] for GST–HST purposes. Financial services

---

[306] Fin. Action Task Force, FATF Report: Virtual Currencies—Key Definitions and Potential AML/CTF Risks 8 (2014), *available at* http://www.fatf-gafi.org/media/fatf/documents/reports/Virtual-currency-key-definitions-and-potential-aml-cft-risks.pdf.
[307] Excise Tax Act, R.S.C. 1985, c. E-15, Sched. V, Part VII (Can.).
[308] *Id.* Sched. VI, Part IX.

include exchanges or payments of money,[309] among myriad other things. As has been shown, bitcoin is likely not money for purposes of the Currency Act or the Bills of Exchange Act, and would appear not to be money for purposes of the Excise Tax Act. But any answer here will be less certain until some further GST–HST guidance is issued or there is a judicial determination of the matter.

Another interesting issue arises in the context of the specified foreign property reporting rules. Any resident person or corporation having specified foreign property equal to C$100,000 at any time during a taxation year must make certain disclosures to the CRA[310] to meet their tax reporting obligations. Are bitcoins held by a taxpayer specified foreign property? The definition includes "funds or intangible property which are situated, deposited or held outside Canada."[311] To the extent that bitcoins are "property," they may be situated or held wherever the wallet containing them is located. If one were to hold one's wallet on a USB drive and have in it C$100,000 or greater, that wallet could travel from and to Canada, so that it could well be located "outside Canada" at some point during the taxation year, triggering the rule. Or, if one were to transfer bitcoins from such a wallet so that the threshold is not met at any time during international travel, then there may be no reporting obligation. We need to wait for the CRA to clarify this and other rules.

Cryptocurrencies have also opened up interesting tax planning opportunities. For example, an estate freeze employing a rollover pursuant to section 85 of the Income Tax Act allows an individual shareholder to 'lock-in' gains by means of preferred shares while transferring future growth, if any, to family members or other favoured parties. The plan requires a taxable Canadian corporation to act as the transferee.[312] Bitcoins can be held by the corporation prior to the freeze or can, if they are eligible property, be transferred into the corporation as part of the freeze transaction. The freeze works best when future growth accrues to common shares. Depending on where the bitcoin price goes in future, undertaking a freeze now may turn out to be savvy tax planning. While work in this area is still in its infancy, future efficient tax structuring of transactions could include individuals, corporations, and trusts holding, lending, and disposing of cryptocurrencies.

---

[309] *Id.* § 123(1).
[310] Income Tax Act, R.S.C. 1985, c. 1, § 233.3(1) (definition of "reporting entity").
[311] *Id.* § 233.3(1) (definition of "specified foreign property").
[312] *Id.* § 85(1).

Among the classes of federal laws touching this subject-matter, cryptocurrency may fit most comfortably in taxation legislation. We continue to have only preliminary guidance about how bitcoins will be taxed as barter or as a commodity, and this piecemeal approach leaves its own questions unanswered, but the current Income Tax Act seems to address many of the initial questions about the taxation of cryptocurrency.

7. Conclusion

Canada is not so unlike other developed countries in its approach to cryptocurrency. Policy makers are seeking to understand more about it. In the interim, regulators are, unsurprisingly, trying to locate cryptocurrencies in the current regulatory structure. The current government has introduced—and Parliament has passed—Bill C-31 in order to expressly address virtual currencies in the PCA and the PCA Regulations. Time will tell what those regulations will say and how far they will extend.

We have looked at some of the federal and provincial laws and regulations that affect cryptocurrency. This examination has been by no means exhaustive, but we hope that we have at least begun to address some of the salient issues in cryptocurrency under Canadian law. In some legal areas, cryptocurrencies appear to fit reasonably well. In others, the current law does not seem to know how to address cryptocurrency. In the history of technological innovation and its intersection with law, this perhaps is not surprising.

More research, discussion, and debate in this area are required and welcome. We view this chapter as the start—or part of the start—of a bigger and more robust discussion, not as the end. This discussion should involve consumers, merchants, regulators, policy makers, advocates for cryptocurrencies, and sceptics. Parties in Canada should begin by understanding the full suite of legal rights and limitations on their use of cryptocurrencies.

GERMANY

CHRISTOPH-NIKOLAUS VON UNRUH

Introduction

It was not until December 2011 that cryptocurrencies were first mentioned by a German governmental body.[1] The statement came from the Federal Financial Supervisory Authority ("**BaFin**") in a publication generally addressing how it would interpret section 1(11) no. 7 of the Banking Act[2] and pursuant to a reform measure to harmonize German banking legislation with European law. The article stated that bitcoin would be interpreted as a "unit of account" within the meaning of section 1(11) of the Banking Act. BaFin subsequently confirmed its opinion on how to treat bitcoin in a number of other publications.[3]

While BaFin may have been the first public body to opine on bitcoin, others have since followed. Following several questions by Members of Parliament regarding bitcoin in taxation matters, the Federal Ministry of Finance issued a statement in the summer of 2013.[4] That statement set out that the income tax and value added tax ("**VAT**") laws generally apply as and where businesses accept bitcoin. In the German legal academic literature, bitcoin was mentioned for the first time in 2012 in an essay. Although the topic of bitcoin was

---

[1] BaFin, *Hinweise zu Finanzinstrumenten nach § 1 Abs. 11 Satz 1 Nummern 1 bis 7 KWG (Aktien, Vermögensanlagen, Schuldtitel, sonstige Rechte, Anteile an Investmentvermögen, Geldmarktinstrumente, Devisen und Rechnungseinheiten)*, (Dec. 20, 2011) *available at* http://www.bafin.de/SharedDocs/Veroeffentlichungen/DE/Merkblatt/mb_111220_finanzinstrumente.html?nn=2818474.
[2] Kreditwesengesetz [KWG] [Banking Act], Jul. 10, 1961, Bundesgeseztblatt, Teil I [BGBL. I] at 2776.
[3] BaFin, *Bitcoins: Supervisory Assessment and Risks to Users*, (Feb. 2, 2014) *available at* http://www.bafin.de/SharedDocs/Veroeffentlichungen/EN/Fachartikel/2014/fa_bj_1401_bitcoins_en.html [hereinafter *Supervisory Assessment*]; 2013 BAFIN ANN. REP. 58.
[4] DEUTSCHER BUNDESTAG: DRUCKSACHEN UND PROTOKOLLE [BT] 17/14062, at 25.

scarcely mentioned in the academic legal literature between 2012 and 2013, it has since become a more popular research subject.[5]

Most legal articles and state comments on bitcoin, such as those from BaFin, appear to take the position that the use of cryptocurrencies is legal in Germany.[6] However, the fact that cryptocurrencies are not issued by any governmental entity results in a need for further analysis on this point. The right to issue money is generally regulated under the Bundesbank Act.[7] Section 14(1) of the Bundesbank Act states that only the Deutsche Bundesbank (the central bank of the Federal Republic of Germany) has the right to issue coins or banknotes. Furthermore, it is a crime according to section 35 to issue stamps, coins, banknotes or other certificates that can be used instead of euros. It is also a crime to use "private money" instead of the euro. The intention of this law is to maintain a state monopoly over the issuance of money and to prevent the creation of private money in Germany.[8]

Nevertheless, over the last few years, some private local currencies have been issued in the form of coins and banknotes, and are used in some parts of Germany with the aim of strengthening the local economy (e.g., Chiemgauer in parts of Bavaria).[9] These notes and coins are typically issued by a central authority (e.g., a club, here Chimgauer e.V.) and purchased at a fixed exchange rate (i.e., 1 euro = 1 Chiemgauer).[10] Merchants accepting this regional currency can then exchange it for euros at a discounted rate of 5 per cent at the private club that issued the coins.[11] Although these private coins and banknotes are not legal according to section 35 of the Bundesbank Act, it is tolerated by the Deutsche Bundesbank and law enforcement

---

[5] Christoph Sorge & Artus Krohn-Grimberghe, *Bitcoin: Eine erste Einordnung*, 36 DATENSCHUTZ UND DATENSICHERHEIT 479 (2012); Kim-Patrick Eckert, *Steuerliche Betrachtung elektronischer Zahlungsmittel am Beispiel sog. Bitcoin-Geschäfte*, 38 DER BETRIEB 2108 (2013); Alexander Djazayeri, *Die virtuelle Währung Bitcoin - Zivilrechtliche Fragestellungen und internationale regulatorische Behandlung*,6/2014 JURIS PRAXISREPORT BANK- UND KAPITALMARKTRECHT (2014); Gerald Spindler & Martin Bille, *Rechtsprobleme von Bitcoins als virtuelle Währung*, 29 WERTPAPIER-METTEILUNGEN 1357 (2014).
[6] BAFIN ANN. REP., *supra* note 3.
[7] Gesetz über die Deutsche Bundesbank [BBankG] [Bundesbank Act], Jul. 26, 1957, BUNDESGESEZTBLATT, Teil I [BGBL. I] at 1782.
[8] ULRICH HÄDE & HUGO J. HAHN, WÄHRUNGSRECHT § 23 no. 96 (2d ed. 2010).
[9] MARIT SADEMACH, REGIONALWÄHRUNGEN 1 ff. (2012).
[10] KRISTER VOLKMANN, REGIONAL - UND TROTZDEM GLOBAL 37 ff. (2009).
[11] Christian Gelleri, *Chiemgauer Regiomoney: Theory and Practice of a Local Currency*, 13 INT'L J. COMMUNITY CURRENCY RES. 61, 71 (2009).

agencies that simply view it as a minor phenomenon and therefore not a threat to the state monopoly over the issuance of currency.[12]

Though section 35 of the Bundesbank Act may be clear with respect to privately issued coins and notes, it is the author's view that this provision does not apply to cryptocurrencies as they are not issued as coins, banknotes, certificates, or anything of the kind. Premising this analysis on article 2(1) of the Basic Law of the Federal Republic of Germany (the Constitution of Germany), any behavior relating to the creation or acceptance of cryptocurrencies can only be prohibited by law if such a prohibition expressly exists in a law. Article 2(1) provides that every person shall have the right to the free development of her personality insofar as she does not violate the rights of others or offend the constitutional order or the moral law. In other words, absent a specific and valid restriction, a person is free to do what she wants. To take a common example in Germany: it is said that a person is free to ride a horse in a forest pursuant to article 2(1). However, legislators are also free to specifically prohibit horse-riding in forests as an environmental protection measure.[13] This principle applies in respect of cryptocurrencies, i.e., the use of cryptocurrencies is in principle permitted by law in Germany, and subject only to specific limits and restrictions enacted by policymakers. In the event that cryptocurrencies are considered to pose a threat to state control of money, it is foreseeable that section 35 of the Bundesbank Act may be amended to expand the prohibition to the use of electronic units of account.

Based on the view that the creation and possession of cryptocurrencies are permitted under German law, cryptocurrencies are property with associated rights that are protected by article 14(1) of the Basic Law. According to this article, property and the right of inheritance shall be guaranteed and their content and limits shall be defined by law. Property, within the meaning of this article, can be interpreted broadly, and the prevailing view defines property as a valuable and legal asset that is tangible or intangible and belongs to one person.[14] Therefore, not only items but also intangible property and rights are protected.[15] As such, cryptocurrencies can be defined

---

[12] SADEMACH, *supra* note 9, at 288 ff.
[13] BVerfG 80, 137.
[14] Peter Axer, *Einleitung Art. 14* in VOLKER EPPING & CHRISTIAN HILLGRUBER, BECK'SCHER ONLINE-KOMMENTAR GRUNDGESETZ (GG) (22d ed. 2014); HANS-JÜRGEN PAPIER, GRUNDGESETZ, art. 14 no. 160-164 (Theodor Maunz & Günter Dürig, eds., 72d ed. 2014).
[15] Axer, *supra* note 14, art. 14 no. 49-50.

as property because other people are willing to pay to receive it.[16] If cryptocurrencies are legal and protected in some way by the Basic Law, then it may be unclear how cryptocurrencies fit within the established German legal system. The following section aims to address this issue.

1. Cryptocurrencies and Financial Institutions

1.1. Cryptocurrency As a Unit of Account.

Even if cryptocurrencies are legal, this does not mean that they are free from regulatory supervision. As indicated above, the relevant finance regulatory entity in Germany is BaFin. BaFin defines cryptocurrencies as neither money nor electronic money, but as a "unit of account" and therefore as a financial instrument under section 1(11) no. 7 of the Banking Act.[17] A "unit of account" is something that has a nominal value and is comparable to foreign currencies, but does not have status as legal tender,[18] yet can serve as a private means of payment in barter transactions.[19] The common example of a unit of account is the special drawing right of the International Monetary Fund.[20] Therefore, even though cryptocurrencies are not legal tender,[21] they are comparable to foreign currencies in the sense that they contain value and serve as means of payment. Note that even though BaFin interprets cryptocurrencies as units of account, this has not yet been reviewed yet by a judicial authority. It remains to be seen whether Germany's courts will also see cryptocurrencies as units of account. Nevertheless, the prevailing view in the literature is that cryptocurrencies should be treated as units of account under German law.[22]

Furthermore, it appears to be the prevailing view that cryptocurrencies are not considered ordinary currencies, as only legal

---

[16] FRANK BROGL, KREDITWESENGESETZ (KWG) § 1 no. 447 (Friedrich Reischauer et al. eds., 2014).
[17] Kreditwesengesetz [KWG] [Banking Act], Jul. 10, 1961, BGBL. I at 2776, § 1(11) no. 7.
[18] FRIEDRICH REISCHAUER & JOACHIM KLEINHANS, KREDITWESENGESETZ (KWG) § 1 no. 447 (14th ed. 2014).
[19] BAFIN ANN. REP., *supra* note 3, at 58.
[20] MAX WEBER & SUSANNE SEIFERT, KREDITWESENGESETZ (KWG) § 1 no. 107 (Günter Luz et al. eds., 2d ed. 2011).
[21] BAFIN ANN. REP., *supra* note 3.
[22] Djazayeri, *supra* note 5.

tender is currency within the meaning of the Banking Act.[23] Legal tenders are instruments of payment that the law requires a creditor to accept as payment from a debtor.[24] For the euro, this requirement is provided under section 14 of the Bundesbank Act in conjunction with section 292 of the Civil Code, which states that only the Deutsche Bundesbank can issue coins and banknotes, and that creditors must accept banknotes in satisfaction of obligations.[25]

Cryptocurrencies do not appear to be considered electronic money under section 1a(3) of the Payment Services Oversight Act.[26] Under this law, electronic money is defined as monetary value represented by a claim on the issuer that is stored on an electronic device. At first glance, it might appear as though this rule could apply, since parts of cryptocurrencies may be said to be stored on electronic devices. The decentralized saving of the block chain would fulfill the requirement of "saved on electronic devices." However, the storage of value on one or several devices is not a *necessary* component of bitcoin.[27] Moreover, the fact that private keys do not necessarily have to be saved on an electronic device (but can be recorded on paper, for example) would not prevent the categorization of cryptocurrency as electronic money because the access authorization to the electronic saved asset does not need to be electronic.[28] Further, papers or vouchers can work as access authorization for electronic money.[29] Despite satisfying these initial qualifications, cryptocurrencies cannot be interpreted as electronic money as they do not represent a claim on any issuer.[30] One of the defining elements of electronic money is that the assets representing electronic value must exist pursuant to an issuance by an issuer and

---

[23] FRANK SCHÄFER, KREDITWESENGESETZ (KWG) § 1 no. 34 (Karl-Heinz Boos et al. eds., 4th ed. 2012); Eckert, *supra* note 5, at 2109.

[24] STEFAN GRUNDMANN, MÜNCHENER KOMMENTAR BÜRGERLICHES GESETZBUCH § 245 no. 48 (Franz Jürgen Säcker et al. eds., 5th ed. 2010); STEFAN SCHAUB, ERMAN BÜRGERLICHES GESETZBUCH § 244 BGB no. 2d (Barbara Grunewald et al. eds., 14th ed. 2014).

[25] SADEMACH, *supra* note 9, at 122 ff.

[26] Zahlungsdiensteaufsichtsgesetz [ZAG] [Payment Services Oversight Act] Jun. 25, 2009 BUNDESGESETZBLATT, Teil I [BGBL. I] at 1506, § 1a(3); BaFin, *Merkblatt - Hinweise zum Zahlungsdiensteaufsichtsgesetz (ZAG)*, (Dec. 22, 2011) available at http://www.bafin.de/SharedDocs/Veroeffentlichungen/DE/Merkblatt/mb_111222_zag.html.

[27] MATTHIAS TERLAU, ZAHLUNGSDIENSTEAUFSICHTSGESETZ (ZAG) § 1a no. 44 (Matthias Caspar & Matthias Terlau, eds. 2014).

[28] *Id.*

[29] *Id.*

[30] Eckert, *supra* note 5, at 2109.

result in a claim against that issuer.[31] An example of electronic money would be prepaid mobile cards.[32] Cryptocurrencies do not fit within this definition. The bitcoin miner does not "issue" cryptocurrency. There is no claim on the miner to pay the value of the cryptocurrency, nor is there any promise linked to a cryptocurrency unit.[33] In contrast, a mobile prepaid card is linked with the undertaking by the telecom operator that the value on the card can be used to make phone calls.

Incidentally, it would be problematic to categorize cryptocurrencies themselves as securities in Germany. According to section 2(1) of the Securities Trading Act, securities are shares in companies or debt securities. Debt securities arise when one promises something related to that security. With cryptocurrencies per se, no-one can be said to promise anything. Accordingly, they should not be interpreted as securities.

The interpretation of cryptocurrencies as units of account suggests that companies whose business models are related to cryptocurrencies may be considered to be credit or financial services institutions within the meaning of sections 1(1) and (2) of the Banking Act. Stating that cryptocurrencies are units of account according to section 1(11) no. 7 of the Banking Act implies that cryptocurrencies are financial instruments within the meaning of section 1(11) of the Act. As a corollary, sections 1(1) and 1(2) of the Act provide that a business that deals with financial instruments is in most cases defined as a credit service or financial services institution.

If a business is interpreted as a credit service or financial services institution and has a presence in Germany, it will need an accreditation issued by the BaFin according to section 32 of the Banking Act. To receive such an accreditation, a company has to file an application that includes, for example, a business plan and proof that the responsible persons are reliable. Furthermore, to process such an application, the applicant has to pay an administration fee, which can range from €1,000 to €50,000.[34]

---

[31] Terlau, *supra* note 27.
[32] *Id.*, § 1a no. 45.
[33] Eckert, *supra* note 5, at 2109.
[34] Verordnung über die Erhebung von Gebühren und die Umlegung von Kosten nach dem Finanzdienstleistungsaufsichtsgesetz [FinDAGKostV] [Ordinance on the imposition of fees and allocation of costs pursuant to the Act establishing the Federal Financial Supervisory Authority], Apr. 29, 2002, Bundesgesetzblatt, Teil I [BGBl. I] at 1504, § 1.

1.2. Domestic Relations

The general consensus is that the jurisdictional scope of German regulatory reach is limited to activities or situations related to Germany.[35] Such a relation is considered to exist where a credit institution or financial institution has a physical office in Germany.[36] However, a company having no physical presence in Germany might still have a nexus due to other circumstances, though this view is far from settled.[37]

One view is that only a domestic presence establishes a relation to Germany and the application of German law, as this was the intention of the lawmakers when the supervisory law came into force.[38] The opposing view is that a physical presence is no longer necessary, as services for German customers can be provided through modern communication forms from outside Germany's borders.[39] This argument is particularly relevant for cryptocurrencies. If an online service is designed for Germans, it makes no difference to the German customer whether the physical office of the business is located in Germany. From this, it follows that if the services are being marketed to German consumers, these services should be regulated to protect stability in the financial marketplace. BaFin interprets the Banking Act in accordance with the latter view[40] and this interpretation has been reinforced by decisions of the Federal Administrative Court.[41] In one noteworthy case, a Swiss bank targeted German customers with a German website and offered credit services without having a license as required under the Banking Act. Furthermore, German finance

---

[35] Spindler & Bille, *supra* note 5, at 1363; AXEL VON GOLDBECK, KREDITWESENGESETZ (KWG) § 32 no. 12 (Günter Luz et al. eds., 2d ed. 2011); ANDREAS SCHWENNICKE, *Kreditwesengesetz (KWG) mit Zahlungsdiensteaufsichtsgesetz (ZAG) KWG* § 32 no. 8 (Andreas Schwennicke et al. eds., 2d ed. 2013); REINFRID FISCHER, KREDITWESENGESETZ (KWG) § 32 no. 15 (Karl-Heinz Boos et al. eds., 4th ed. 2012).

[36] Kreditwesengesetz [KWG] [Banking Act], Jul. 10, 1961, BGBL. I at 2776, § 53.

[37] Spindler & Bille, *supra* note 5, at 1364.

[38] SCHWENNICKE, *supra* note 35, § 32 no. 14.

[39] Spindler & Bille, *supra* note 5, at 1364.

[40] BaFin, *Notes regarding the licensing requirements pursuant to section 32 (1) of the German Banking Act (Kreditwesengesetz—KWG) in conjunction with section 1 (1) and (1a) of the KWG for conducting cross-border banking business and/or providing cross-border financial services*, (Apr. 5, 2005) *available at* http://www.bafin.de/SharedDocs/Veroeffentlichungen/EN/Merkblatt/mb_050400_crossborder_en.html.

[41] Bundesverwaltungsgericht [BVerwG] [Federal Administrative Court] Apr. 22, 2009, WERTPAPIERMITTEILUNGEN [WM] 1553 ff, 2009.

agents offered credit services to German customers. BaFin prohibited the Swiss bank from undertaking further economic activities. The bank claimed it did not need a license under the Banking Act because it did not have an office physically located within Germany. The Federal Administrative Court backed the decision of BaFin stating that a German presence existed because the website was in German and agents in Germany worked for the Swiss bank.

The principles that can be taken from the court's interpretation are that a domestic relation is seen to exist when German customers are targeted by a business. Indicators for this might be that the website is in German, the website's homepage is using the German country code top-level domain (.de), or the service accepts euro as a means of payment.[42] Another indicator might be the proportion of German customers who make up the customer base. If, for example, 90% of the customers are German, a German relation is considered to exist, thus triggering the application of German law.[43]

Not every service that attracts German customers and is available online is required to abide by German regulations.[44] According to section 2(1) of the Basic Law, citizens are allowed to use services that are based outside of Germany and that do not follow German regulations.[45] Therefore, whether a domestic presence exists is decided on a case-by-case basis looking at all relevant factors as opposed to following a pre-determined set of criteria.

Another exception to the application of German regulatory law is that of businesses holding a license to conduct business within the European Economic Area. License holders may operate in Germany without further licensing requirements according to section 53b of the Banking Act.

1.3. Business Models That Qualify As Credit Institutions

Cryptocurrency-based businesses that buy and sell cryptocurrencies for commission are considered to be credit institutions pursuant to section 1(1), sentence 1, no. 4 of the Banking Act.[46] This section provides

---

[42] Spindler & Bille, *supra* note 5, at 1364.
[43] Bundesverwaltungsgericht [BVerwG] [Federal Administrative Court] Apr. 22, 2009, WERTPAPIERMITTEILUNGEN [WM] 1557, 2009.
[44] SCHWENNICKE, *supra* note 35, § 32 no. 12.
[45] Bundesverwaltungsgericht [BVerwG] [Federal Administrative Court] Apr. 22, 2009, WERTPAPIERMITTEILUNGEN [WM] 1557, 2009.
[46] Kreditwesengesetz [KWG] [Banking Act], Jul. 10, 1961, BGBL. I at 2776, § 1(1) sentence 1 no. 4; Djazayeri, *supra* note 5.

that a credit institution is a company that buys and sells financial instruments for the accounts of others. Because cryptocurrencies are considered financial instruments, businesses engaged in the purchase and sale of these assets on behalf of others would qualify as credit institutions under the law. The gains and losses that arise out of such transactions are borne by the client. Nevertheless, the business must appear as a business of that commission agent to outsiders, i.e., outside third parties are not to know that the commission agent sells and buys cryptocurrencies for and on others' behalf.[47] Businesses that offer to buy and sell cryptocurrencies in order to hide the identity of the real owner qualify as credit institutions.

1.4. Business Models That Qualify As Financial Services Institutions

The different cryptocurrency-based business models that are interpreted as financial services institutions in accordance with section 1(1a) of the Banking Act will be discussed below.

1.4.1. Arranging Dealings to Buy and Sell Cryptocurrencies

According to Section 1(1a) 2 no. 1 of the Banking Act, a company is a financial services institution when it arranges the sale of financial instruments.[48] This definition includes those businesses, whether they deal with cryptocurrency or not, whose exchange operations are limited to providing a marketplace platform for the buyer and seller. This is the case even if there is no requirement that the buyer and seller sign a written contract. While such a business would be considered a financial services institution under the law, BaFin has specified that the arranging of meetings between buyers and sellers only becomes a business (and therefore a financial services institution) when 25 or more transactions are arranged per month.[49] In Germany, the leading exchange, bitcoin.de, is qualified as a financial services institution according to Section 1 (1a) 2 no. 1 of the Banking Act, and is licensed by BaFin.

---

[47] SCHÄFER, *supra* note 23, § 1 no. 57.
[48] *Id.*, § 1 no. 123k.
[49] *Id.*, § 1 no. 122a.

1.4.2. Operating a Multilateral Trading System

Companies that operate multilateral trading facilities ("MTFs") are considered to be financial services institutions within the meaning of section 1(1a) 2 no. 1 b of the Banking Act. A multilateral trading facility is a facility that brings together multiple third-party buyers and sellers interested in financial instruments offered by the platform. Transactions occur in a non-discretionary way, resulting in a purchase agreement for those financial instruments. Interest in buying and selling on the platform creates an obligation for the buyer and seller to complete the transaction.[50] Regulations address a number of MTF elements, including membership, and the negotiation and closing of deals.[51] For example, the law prohibits anyone from encumbering the closing of a deal once a buyer has been matched with a seller.[52] It is irrelevant whether the execution of the contract is carried out within the platform or outside: if the closing of the contract happened within the MTF, the relevant regulations apply.[53] Typical examples for multilateral trading systems are stock exchanges.[54] Based on this analysis, it may be that cryptocurrency exchanges such as cryptsy.com or bitstamp.net are multilateral trading facilities.

1.4.3. Trading on a Continuous Basis on Organized Markets and Unregulated Exchanges

There are other business models that would also qualify a business as a financial services institution. For example, a business engaged in the purchase and sale of cryptocurrencies on a continuous basis, on its own account, against its own proprietary capital, at prices defined by itself on an organized market or on a multilateral trading system, will also be considered a financial services institution within the meaning of section 1(1a) no. 4a of the Banking Act.[55]

---

[50] *Id.*, § 1 no. 123j.
[51] *Id.*, § 1 no. 123j.
[52] *Id.*, § 1 no. 123k.
[53] BaFin, *Supervisory assessment*, *supra* note 3.
[54] WEBER & SEIFERT, *supra* note 20, § 1 no. 41.
[55] Kreditwesengesetz [KWG] [Banking Act], Jul. 10, 1961, BGBL. I at 2776, § 1(1a) no. 4a.

An organized market, defined under section 2(5) of the Securities Trading Act[56] is a multilateral trading system operated and managed within the European Economic Area by a market operator that brings together multiple third parties buying and selling cryptocurrencies and that is authorized and supervised by a governmental body. Buying and selling on a continuous basis is not a necessary condition for an organized market to be in existence.

The European Securities and Market Authority publishes a list of markets that fulfill these requirements.[57] At the time of writing, there are no regulated markets in which cryptocurrencies are traded pursuant to the German Banking Act. An exchange that only arranges the contact between the seller and the buyer, e.g., bitcoin.de, is not a regulated market within the meaning of this law. However, MTFs (possibly bitstamp and cryptsy) provide similar, though less regulated, services through which persons can buy and sell cryptocurrency on an ongoing basis.

Buying and selling on an ongoing basis is considered to occur if a person, in accordance with market regulations, offers to transact with cryptocurrencies.[58] However, not every person that buys and sells on a regular basis on a regulated market is a financial services institution. The administration of private assets does not require the administrator to act as a financial services institution.[59] The same exclusion would apply to someone dealing on his or her own behalf, thus exempting a day trader from the need to obtain a license.[60] Nevertheless, BaFin interprets "continuous" as 25 transactions per month.[61] This interpretation has not yet been reviewed by any court. Such a business thus becomes a financial services institution regardless of whether the business is a company or an individual enterprise. Thus, someone who trades cryptocurrencies more than 25 times per month

---

[56] Wertpapierhandelsgesetz [WpHG] [Securities Trading Act], Jul. 27, 1994, BUNDESGESETZBLATT, Teil I [BGBL. I] at 2708, § 2(5); SCHÄFER, *supra* note 23, § 1 no. 133 a.

[57] European Securities and Market Authority, Multilateral Trading Facilities, http://mifiddatabase.esma.europa.eu/Index.aspx?sectionlinks_id=22&language=0&pageName=MTF_Display&subsection_id=0 (last visited Feb. 12, 2015).

[58] BaFin, *Merkblatt - Hinweise zu den Tatbeständen des Eigenhandels und des Eigengeschäfts*, (Oct. 24, 2014) *available at* http://www.BaFin.de/SharedDocs/Veroeffentlichungen/DE/Merkblatt/mb_110322_eigenhandel_eigengeschaeft_neu.html [hereinafter *Merkblatt*].

[59] SCHWENNICKE, *supra* note 35, § 1 no. 126.

[60] *Id.*

[61] SCHÄFER, *supra* note 23, § 1 no. 134.

would automatically become a financial services institution and need to be licensed.

1.4.4. Regulatory Exchange of Cryptocurrencies Against Fiat

If a business is limited to exchanging cryptocurrencies to fiat, and engages in this activity on a continuous basis, this business will also be categorized as a financial services institution in accordance with section 1(1a) no. 4b of the Banking Act.[62] This section states that a person who provides a system that enables the sale and purchase of financial instruments on a regular basis outside of a regulated market or an MTF is defined as a finance services institution, even though "regular basis" means a less than continuous basis.[63] It is not necessary that a system be operated automatically.[64] BaFin interprets that dealings occur on a continuous basis, within the meaning of section 1(1a) no. 4b of the Banking Act, when the execution of the deals works in an established and repetitive way.[65] Thus, it may be that a company operating a cryptocurrency ATM where bitcoins are sold on a continuous and repetitive basis is a financial services institution.

1.5. Business Models That Do Not Qualify As Credit or Financial Services Institutions

Not all companies whose business models are related to cryptocurrencies are defined as credit or financial services institutions. For example, a bitcoin mining business would not likely be considered to be a financial services institution by BaFin because it does not satisfy the basic prerequisite of holding deposits or other repayable funds. Nor does a miner issue any cryptocurrencies under the ordinary understanding of "issuing."[66] Furthermore, the activity of bitcoin mining is not involved in the trade of goods because miners do not buy or sell cryptocurrencies, at least not in their capacities as miners.

However, bitcoin mining businesses usually do not limit their activities to the mining of "new coins." They also often facilitate the transfer of bitcoins between other users through the act of broadcasting these transactions onto the block chain. Neither BaFin nor any judicial

---

[62] Kreditwesengesetz [KWG] [Banking Act], Jul. 10, 1961, BGBL. I at 2776, § 1(1a) no. 4b.
[63] SCHÄFER, *supra* note 23, § 1 no. 133 b.
[64] BaFin, *Merkblatt*, *supra* note 58.
[65] *Id.*
[66] BAFIN ANN. REP., *supra* note 3.

literature for that matter has publicly opined on this particular activity, thus leaving it open to speculation as to if and how it will be regulated. According to section 1(2) no. 2b of the Payment Services Oversight Act, the execution of a transfer of a financial instrument is a financial service.[67] Companies offering financial services within the meaning of section 1(2) require permission to do so.[68] Perhaps the reason why BaFin has not commented on this issue is the "transfer" referred to in section 1(2) no. 2b of the Payment Services Oversight Act refers to a transfer of legal tender pursuant to section 675c and other sections of the Civil Code.[69] In addition, the writing or broadcasting of a transaction on the block chain does not constitute a transfer within the meaning of section 675 *et seq.* of the Civil Code. This is because those sections merely codify how an owner's claim of legal tender against one bank is transferred to another person, so that the transferee has a claim against the bank.

Furthermore, section 1(10) no. 9 of the Payment Services Oversight Act states that services provided by technical service providers are not considered to be financial services as long as they support the provision of payment services without themselves entering at any time into possession of the funds.[70] As a miner never comes into the possession of the funds in a transfer activity, this exemption regarding technical service providers may be a more appropriate fit for those engaged in actual bitcoin mining as opposed to qualifying their activities as financial services.

There may appear to be some similarities between portfolio management (a regulated activity) and the provision of cryptocurrency wallet services. However, in the author's view, it is unlikely that the operation of cryptocurrency wallet services or wallet security services would require a licence according to section 32 of the Banking Act under the current legislation.[71] Such activity would fall short of the definition of portfolio management within the meaning of section 1(1a) sentence 2 no. 3 of the Banking Act, which requires a license because the management of a portfolio is considered to be a financial

---

[67] Zahlungsdiensteaufsichtsgesetz [ZAG] [Payment Services Oversight Act] Jun. 25, 2009, BGBL. I at 1506, § 1(2) no. 2b.

[68] Zahlungsdiensteaufsichtsgesetz [ZAG] [Payment Services Oversight Act] Jun. 25, 2009 BUNDESGESETZBLATT, BGBL. I at 1506, § 8.

[69] SCHWENNICKE, *supra* note 35, § 1 no. 126.

[70] Zahlungsdiensteaufsichtsgesetz [ZAG] [Payment Services Oversight Act] Jun. 25, 2009 BUNDESGESETZBLATT, BGBL. I at 1506, § 1(1) no. 9.

[71] Spindler & Bille, *supra* note 5, at 1365.

service.[72] The activity of managing a portfolio implies that the portfolio manager has the right to trade the financial instruments that are being managed.[73] This ability is not one that is possessed by typical online cryptocurrency wallet providers. In many business models that have been analyzed, for instance, blockchain.info, the operator of the online wallet does not have the right to trade with the cryptocurrencies under their care. Wallet services would not likely be considered to be security depositing businesses either, because cryptocurrencies (as discussed above) are likely not securities under German law.[74]

Finally, no permission is needed if a company only receives cryptocurrencies in exchange for its services or goods.[75] This is because a company that only receives cryptocurrencies does not bring any services that qualify this company as a credit or financial services institution. It should be self-evident that a customer who pays in cryptocurrency does not require permission to do so.[76]

2. Cryptocurrencies and Taxation

Like many economic activities, those that involve cryptocurrencies are subject to tax regulation. The most relevant taxation laws in Germany for cryptocurrencies are the Value Added Tax Act and the Income Tax Act.[77]

2.1. Cryptocurrencies and VAT

The Value Added Tax Act is based on European Union directives.[78] As there is no decision by the European Court of Justice (the "**ECJ**") at the time of writing about how to interpret the EU Directives with reference to cryptocurrencies, each EU member state is free to interpret those directives as it sees fit. There are some differences between the EU Directives and the Value Added Tax Act. The question as

---

[72] Kreditwesengesetz [KWG] [Banking Act], Jul. 10, 1961, BGBL. I at 2776, § 1(1a) sentence 2 no. 3; Gerald Spindler & Martin Bille, *supra* note 5, at 1365.
[73] Schwennicke, *supra* note 35, § 1 no. 113.
[74] Spindler & Bille, *supra* note 5, at 1365.
[75] BaFin Ann. Rep., *supra* note 3.
[76] Djazayeri, *supra* note 5.
[77] Umsatzsteuergesetz [UStG] [Value Added Tax Act] Nov. 26, 1979, Bundesgesetzblatt, Teil I [BGBL. I] at 386; Einkommensteuergesetz [EStG] [Income Tax Act] Oct. 16, 1934, Bundesgesetzblatt, Teil I [BGBL. I] at 3366.
[78] See e.g. Council Directive 2006/112/EC.

to whether cryptocurrency transactions are subject to VAT is also pending at the ECJ.[79]

2.1.1. Definition

VAT rules distinguish between a special commodity and a regular commodity. The appropriate place to begin our analysis is to examine whether cryptocurrencies are considered to be private money, which is a special commodity, or are within the regular commodity category. The consequences of treating cryptocurrency as private money or as a regular commodity are significant.

The Ministry of Finance has sent mixed messages about the qualification of cryptocurrencies. In response to a parliamentary question in August 2013, the Ministry of Finance stated that cryptocurrencies are to be treated as money, but not as legal tender, and that the purchase of goods with cryptocurrencies is not an exchange contract within the meaning of section 3(12) of the Value Added Tax Act.[80] In another reply to a parliamentary question in October 2014, another representative of the Ministry stated that cryptocurrencies must be treated as a regular commodity.[81] That cryptocurrencies should be treated as money, but not as legal tender, as was suggested by the Ministry in its first response to Parliament, has important consequences. An analysis of the text of the legislation reinforces this view.

In the Value Added Tax Act, the word "currency" is mentioned twice, first under section 11(5) and later under section 16(6). The term "legal tender" is also mentioned under section 4 no. 8b, as a sub-category of the term "currency," and in section 25c (2) no. 2. Sections 11(5) and 16(6) of the Value Added Tax Act relate to the taxation of goods or services that are not paid in euros. Section 4 no. 8b of the Value Added Tax Act provides that a service to exchange legal tender is VAT-free. Section 25c (2) no. 2 describes that the importation of gold coins, which have been used once as legal tender, is VAT-free. It is possible to interpret this taxonomy as suggesting that sections 11(5) and 16(6) apply to both legal tender and private money, which include

---

[79] Case C-264/14, Skatteverket v. David Hedqvist, *available at* http://eur-lex.europa.eu/legal-content/EN/TXT/PDF/?uri=OJ:C:2014:245:FULL&from=EN.

[80] DEUTSCHER BUNDESTAG: DRUCKSACHEN UND PROTOKOLLE [BT] 17/14530 at 41 and 17/14803, at 25.

[81] DEUTSCHER BUNDESTAG: DRUCKSACHEN UND PROTOKOLLE [BT] Plenarprotokoll 18/59, at 5478.

cryptocurrencies, and that sections 4 no. 8b and 25c(2) no. 2 apply only to legal tender. Such an interpretation would be in accordance with the structure of the law. Sections 11(5) and 16(6) are relevant if cryptocurrencies are treated as currencies, because a cryptocurrency would be simply another currency in addition to the euro. Furthermore, section 4 no. 8b of the Value Added Tax Act would still apply to activities relating to cryptocurrency. Only the service to exchange legal tender would be VAT-free. Since cryptocurrency is not legal tender, the service and the service fee to exchange cryptocurrencies to euros or vice versa would be subject to VAT.

It is important to bear in mind that Ministry of Finance responses to parliamentary questions do not bind the local finance authorities, though the Ministry could decide to provide binding notice. If the Ministry were to provide binding notice to the local finance authorities to treat cryptocurrencies as a commodity, the formal position taken in such a notice could be challenged through judicial review.

2.1.2. Customer Payment in Cryptocurrency to a Business for the Provisions of Goods or Services

According to section 1 no. 1 of the Value Added Tax Act, a person paying in cryptocurrency for a good or service provided by a business must pay VAT on the transaction. The determination of the VAT owed from the transaction is contingent on how cryptocurrency is classified. This section will examine VAT for payments made in cryptocurrency under different classification scenarios.

2.1.2.1 Cryptocurrency As Private Money

If cryptocurrencies are treated as private money in exchange for which a consumer receives a good or a service, VAT will be based on the amount of cryptocurrency that the consumer pays.[82] To calculate the VAT, the received cryptocurrency has to be hypothetically converted into euros.[83] It is an open question whether the conversion to other currencies occurs at the moment when the customer receives the good or service or at the moment when the business receives the cryptocurrency

---

[82] Umsatzsteuergesetz [UStG] [Value Added Tax Act] Nov. 26, 1979, BGBL. I at 386, § 10(1) no. 2.

[83] Umsatzsteuergesetz [UStG] [Value Added Tax Act] Nov. 26, 1979, BGBL. I at 386, § 16(6).

as payment.⁸⁴ For transactions involving cryptocurrencies, this is important because the value of the cryptocurrency may fluctuate from the moment the customer receives the good or service and the moment the business owner receives the cryptocurrency. The Value Added Tax Act appears to state that the moment the customer receives the good or service is the moment when the VAT is calculated.⁸⁵ However, this interpretation would not be in accordance with the EU VAT Directive. According to article 73 of the EU VAT Directive, the basis for calculating VAT should only be the consideration that the business owner actually obtained.⁸⁶ Therefore, the Value Added Tax Act should be interpreted such that the calculation of VAT, and thus the conversion to euros for this purpose, occurs at the moment when the business receives the cryptocurrency.⁸⁷

If cryptocurrency were treated as private money, transactions exchanging cryptocurrency to legal tender would not be subject to VAT within the meaning of section 1(1) no. 1 of the Value Added Tax Act. The exchange of money is not a transaction on which VAT has to be paid.⁸⁸ Only transactions for goods or services are subject to VAT regulation.⁸⁹ The exchange of money to other currencies for personal benefit is not such a taxable service. However, the exchange of money may be defined as a service only when the aim is to provide an exchange service to customers.⁹⁰ This is usually not the case if cryptocurrencies received by a business for the delivery of goods or services are exchanged for legal tender.

2.1.2.2 Cryptocurrency As an Ordinary Commodity

If cryptocurrencies are treated as commodities, a consumer's payment in cryptocurrency is a transaction on which VAT must

---

[84] Christian Korn, Umsatzsteuergesetz § 16 no. 157 (Johann Bunjes, ed., 12th ed. 2012).
[85] Id., § 16 no. 35.
[86] Council Directive 2006/112/EC, art. 73.
[87] Holger Stadie, Umsatzsteuergesetz § 16 No. 157 (Günter Rau & Erich Dürrwächter, eds., 2014).
[88] Id., § 1 no. 10.
[89] Martin Robisch, Umsatzsteuergesetz § 1No. 10, (Johann Bunjes, 12d ed. 2012).
[90] Case C-172/96, Comm'rs of Customs and Excise v. First National Bank of Chicago, 1998 E.C.R. I-4413; Matthias Geurts, *Anmerkung: Devisengeschäfte mehrwertsteuerpflichtig*, 474 (1998).

be paid according to the VAT rules on exchange contracts.[91] With exchange contracts, the VAT is based on the value of the obtained consideration.[92] Whether the VAT should be calculated based on the objective or subjective value of the obtained consideration remains a subject for debate.[93] For cryptocurrencies, the objective value is the average exchange rate of the cryptocurrency from several exchanges (e.g., Bitcoin Average). In contrast, the subjective value would be the exchange rate of the cryptocurrency on the exchange that the business regularly uses. This question has been adjudicated by the ECJ and the Federal Fiscal Court (FFC), which both found that only the subjective values are necessary to calculate the VAT on exchange contracts.[94]

If cryptocurrencies are treated as commodities, then for a business each and every exchange of cryptocurrencies is a sale of commodities. On such a transaction, VAT is payable by the business receiving payment.[95]

2.1.2.3. Conclusion

There is ultimately no de facto distinction between qualifying cryptocurrencies as private money or ordinary commodities when a consumer purchases a good or a service. VAT is due on the transaction on the amount of the cryptocurrency that is received. However, things are different when cryptocurrencies are treated as commodities and the business sells the cryptocurrencies. When this occurs, the business would have to pay VAT on the amount of money received in exchange for the cryptocurrencies. This means that a business that sells 100 euros worth of cryptocurrencies has to pay €19 in VAT.[96] In contrast, if cryptocurrencies are treated as money, no VAT is due for the sale of the cryptocurrency, unless the aim of the sale of cryptocurrency is to provide an exchange service for others (as opposed to it being on one's own account).

---

[91] Umsatzsteuergesetz [UStG] [Value Added Tax Act] Nov. 26, 1979, BGBL. I at 386, §§ 1(1) no. 1, 3(12).

[92] Umsatzsteuergesetz [UStG] [Value Added Tax Act] Nov. 26, 1979, BGBL. I at 386, § 10(2) no. 2.

[93] HELMUT SCHUHMANN, UMSATZSTEUERGESETZ § 10 no. 335 (Günter Rau & Erich Dürrwächter, eds., 2014).

[94] Bundesfinanzhof [BFH] [Federal Tax Court], DEUTSCHES STEUERRECHT - ENTSCHEIDUNGSDIENST [DStRE] at 369-370, 2007; Case C-380/99, Bertelsmann AG v. Finanzamt Wiedenbrück, 1999 E.C.R. I-5176.

[95] Umsatzsteuergesetz [UStG] [Value Added Tax Act] Nov. 26, 1979, BGBL. I at 386, § 1(1) no. 1, 10(1).

[96] Umsatzsteuergesetz [UStG] [Value Added Tax Act] Nov. 26, 1979, BGBL. I at 386, § 1(1) no. 1, § 1(1) no. 10, § 1(1) no. 12.

2.1.3. Mining the Block Reward

For reasons set out below, it is the author's belief that bitcoin mining, which is the rewarding of cryptocurrency for mining a block, is a VAT-free transaction. This is true regardless of whether cryptocurrencies are treated as money or as commodities under German tax law. The primary basis for this conclusion is the view that the mining activity is neither a supply of goods nor a delivery of services under German tax law.[97] However, this position is speculative and debatable. According to one opinion, there is an insufficient link between any services provided by a miner and any consideration received for a mining activity to qualify as the provision of a good or service.[98] Another argument for this is that a purpose of the block reward is to create new coins.[99] However, a counterargument suggests that the requisite link does exist. The purpose of the block reward is not only to create new coins but also to reward the miners, as they are supporting and stabilizing the network.[100] Perhaps the strongest case against mining being a VAT taxable transaction is that it lacks two identifiable parties as participants in the transaction. Transactions for the benefit of the unknown and unidentifiable are not subject to VAT.[101] The recipients or beneficiaries of the service, where the service is the adding of blocks to the block chain, is not an identifiable person or body of persons.[102] The bitcoin network does not identify miners or users, and nobody knows which computers are participating in the network.

2.1.4. Receiving the Mining Fee

In addition to the mining reward, miners often receive a fee for the intake of transactions into the block. Whether this fee is a VAT-taxable

---

[97] Umsatzsteuergesetz [UStG] [Value Added Tax Act] Nov. 26, 1979, BGBL. I at 386, § 1(1) no. 1.
[98] HM REVENUE & CUSTOMS, REVENUE AND CUSTOMS BRIEF 9 (2014): BITCOIN AND OTHER CRYPTOCURRENCIES (2014), available at https://www.gov.uk/government/publications/revenue-and-customs-brief-9-2014-bitcoin-and-other-cryptocurrencies/revenue-and-customs-brief-9-2014-bitcoin-and-other-cryptocurrencies.
[99] SATOSHI NAKAMOTO, BITCOIN: A PEER-TO-PEER ELECTRONIC CASH SYSTEM 4 (2008), https://bitcoin.org/bitcoin.pdf.
[100] *Id.*
[101] STADIE, *supra* note 87, § 1 no. 40.
[102] ALEXANDER OELMEIER, UMSATZSTEUERGESETZ (UStG) § 1 no. 4 ff. (Wilfried Wagner et al. eds., 72d ed. 2014).

transaction depends on whether cryptocurrencies are treated as private money or as a commodity. If cryptocurrencies are treated as private money, then this transaction is VAT-free.[103] If cryptocurrencies are treated as a commodity, this transaction would be subject to VAT according to section 1 (1) no. 1, 3(12) because the broadcasting or writing of the transaction into the block chain is a service provided to the two parties involved in the transfer of the cryptocurrency.

2.1.5. Trading with Cryptocurrencies (Exchanges)

For businesses engaged in the business of trading cryptocurrencies, whether cryptocurrencies are treated as private money or as commodities is significant. Also, natural persons that trade in cryptocurrencies can become businesses (for purposes of VAT) where their trades can be characterized as sustainable actions to generate income according to section 2(1). For example, a private individual selling more than 200 items on eBay may be categorized as a business in the sense of the VAT law.[104]

When cryptocurrencies are treated as commodities, cryptocurrencies purchased from a non-VAT-taxable person, such as a private person, are VAT-free. Only the delivery of goods or the provision of services are subject to VAT. However, if the business sells the cryptocurrency, it has to pay VAT on the basis of the money received, as the business is selling a commodity.[105] Also note that if a business resells items that were bought initially from a non-taxable person, then only the profit margin is subject to VAT.[106] This exception does not currently apply to cryptocurrencies, since they are not identified as commodities under the Value Added Tax Act.[107] Therefore, the received price for the cryptocurrency is the basis on which to calculate the VAT.

Alternatively, if cryptocurrencies are treated as private money, a business exchanging private money to legal tender on a regular basis

---

[103] Umsatzsteuergesetz [UStG] [Value Added Tax Act] Nov. 26, 1979, BGBL. I at 386, § 4 no. 8d, § 4 no. 5.
[104] Bundesfinanzhof [BFH] [Federal Tax Court], BUNDESTEUERBLATT II [BStBl II] at 634, 2012.
[105] Umsatzsteuergesetz [UStG] [Value Added Tax Act] Nov. 26, 1979, BGBL. I at 386, § 10(2).
[106] Umsatzsteuergesetz [UStG] [Value Added Tax Act] Nov. 26, 1979, BGBL. I at 386, § 25a.
[107] Umsatzsteuergesetz [UStG] [Value Added Tax Act] Nov. 26, 1979, BGBL. I at 386, § 25a.

could be considered to be providing a service.[108] The consideration for this service is either the administration fee or the margin between the buying and selling price.[109] This service is not subject to an exemption because it is not legal tender (within the meaning of section 4 no. 8b of the Value Added Tax Act) that is being exchanged, but rather private money. There is some uncertainty as to whether the basis for calculating the VAT is the difference between the buying and selling price at the moment of the transaction, or the difference between the selling price and average market price at the moment of transaction.[110] An argument for calculating the VAT based on the difference between the selling price and average price with this method is that only the service of buying or selling the cryptocurrency at values below or above the average price is taxed. In cases where the whole margin is subject to VAT for every transaction, the profit will be taxed double for each unit bought and sold.[111] The ECJ tends to calculate the VAT on the basis of the margin between buying and selling price.[112]

2.2. Cryptocurrencies and Income Tax

The prevailing view for cryptocurrencies with respect to income tax is that they should be treated as non-depletable assets, similar to the treatment given to legal tender. Profits arising out of trading with any commodities, special or regular, are subject to income tax. This would apply to cryptocurrencies regardless of their classification as special or regular commodities. The way in which the Income Tax Act applies to the profits generated from trading with cryptocurrencies depends on whether the taxpayer generates the income from private activities or economic activities.

---

[108] Case C-172/96, Comm'rs of Customs and Excise v. First National Bank of Chicago, 1998 E.C.R. I-4413; Rüdiger Philipowski, *Anmerkung: Umsatzsteuerliche Behandlung von Devisengeschäften einer Bank*, UR 459 (1998).
[109] Case C-172/96, Comm'rs of Customs and Excise v. First National Bank of Chicago, 1998 E.C.R. I-4413; Rüdiger Philipowski, *supra* note 108.
[110] Rüdiger Philipowski, *Anmerkung: Zur umsatzsteuerlichen Beurteilung von Devisengeschäften und zur Frage des Vorsteuerabzuges*, WUB I K 3 56 (1999).
[111] *Id.*
[112] Case C-172/96, Comm'rs of Customs and Excise v. First National Bank of Chicago, 1998 E.C.R. I-4413;

2.2.1. Distinction between Income Arising from Private Activities and Economic Activities

Income from incorporated businesses is usually qualified as income arising from economic activities according to section 8 of the Corporate Tax Act.[113] Income from unincorporated firms and natural persons is qualified as income from economic activity if the activity is independently sustainable and comprises more than mere asset management according to section 14 of the Fiscal Code.[114] The line between income out of asset management and income out of economic activities is thin and the distinction has to be made on a case-by-case basis.[115] An indicator that income is derived from economic activities would be where the same activity is repeated over and over.[116] One example is the income derived from the permanent buying and selling of assets.[117] In contrast, income from a private person selling her commodities would usually be qualified as income arising out of private activities. However, this can always be re-qualified as income from economic activities if the selling process is handled in many small transactions rather than one large transaction.

2.2.2. Private Activities

Where the selling of cryptocurrency is qualified as a private activity and where cryptocurrencies are defined as a commodity, profits arising out of the sale of cryptocurrencies would be income tax free if the owner held the cryptocurrency for at least one year from the time of acquisition.[118] There are exceptions to this law that apply to items of daily use as defined in the Income Tax Act. However, it is unlikely that cryptocurrencies would qualify as items under the

---

[113] Körperschaftsteuergesetz [KStG] [Corporate Tax Act] Aug. 31, 1976, BUNDESGESETZBLATT, Teil I [BGBL. I] at 4144, § 8 (exception for non-profit corporations).
[114] Abgabenordnung [AO] [Fiscal Code] Oct. 1, 2002, BUNDESGESETZBLATT, Teil I [BGBL. I] at 3866, § 13.
[115] EVA-MARIA GERSCH, ABGABENORDNUNG (AO), § 14 no. 13 (Franz Klein et al. eds., 12th ed. 2014).
[116] ULRICH KOENIG, ABGABENORDNUNG (AO), § 14 no. 15 (Armin Pahlke et al. eds., 2d ed. 2009).
[117] EVA-MARIA GERSCH, *supra* note 115, § 14 no. 14.
[118] Einkommensteuergesetz [EStG] [Income Tax Act] Oct. 16, 1934, BGBL. I at 3366, § 23(1) no. 2(1); DEUTSCHER BUNDESTAG: DRUCKSACHEN UND PROTOKOLLE [BT] 17/14062, at 25.

law.[119] Income arising out of other private service activities relating to cryptocurrencies, such as acting as an agent, would be taxable according to section 22 no. 2 if the income exceeds €256 per year.[120]

The profit is calculated as the margin between the buying and selling price.[121] Any loss arising out of trading with cryptocurrencies can be allocated only to profits arising out of trading with cryptocurrencies from the same year.[122] Here, it is irrelevant whether the loss occurred out of a transaction of different cryptocurrencies (e.g., profits generated through trades with Dogecoins versus losses incurred through trades with bitcoins). In the case that cryptocurrencies are sold less than one year after acquisition, the whole of the profit is taxable if the profit reaches or exceeds €600 per year.[123]

It remains unsettled as to how to calculate the one-year period for cryptocurrencies that were purchased at different times. The German government has not yet decided whether the one-year period should be based on the First-in-First-out-Method, Last-in-First-out-Method or in a different way.[124] Uncertainty arises out of the fact that the relevant article in the law was changed recently and the amendments did not expressly consider cryptocurrencies. However, the prevailing view in the academic literature is that the taxpayer has to prove that he or she has owned the cryptocurrencies for at least one year.[125] This proof cannot be provided if cryptocurrencies purchased on several dates are deposited together in one wallet. However, it may be possible to provide this proof through the block chain, although this would depend on the protocol of each cryptocurrency. For bitcoin, a timestamp in the block chain indicating when the bitcoin was transferred might be considered as a valid proof of the date of acquisition.

---

[119] Einkommensteuergesetz [EStG] [Income Tax Act] Oct. 16, 1934, BGBL. I at 3366, § 23(1) no. 2(2).

[120] Einkommensteuergesetz [EStG] [Income Tax Act] Oct. 16, 1934, BGBL. I at 3366, § 22 no. 2; Deutscher Bundestag: Drucksachen und Protokolle [BT] 17/14062, at 25.

[121] Einkommensteuergesetz [EStG] [Income Tax Act] Oct. 16, 1934, BGBL. I at 3366, § 23(3).

[122] Einkommensteuergesetz [EStG] [Income Tax Act] Oct. 16, 1934, BGBL. I at 3366, § 23(3) no. 7; Rudolf Mellinghoff, Einkommenssteuergesetz (EStG) § 23 No. 22 (Paul Kirchhof et al. eds., 2014).

[123] Einkommensteuergesetz [EStG] [Income Tax Act] Oct. 16, 1934, BGBL. I at 3366, §23(3) no. 5; Mellinghoff, *supra* note 122, § 23 no. 23.

[124] Deutscher Bundestag: Drucksachen und Protokolle [BT] 17/14530, at 41.

[125] Andreas Musil, Einkommensteuer- und Körperschaftssteuergesetz (EStG, KStG) § 23 no. 153 (Carl Herrmann et al. eds., 2014); Hanno Kube, Einkommenssteuergesetz (EStG) § 23 no. 7 (Paul Kirchhof et al. eds., 2014).

2.2.3. Economic Activities

In cases where an activity is defined as an economic activity, only the profit is subject to income tax.[126] How the profit is calculated depends on several parameters such as the transaction volume or annual profit of the company, and the rules are set out in the Fiscal Code.[127] The intention of the law is that the differences in whichever way the profit is calculated should be marginal in the long run.[128]

If the company has a yearly transaction volume of equal to or less than €500,000 and a profit equal to or less than €50,000, profit will be calculated as "earnings less expenses."[129] Earnings arising out of the sale of cryptocurrencies are therefore fully considered in this calculation for the profit, regardless of how long ago the business acquired the cryptocurrency.

If the company's transaction volume exceeds €500,000 or profit exceeds €50,000, the profit is calculated by comparing the value of the business to the previous year.[130] The difference in the value is the profit or loss. In this case, the cryptocurrency can be valued at the buying price or lower, if appropriated.[131] A valuation above the buying price is not possible under German law to prevent auditing fraud. When the cryptocurrency is sold, the whole selling price that goes to the company will raise or decrease the value of the company and therefore influence the profit, regardless of whether the cryptocurrency was held for more or less than one year.

3. Cryptocurrencies and Criminal Law

Activities related to cryptocurrencies may violate several laws and therefore be subject to criminal prosecution. The following section reviews aspects of German law that may apply depending on the particular activity or use of cryptocurrency. The main operative statute

---

[126] Einkommensteuergesetz [EStG] [Income Tax Act] Oct. 16, 1934, BGBl. I at 3366, §2(2) no. 1.
[127] Einkommensteuergesetz [EStG] [Income Tax Act] Oct. 16, 1934, BGBl. I at 3366, §4; Abgabenordnung [AO] [Fiscal Code] Oct. 1, 2002, BGBl. I at 3866, § 141.
[128] EBERHARD LITTMANN, DAS EINKOMMENSTEUERRECHT § 4 no. 2 (Horst Bitz et al. eds., 2014).
[129] Einkommensteuergesetz [EStG] [Income Tax Act] Oct. 16, 1934, BGBl. I at 3366, §4(3) no. 1.
[130] Einkommensteuergesetz [EStG] [Income Tax Act] Oct. 16, 1934, BGBl. I at 3366, §4(1).
[131] Einkommensteuergesetz [EStG] [Income Tax Act] Oct. 16, 1934, BGBl. I at 3366, §6(1) no. 2.

is the Criminal Code StGB, which codifies the basic principles of German criminal law. However, many other laws regulate behavior separate and apart from the main criminal realm, e.g., the Bundesbank Act and the Banking Act.

3.1. Creation and Use of Coins and Paper Money/Paper Wallets

As discussed above, it is illegal to distribute coins or bills to third parties for use instead of legal tender. This crime is punishable by up to five years' imprisonment.[132] Accordingly, one may interpret this prohibition as rendering the distribution of cryptocurrency in the form of coins or notes a criminal act, extending as well to regional currencies.[133] However, this prohibition does not appear to be publicly recognized and it is not enforced against regional currencies. The issuers of those currencies are typically not guilty, as they may not know that their actions are illegal, i.e., there is a lack of mens rea.[134] In the past, the prohibition has been applied to gold certifications. In the 1960s, companies wanted to issue certificates for gold, which could have been transferred freely.[135] The Bundesbank prohibited this, claiming that those certificates would be legal tender documents within the meaning of section 35 of the Bundesbank Act.[136]

While a cryptocurrency unit existing as a digital asset would not qualify as legal tender, as it does not exist in physical form, there are physical manifestations of cryptocurrency that may be subject to this section of the law (e.g., paper bitcoin wallets). Note that according to the text of the Federal Bank Law, only the distribution of these documents is a crime.[137] This means that, in principle, the creation, storage, transport, possession, or collecting of items similar to legal tender is not prohibited.[138] Therefore, the creation of paper wallets is, in the view of the author, not covered under section 35(1) no. 1 of the Bundesbank Act and is legal.

---

[132] Gesetz über die Deutsche Bundesbank [BBankG] [Bundesbank Act], Jul. 26, 1957, BGBL. I at 1782, § 35(1) no. 1.
[133] HÄDE & HAHN, *supra* note 8, § 23 no. 100.
[134] SADEMACH, *supra* note 9, at 230.
[135] *Id.* at 167.
[136] *Id.*
[137] Gesetz über die Deutsche Bundesbank [BBankG] [Bundesbank Act], Jul. 26, 1957, BGBL. I at 1782, § 35; SADEMACH, *supra* note 9, at180; HEINZ BECK, GESETZ ÜBER DIE DEUTSCHE BUNDESBANK § 35 no. 936.
[138] HEINZ BECK, GESETZ ÜBER DIE DEUTSCHE BUNDESBANK § 35 no. 936 (1959).

The use of coins or documents that are not qualified by the state as legal tender for payment is a crime.[139] Therefore, it is the author's belief that the use of cryptocurrency in the form of physical coins and notes as a method of payment may be a violation of this section of the Bundesbank Act. The Federal Bank and other financial institutions are obligated to collect any coins and papers which are not legal tender but are being used as such, and must notify law enforcement agencies.[140] An argument may be made that the mere purchase of such coins or paper manifestations of cryptocurrency for collection reasons might not be defined as a crime under section 35 of the Bundesbank Act where the intention is simply to purchase the item (cryptocurrency coin) rather than to commercially circulate it as a payment method.

3.2. Acting as a Finance or Financial Services Institution

As mentioned above, several cryptocurrency-related activities, such as the operation of exchanges or automated teller machines ("ATMs"), require the permission of BaFin.[141] The penalty for operating such activities without formal permission from BaFin is imprisonment not exceeding five years or a fine.[142] In Germany, a legal entity cannot be penalized by criminal law; instead, the natural persons representing the entity will be penalized.[143] The representative person in such cases will be the person responsible for operating the activity for which permission is needed.[144]

There are differing degrees for the penalty of not obtaining the proper permission to operate a financial service. Where the omission is as a result of negligence, the penalty is reduced to imprisonment not exceeding three years or a fine.[145] An example of negligence with respect to this law would be a person who knows that he or she might need permission but acts in the expectation that no permission is

---

[139] Gesetz über die Deutsche Bundesbank [BBankG] [Bundesbank Act], Jul. 26, 1957, BGBL. I at 1782, § 35(1) no. 2.
[140] Gesetz über die Deutsche Bundesbank [BBankG] [Bundesbank Act], Jul. 26, 1957, BGBL. I at 1782, § 36.
[141] Kreditwesengesetz [KWG] [Banking Act], Jul. 10, 1961, BGBL. I at 2776, § 1, § 32.
[142] Kreditwesengesetz [KWG] [Banking Act], Jul. 10, 1961, BGBL. I at 2776, § 52(1) no. 2.
[143] Strafgesetzbuch [StGB] [Criminal Code], Nov. 13, 1998, BUNDESGESETZBLATT, Teil I [BGBL. I] at 945, § 14; HENNING LINDEMANN, KREDITWESENGESETZ (KWG) § 54 no. 10 (Karl-Heinz Boos et al. eds., 4th ed. 2012).
[144] SCHWENNICKE, *supra* note 35, § 54 no. 12.
[145] Kreditwesengesetz [KWG] [Banking Act], Jul. 10, 1961, BGBL. I at 2776, §§ 52(1) no. 2, 52.

needed.[146] This might occur where such a person mistakenly assumes that he or she is not acting as a commercial enterprise.[147]

3.3. Mining Cryptocurrencies Using Botnets

Cryptocurrencies can be mined by a personal computer, server farms, and with botnets.[148] Botnets are malware that exploit the computing capacity and energy of unsuspecting Internet users. In the case of mining, a botnet uses a collection of PCs connected to the Internet to operate the mining process. This is done without the knowledge or permission of the computer users as the botnet software works inconspicuously in the background.[149] This behavior violates several criminal laws.[150]

The act of programming software for the purpose of data espionage and phishing is a crime in Germany. It is punishable by imprisonment not exceeding one year or a fine.[151] The programming of botnet software is captured by this law as its operation is based on the use of espionage to target the unsuspecting PC user.[152] A person who illicitly installs malware is liable for the damage caused.[153] This section stipulates that a person that unlawfully obtains data not intended for himself (especially if he circumvented protections against unauthorized access) shall be liable to imprisonment not exceeding three years or a fine. The person does not have to have read the data in order for the act of obtaining unauthorized data to materialise. Even having access to that data is sufficient for a finding that the crime has been committed.[154] Further evidence that this section has been violated can include the use of malware to spy on the data of a PC simply to

---

[146] LINDEMANN, *supra* note 143, § 54 no. 10.
[147] SCHWENNICKE, *supra* note 35, § 54 no. 18
[148] *ZeroAccess botnet*, WIKIPEDIA, http://en.wikipedia.org/wiki/ZeroAccess_botnet (last visited Feb. 12, 2015); Robert Lemos, *Cyber-criminals putting botnets to work on bitcoin mining*, EWEEK, Apr. 12, 2013, http://www.eweek.com/security/cyber-criminal-putting-botnets-to-work-on-bitcoin-mining.
[149] *ZeroAccess botnet*, *supra* note 148.
[150] Franziska Boehm & Paulina Pesch, *Bitcoins: Rechtliche Herausforderungen einer virtuellen Währung*, MULTI MEDIA UND RECHT 75, 77 (2014).
[151] Strafgesetzbuch [StGB] [Criminal Code], Nov. 13, 1998, BGBL. I at 945, § 202c (1) no. 2.
[152] Philipp Roos & Philipp Schumacher, *Botnetze als Herausforderung für Recht und Gesellschaft*, MULTI MEDIA UND RECHT 377, 379 (2014).
[153] Strafgesetzbuch [StGB] [Criminal Code], Nov. 13, 1998, BUNDESGESETZBLATT, Teil I [BGBL. I] at 945, §§ 202a, 303a; Roos & Schumacher, *supra* note 152.
[154] *Id.*

determine the available space on a hard disk and what processes are operated on the PC.[155]

However, *quaere* whether the element of "altering" under section 303a is fulfilled if the malware is only installed on an empty hard drive. One opinion is that doing so constitutes an alteration committed on the hard drive, bringing this activity within section 303a.[156] However, the prevailing view is that an alteration under section 303a occurs with each installation of a program *and* where the hardware of the host PC has been altered.[157] Therefore, any installation of malware against the will of the other PC user is likely to fulfill the element of "altering" under section 303a, irrespective of whether or not the installation has been made on an empty hard drive.

In certain cases, the installation of malware may also come within the ambit of section 303b of the Criminal Code. This provision states that a person will be liable to imprisonment not exceeding three years or to a fine if he or she commits a crime pursuant to section 202a and 303a of the Criminal Code and, in so doing, causes extensive interference with the data processing operations of a PC that is substantially important to another.[158] Where a PC no long works properly, extensive intervention in the data processing operation can be said to have occurred.[159] The elements of 303b of the Criminal Code are only fulfilled when the installation of the malware makes the PC slower or interferes with the usability of the PC.[160] However, the perpetrator is only liable if he or she acts with intent.[161] Therefore, in cases that fall under section 303b of the Criminal Code, if the program was not designed to interfere with the system of the host PC, there is no intent and hence no liability.[162] As the aim of a mining botnet software is not to interfere with the processes of the host PC, and because the mining software should operate undiscovered in the background of the host PC, the requisite intent to cause damage may be absent from the person operating a mining botnet, thus relieving the individual committing the act of liability under section 303b of the Criminal Code.

---

[155] THOMAS FISCHER, STRAFGESETZBUCH (STGB) § 202 a no. 11 (61st ed. 2014).
[156] *Id.* § 303a no. 12.
[157] MATTHIAS WEIDEMANN, BECK'SCHER ONLINE-KOMMENTAR STRAFGESETZBUCH (STGB) § 303a no. 13 (Bernd von Heintschel-Heinegg, 24th ed. 2014).
[158] *Id.* § 303 b no. 6.
[159] *Id.* § 303 b no. 14.
[160] FISCHER, *supra* note 155, § 303b no. 9.
[161] Strafgesetzbuch [StGB] [Criminal Code], Nov. 13, 1998, BGBL. I at 945, § 15.
[162] WEIDEMANN, *supra* note 157, § 303b no. 14.

Although the operator of mining botnet software is liable for espionage and alteration of the host PC, it is perhaps paradoxical that he or she would not be criminally responsible for the act that constitutes his or her main objective: the unpermitted use of computing capacity and electricity belonging to the victims. The use of the computing capacity of a hacked PC is not a criminal act, given that the act in question is not codified in the criminal law. According to section 1 of the Criminal Code, an act may only be punished if criminal liability is established by law. Until such behavior is codified, offenders cannot be prosecuted for merely using the computer capacity and electricity of a hacked PC.

While the theft of electricity would be a crime according to the general section 248c of the Criminal Code, the offender would need to take the electricity directly from the victim.[163] In the case of botnet mining, the electricity is delivered to the hacked host PC and used in that location; it is not taken directly by the mining operator. It is the author's belief that since the operator only receives the data, but not electrical energy, it would be difficult to find that his or her actions are sufficient for finding the commission of the crime under section 248c as it is currently drafted.

3.4. Theft of Cryptocurrencies

Reports of bitcoin theft have been made on several occasions, yet the question as to what legal framework applies to stolen cryptocurrency remains unsettled among legal experts.[164] The crime of theft is codified in section 242 of the Criminal Code. According to this section, a person who takes away chattels belonging to another person with the intention of unlawfully appropriating them for herself shall be liable to imprisonment not exceeding five years or to a fine. Chattels are defined as physical, movable property, meaning that cryptocurrencies are excluded from this category of property since they are not physical. This makes it difficult to argue that the general law against theft extends to the theft of cryptocurrency.[165]

When cryptocurrencies are stolen, usually it is by way of theft of the private key. However, in the author's view, it is unlikely that the mere act of copying the private key from a paper wallet would result in a criminal offence. This conclusion is supported by analogy to the

---

[163] FISCHER, *supra* note 155, § 248 c No. 2.
[164] Boehm & Pesch, *supra* note 150.
[165] *Id.*

act of copying a private pin number from a payment card. Under German law, the act of copying this type of information is not in itself a crime. Rather, additional circumstances surrounding the theft or unauthorized copying of a private key will bring the activity under the scrutiny of the criminal law. For example, a common technique used to steal private keys is the use of phishing attacks whereby malware is inconspicuously installed on the victim's PC to spy for the private key. Once in possession of the private key, the thief transfers the victim's bitcoins to another wallet. As noted above, the development of malware software (section 202c),[166] cyber-espionage (section 202a), and the installation of malware (section 303a) are all criminal acts punishable by imprisonment of up to three years or a fine.[167] It is likely through these criminal acts that unauthorized copying of a private key would be prosecuted.

There are other criminal law provisions that may capture the theft of bitcoins. Section 263a of the Criminal Code makes it a crime for a person to obtain a material benefit through the unauthorized use of data to influence the result of a data processing operation, and the punishment for this offence is imprisonment not exceeding five years or a fine.[168] The following will explain the view that if a private key that has been copied is subsequently used to transfer bitcoins to another address controlled by the thief, then the elements of section 263a are satisfied.

A material benefit within the meaning of this law is anything that has an economic value.[169] As cryptocurrencies have an economic value, a material benefit is present.[170] Data processing operations are automatic operations that perform data acquisitions and create results with the acquired data.[171] Thus, a bitcoin miner who adds a transaction to the block chain undertakes such a data processing operation. The creation of the block with new transactions is an automatic operation. Through this data acquisition operation (i.e., the order to transfer the cryptocurrency from one wallet to another, signed with a private key), new data is generated: the block containing the transaction.

---

[166] Boehm & Pesch, *supra* note 150.
[167] *Id.*
[168] Strafgesetzbuch [StGB] [Criminal Code], Nov. 13, 1998, BUNDESGESETZBLATT, Teil I [BGBL. I] at 945, § 263a.
[169] STEPHAN BEUCKELMANN, BECK'SCHER ONLINE-KOMMENTAR STRAFGESETZBUCH (STGB) § 263 no. 40 (Bernd von Heintschel-Heinegg, 24th ed. 2014).
[170] Eckert, *supra* note 5, at 2109.
[171] KATHARINA BECKEMPER, BECK'SCHER ONLINE-KOMMENTAR STRAFGESETZBUCH (STGB) § 263 a no. 7 (Bernd von Heintschel-Heinegg, 24th ed. 2014).

The question of when the use of data can be considered unauthorized has been widely discussed in the literature.[172] The prevailing view is that when the offender is not legitimized to use the data and that he or she received the data in an unlawful way, the use of the data is unauthorized.[173]

4. Cryptocurrencies and the Civil Law

4.1. Definition

The definition of cryptocurrencies in the civil law in Germany is unsettled. At the time of writing, there are no court decisions on the subject. The scholarly essays addressing the civil law definition of cryptocurrencies present a range of views.[174] The question is an important one, as the answer will dictate the legal framework applicable to contracts involving cryptocurrency and how cryptocurrency can be protected as an asset. One opinion argues that, for cryptocurrencies, the laws of material property and immaterial property do not apply.[175] Nor are cryptocurrencies to be characterized as immaterial properties in their own class (*sui generis*).[176] Under this view, a contract involving cryptocurrencies is not a sales contract or an exchange contract, but is rather an atypical work-for-hire contract to which section 631 *et seq.* of the Civil Code apply.[177] This law states that the subject matter of a contract to produce a work may be either the production or alteration of a thing or some other result to be achieved through the work or service. A contract involving cryptocurrencies may be a contract to produce a work inasmuch as one party is committing to recording the transmission of the cryptocurrency in the block chain. Another opinion might posit cryptocurrencies as species of rights, or at least as an immaterial property.[178] According to this perspective, contracts in which cryptocurrencies are involved are usually exchange contracts

---

[172] *Id.* § 263a no. 19-24.
[173] *Id.*
[174] Djazayeri, *supra* note 5.; Boehm & Pesch, *supra* note 150, at 75; Christian Engelhardt & Sascha Klein, *Bitcoins - Geschäfte mit Geld, das keines ist*, MULTI MEDIA UND RECHT 355 (2014); Moritz Schroeder, *Bitcoin: Virtuelle Währung - reelle Problemstellungen*, JURPC WEB-DOK 104/2014, 1.
[175] Djazayeri, *supra* note 5.
[176] Djazayeri, *supra* note 5.
[177] BÜRGERLICHES GESETZBUCH [BGB] [Civil Code], Aug. 18, 1896, REICHSGESETZBLATT [RGBL.] 195, as amended, § 631; Djazayeri, *supra* note 5.; Boehm & Pesch, *supra* note 150, at 78.
[178] Schroeder, *supra* note 174, at 60.

under section 480 of the Civil Code, which says that the provisions relating to purchase apply, *mutatis mutandis*, to exchange contracts.[179]

4.1.1. Cryptocurrencies as Currencies

As mentioned above, it is the author's view that cryptocurrencies are private money and should be treated as such. Furthermore, the relevant civil law provisions only demand a payment; they do not specify that legal tender is required to be used for payments (see, for example, section 433 of the Civil Code regarding purchase agreements and section 632a of the Civil Code regarding contracts to produce a work). Thus, where the obligation of a party to a contract is to pay a price, it is not necessary that the payment be made in legal tender in order to satisfy the legal conditions imposed by law. The legal requirement to use legal tender arises with the payment of damages under tort law or if parties do not provide for a currency of payment in their agreements. If the contractual parties mention the currency or method of payment, for example, bitcoin, in a private contract, then it would be defined as a purchase agreement (if one of the parties purchases something), or as an exchange contract (if one of the parties exchanges a cryptocurrency to fiat). Despite the range of opinions and unsettled nature of the matter, it appears as though the prevailing view in Germany is that cryptocurrencies are not money, as they are not legal tender.[180] Therefore, other opinions about what cryptocurrencies are under the civil law and what consequence this has for different types of legal contracts will be presented and discussed.

4.1.2. Cryptocurrencies As a Thing or a Right

According to section 90 of the Civil Code, only corporeal objects can be "things."[181] Corporeal means that the object has to be physical and that it has fixed dimensions. Hence, cryptocurrencies cannot qualify as things under this definition; they are only digital and do not have fixed dimensions pursuant to our current understanding of dimensions.[182] Nor can cryptocurrencies be considered to be a right. Only those rights explicitly recognized by law can be identified as

---

[179] BÜRGERLICHES GESETZBUCH [BGB] [Civil Code], Aug. 18, 1896, REICHSGESETZBLATT [RGBL.] 195, as amended, § 480.
[180] Engelhardt & Klein, *supra* note 174, at 356.
[181] BÜRGERLICHES GESETZBUCH [BGB] [Civil Code], Aug. 18, 1896, RGBL. 195, as amended, § 90.
[182] Djazayeri, *supra* note 5.

rights.[183] As a result, cryptocurrencies are not rights as they are not explicitly recognized as such by the civil law.[184]

4.1.3. Cryptocurrencies As Immaterial Goods

Another category of property is that of immaterial goods. While it may be difficult to qualify cryptocurrencies under the first two above-mentioned categories, cryptocurrencies appear to find safe haven in the category of immaterial goods.[185] Immaterial goods are goods that are not things and yet have monetary or non-monetary value. Examples of immaterial goods are freedom, ideas or inventions. Certain immaterial goods are afforded some legal protections. For example, some immaterial goods and properties are transferable,[186] and only certain types of intellectual property give the owner intellectual property rights. The rights associated with different types of immaterial property are stipulated in various laws,[187] such as the Patent Act,[188] the Trademark Act,[189] and the Copyright Act.[190] Although there has been discussion about whether copyright laws might apply to cryptocurrencies, the general view in Germany seems to be that IP laws do not extend to them.[191] This conclusion flows from the understanding that cryptocurrencies are not original personal creations, and thus, according to section 2(2) of the Copyright Act, they cannot be protected. Only the source code and software of a cryptocurrency might be protected by the copyright law, but not the currency unit (or a part of a currency unit) evolving out of the source code.[192] The Federal Court of Justice of Germany has decided that new forms of protected immaterial rights can only be established by new

---

[183] Engelhardt & Klein, *supra* note 174, at 357.
[184] *Id.*
[185] Djazayeri, *supra* note 5.
[186] *Id.*
[187] *Id.*
[188] Patentgesetz [PatG] [Patent Act], May 5, 1936, REICHGESETZBLATT, Teil I] [RGBL. I] at 501.
[189] Markengesetz [MarkenG] [Trademark Act], Oct. 25, 1994, BUNDESGESETZBLATT, Teil I [BGBL. I] at 3082.
[190] Urheberrechtsgesetz [UrhG] [Copyright Act], Sep. 9, 1965, BUNDESGESETZBLATT, Teil I [BGBL. I] at 1273.
[191] Boehm & Pesch, *supra* note 150, at 78.
[192] Urheberrechtsgesetz [UrhG] [Copyright Act], Sep. 9, 1965, BUNDESGESETZBLATT, Teil I [BGBL. I] at 1273, § 69; Boehm & Pesch, *supra* note 150, at 78; Djazayeri, *supra* note 4.

laws.[193] The intention behind this is to avoid legal uncertainty. The consequence of this position is that no one can become an owner of virtual property that is not recognized by law, e.g., patents, which are recognized by law and can be owned.[194] Although this legal practice has been criticized, it is still the law in Germany.[195] One opinion states that, as a result of the state of the law, contracts involving cryptocurrencies are neither contracts of exchange nor purchase contracts since cryptocurrencies do not confer any rights.[196] They are only contracts to produce a work because only the success of the transaction of the coins meets the obligation of the person who pays with the virtual currencies.[197] Following this vein of thought, cryptocurrencies do not exist in Civil Law.[198]

4.1.4. Cryptocurrencies As Commodities

Some have argued that cryptocurrencies should be treated like commodities, which are not protected by the civil law of Germany, but are provided for in the criminal law.[199] "Protected" in this context means the right to exclude others from the use of the commodity, i.e., excludability. For example, a patent is a commodity that is protected by civil law, as the owner can exclude others from using the patent. However, if the theft of cryptocurrencies is a crime, then cryptocurrencies are protected by criminal law, but civil remedies may be unavailable. An argument in support of this position is that legal possessions that are neither rights nor objects are mentioned in section 453(1) no. 2 alternative 2 of the Civil Code as "other objects."[200]

---

[193] Bundesgerichtshof [BGH], WERTPAPIERMITEILUNGEN [WM] at 1849, 2005.
[194] Engelhardt & Klein, *supra* note 174, at 357.
[195] Helmut Redeker, *Information als eigenständiges Rechtsgut*, 27 COMPUTER UND RECHT 634, 638 (2011); MATTHIAS BERBERICH, VIRTUELLES EIGENTUM 212 ff., 464 (2010).
[196] Djazayeri, *supra* note 5.
[197] *Id.*
[198] LEGAL TRIBUNE ONLINE, *Zum ersten Mal ein freier Markt der Währungen: Interview mit Julian Schneider* (Oct. 28, 2013), http://www.lto.de/recht/hintergruende/h/bitcoins-waehrung-rechnungseinheit-umsatzsteuer.
[199] Engelhardt & Klein, *supra* note 174, at 358; Schroeder, *supra* note 168, at 31.
[200] Moritz Schroeder, *supra* note 174, at 51; BÜRGERLICHES GESETZBUCH [BGB] [Civil Code], Aug. 18, 1896, RGBL., 195, as amended, §§ 453(1) no. 2 alternative 2.

4.1.5. Conclusion

As it is uncertain what cryptocurrencies are, some opinions in the literature suggest that lawmakers define computer data as an immaterial good.[201] The need to define the rights conferred by the ownership of computer data extends beyond cryptocurrency to items in computer games such as World of Warcraft or Second Life.[202]

4.2. Contract Law

4.2.1. Buying Cryptocurrencies

The type of contract that exists when a consumer purchases cryptocurrency with fiat money has been discussed in the academic literature but not by the courts. The prevailing view is that such a contract is not a purchase agreement within the meaning of section 433 of the Civil Code because cryptocurrency is not a "thing" within the meaning of the law.[203] One opinion defines a contract to buy cryptocurrencies as a "contract to produce a work and similar contracts" within the meaning of section 631 *et seq.* of the Civil Code.[204] According to this provision, a contract to produce a work exists when one party is obligated to produce a result, while the other party has to pay the agreed remuneration. For example, in taxi contracts, the taxi driver has the obligation to drive a customer to the required destination whereas the guest has the obligation to pay the taxi driver. The obligation to produce a result in such a contract is the successful transportation of a person from A to B. In the case of a contract to buy cryptocurrencies, the obligation to provide a result would be the obligation to produce a successful and confirmed transaction on the block chain.[205]

Another perspective, supported by this author, is that for such contracts, the second alternative of section 453(1) of the Civil Code applies. This section states that the provisions on the purchase of things apply, *mutatis mutandis*, to the purchase of rights and other objects. According to this view, a cryptocurrency is an "other object" within

---

[201] Engelhardt & Klein, *supra* note 174, at 359.
[202] Jan-Peter Psczolla, *Virtuelle Gegenstände als Objekte der Rechtsordnung*, JURPC WEB-DOK 17/2009, 1.
[203] Boehm & Pesch, *supra* note 150, at 78.
[204] *Id.*
[205] *Id.*

the meaning of section 453(1) of the Civil Code.²⁰⁶ The classification of an "other object" was added to this section for the specific purpose of defining immaterial goods such as electricity or heating as subjects of a purchase agreement.²⁰⁷ As it was the legislature's intention to create a broad term through its use of the term "special objects," any legal possession could conceivably be an "other object."²⁰⁸ Therefore, data and information can also be special objects within the meaning of section 453(1) of the Civil Code.²⁰⁹ Since section 456 of the Civil Code refers to section 433 of the Civil Code, the provisions in a purchase agreement for "other objects" apply in the same way as for the purchase of any currency. This means that the purchase of other virtual goods, such as items in computer games, would be defined as a contract to purchase a right within the meaning of section 456(1) no. 2. This definition seems to be the most appropriate as the buyer of cryptocurrencies does not only benefit from the success of the transaction, but also receives something (an "other object") that he or she can transfer to another person.

4.2.2. Buying an Item With Cryptocurrencies

Another important transaction to consider is the purchase of goods with cryptocurrency. The prevailing view is that this is not a purchase agreement within the meaning of section 433 of the Civil Code because the buyer does not pay with legal tender, therefore he or she is not paying the purchase price.²¹⁰ Working from the premise that buying cryptocurrency is a contract to produce a work according to section 631 of the Civil Code, it should follow that a payment for goods with cryptocurrency is also a contract to produce a work within the meaning of section 631.²¹¹ Section 631 of the Civil Code provides that a party is obliged to produce the promised work when the other party is obliged to pay the agreed remuneration.²¹² The promised

---

²⁰⁶ Schroeder, *supra* note 174, at 50.
²⁰⁷ DEUTSCHER BUNDESTAG: DRUCKSACHEN UND PROTOKOLLE [BT] 14/6040, at 242.
²⁰⁸ ROLAND MICHAEL BECKMANN, KOMMENTAR ZUM BÜRGERLICHES GESETZBUCH (BGB) MIT EINFÜHRUNGSGESETZ UND NEBENGESETZEN BUCH 2, RECHT DER SCHULDVERHÄLTNISSE § 453 no. 36 (Julius von Staudinger, ed., 12th ed. 2014).
²⁰⁹ Schroeder, *supra* note 174, at 50.
²¹⁰ Boehm & Pesch, *supra* note 150, at 78; Moritz Schroeder, *supra* note 174, at 60.
²¹¹ Boehm & Pesch, *supra* note 150, at 78 (denying this without classifying such transactions).
²¹² BÜRGERLICHES GESETZBUCH [BGB] [Civil Code], Aug. 18, 1896, RGBL. 195, as amended, § 631.

work in this case would be the transaction of the agreed amount of the cryptocurrency. The obligation to pay would accordingly be the delivery of the good. The delivery of the good (cryptocurrency) can also fall under remuneration within the meaning of section 631 of the Civil Code, as remuneration allows for a wider interpretation than the obligation to pay the purchase price in a purchase agreement under section 433 of the Civil Code.[213] The consensus appears to be that remuneration within the meaning of 631 of the Civil Code might refer to money, but could also include other forms of payment, such as the delivery of work or that of other goods.[214] Alternatively, in the event that buying a cryptocurrency is a purchase of rights under section 453 of the Civil Code, then a purchase made with cryptocurrencies is an exchange contract within the meaning of section 480 of the Civil Code.[215]

One characteristic of an exchange contract is that two assets (which do not need to be similar) are exchanged.[216] Some perspectives, interpreting rights and assets narrowly, would deny that cryptocurrencies are such an asset.[217] However, this position ignores the fact that the category of assets under section 480 of the Civil Code must be interpreted broadly, thereby including rights or other legal possessions of value that are transferable.[218] Cryptocurrencies are, at a minimum, a legal possession of value insofar as they are a commodity. Furthermore, cryptocurrencies can be transferred legally, since cryptocurrency transactions do not violate any law.

If buying an item with cryptocurrency is interpreted as an exchange contract within the meaning of section 480 of the Civil Code, the result is that the legal provisions to a purchase contract, including section 433 of the Civil Code (relating to defects), would apply. In such a transaction, it also seems appropriate to interpret the law in a broader way, and not to follow the interpretation that paying for goods with cryptocurrencies is only a "contract to produce a work."

---

[213] WOLFGANG VOIT, BECK'SCHER ONLINE-KOMMENTAR BÜRGERLICHES GESETZBUCH (BGB) § 631 no. 72 (Heinz Georg Bamberger & Herbert Roth, 33d ed. 2014).
[214] Id.
[215] Schroeder, *supra* note 174, at 60.
[216] HARM P. WESTERMANN, MÜNCHENER KOMMENTAR BÜRGERLICHES GESETZBUCH § 480 no. 1 (Franz Jürgen Säcker et al. eds., 6th ed. 2012).
[217] Boehm & Pesch, *supra* note 150, at 78 Djazayeri, *supra* note 4.
[218] WESTERMANN, *supra* note 216, § 480 no. 1.

4.2.3. Other Contracts

If cryptocurrencies are to be considered as a kind of right, then all other civil exchanges that are paid for in cryptocurrencies, such as producing a work, providing a service, and leasing, must be interpreted under the normal legal categories for such contracts. The reason is that these contracts allow for a broader interpretation of the obligation to pay, thus permitting cryptocurrencies to satisfy the payment obligation. Examples of this include: lease agreements under section 535 of the Civil Code (providing an obligation to pay the lessor the agreed rent); service agreements under section 611 of the Civil Code (providing an obligation to grant the agreed remuneration); and contracts to produce a work under section 631 of the Civil Code (providing an obligation to pay the agreed remuneration).[219]

4.3. Legal Acts *Sui Generis*

In German law, when there is an agreement for the transfer of a commodity, the contract and the actual transmission of the commodity are two separate juridical acts. The analysis of what type of legal action characterizes the transfer of cryptocurrency will be premised on the presumption that a contract to buy cryptocurrencies is a contract to buy a right according to section 453 of the Civil Code and that a contract to buy an item with cryptocurrencies is an exchange contract according to section 480 of the Civil Code.[220]

The view that the transfer of cryptocurrencies is a transfer of rights is based on the argument that such a contract is a contract to "purchase rights." Rights are transferred according to sections 398 and 413 of the Civil Code.[221] According to these sections, a right is transferred if the parties agree that the right is transferred. In the author's view, these provisions are not appropriate for cryptocurrencies because a transfer of ownership of cryptocurrencies usually goes hand in hand with, and is arguably synonymous with, a corresponding entry into the block chain (at least as to on-block chain transactions). It is also doubtful that the law relating to the transfer of a thing (section 929 of the Civil Code) would apply to the transfer of cryptocurrency between two

---

[219] Schroeder, *supra* note 174, at 64; Bürgerliches Gesetzbuch [BGB] [Civil Code], Aug. 18, 1896, Reichsgesetzblatt [RGBl.] 195, as amended, §§ 535, 611, 631.

[220] Bürgerliches Gesetzbuch [BGB] [Civil Code], Aug. 18, 1896, RGBl., 195, as amended, §§ 453, 480.

[221] Bürgerliches Gesetzbuch [BGB] [Civil Code], Aug. 18, 1896, RGBl., 195, as amended, §§ 398, 413.

parties. Ownership of property is transferred by delivery of the thing as well as an agreement as to the transfer of ownership according to section 929 of the Civil Code.[222] However, because cryptocurrencies are not things, this law cannot apply directly.[223]

Because the transfer of cryptocurrencies cannot be subsumed either under section 929 on the one hand, or under sections 398 and 413 of the Civil Code on the other hand, the transfer of cryptocurrencies is a legal act *sui generis*. Legal acts *sui generis* are those that cannot be placed into any of the known categories. Therefore, one opinion tends to use section 929 of the Civil Code by analogy.[224] Irrespective of how the contract is categorized, the transfer of cryptocurrencies is only successful if the recipient of the cryptocurrency is registered in the block chain as the new owner of the coins. This means that the seller of cryptocurrencies fulfills his or her obligation of a cryptocurrency purchase agreement when the buyer is registered as the new owner of the coins in the block chain. When there is an exchange contract, the person who pays using cryptocurrency also fulfills his or her obligations when the contracting partner is registered in the block chain as owner of the coins.

4.4. Revocation of the Contract

Juridical consequences follow from a breach of contract. This holds true for contracts involving cryptocurrencies. However, the particular consequences will depend on how that contract is defined.[225] As discussed, contracts involving cryptocurrency will usually qualify as contracts to purchase rights (section 453 of the Civil Code) or as exchange contracts (section 480 of the Civil Code). Here we will discuss the breach of duty or revocation of these types of contracts with regards to cryptocurrencies.

4.4.1. The Delivered Items Have a Defect

The provisions regarding defective goods or services in an exchange contract are similar to those that cover purchase agreements. A person can demand the revocation of a contract under certain circumstances,

---

[222] BÜRGERLICHES GESETZBUCH [BGB] [Civil Code], Aug. 18, 1896, RGBL., 195, as amended, § 929.
[223] Engelhardt & Klein, *supra* note 174, at 357.
[224] Spindler & Bille, *supra* note 5, at 1363; BÜRGERLICHES GESETZBUCH [BGB] [Civil Code], Aug. 18, 1896, RGBL., 195, as amended, § 929.
[225] Boehm & Pesch, *supra* note 150, at 78.

for example if there is a defect with the thing, its specification, or there is an additional period for performance, according to sections 437 and 488 of the Civil Code.[226] If the necessary conditions for the revocation of a contract are fulfilled, each party has to return the received goods and services or payment according to section 346(1) of the Civil Code, which means that one party has to return the item while the other party has to return the received cryptocurrency.[227]

Consequently, a person who demands the revocation of a contract receives the amount of the cryptocurrency paid regardless of differences in the exchange rate at the time of payment and the time of refund. This problem is discussed in the German literature, which posits that where payment is made in stock, then that stock, regardless of the change in valuation, must be returned where the item purchased with them is defective.[228] In older literature and legal decisions, the consensus had been that the risk of loss in returning the stock should be borne by the buyer.[229] However, this position has shifted and more recent opinions have been that profit or loss should be borne by the seller.[230] The reason is that section 346(1) of the Civil Code appears to hold that the buyer has to receive the paid-for performance—here, the amount of cryptocurrency paid over—back.[231] Therefore, where payment is made in cryptocurrency, a change in its value will not be taken into consideration.[232] Furthermore, according to sections 280, 281 and 325 of the Civil Code, the buyer can claim damages for the difference in value between the cryptocurrency paid and that which is returned if the value of the cryptocurrency declines.

---

[226] BÜRGERLICHES GESETZBUCH [BGB] [Civil Code], Aug. 18, 1896, REICHSGESETZBLATT [RGBL.] 195, as amended, §§ 437, 488.
[227] HUBERT SCHMIDT, BECK'SCHER ONLINE-KOMMENTAR BÜRGERLICHES GESETZBUCH (BGB) § 346 no. 31 (Heinz Georg Bamberger & Herbert Roth, 33d ed. 2014).
[228] Id.
[229] WALTHER HADDING, BÜRGERLICHES GESETZBUCH MIT EINFÜHRUNGSGESETZ UND NEBENGESETZEN § 346 no. 6 (Hans Th. Soergel, ed., 12th ed. 1990).
[230] SCHMIDT, *supra* note 227, § 346 no. 31; RAINHARD GAIER, MÜNCHENER KOMMENTAR BÜRGERLICHES GESETZBUCH (BGB) § 346 no. 17 (Franz Jürgen Säcker et al. eds., 6th ed. 2012).
[231] SCHMIDT, *supra* note 227, § 346 no. 31; GAIER, *supra* note 230, § 346 no. 17; BÜRGERLICHES GESETZBUCH [BGB] [Civil Code], Aug. 18, 1896, RGBL., 195, as amended, § 346(1).
[232] SCHMIDT, *supra* note 227, § 346 no. 31; GAIER, *supra* note 230,§ 346 no. 17.

4.4.2. Revocation of Consumer Contracts

Under certain circumstances, according to section 355 of the Civil Code, a consumer has the right to revoke a contract within 14 days of purchase. This rule applies to the purchase of an item that is made online. Similar to a revocation due to defective goods, the seller has to return the paid cryptocurrency notwithstanding the value of the cryptocurrency at the moment of the return. However, the consumer will ultimately have to forgo any claim to damages for breach, because by opting to revoke the contract as of right,[233] thereby having his or her payment returned, this releases the seller of any further obligation initially contained under the now-revoked consumer contract.

4.4.3. Delivery or Payment with Misappropriated Cryptocurrency

Rights, which are involved in a purchase agreement, might be defective in legal terms, according to sections 453 and 435 of the Civil Code. One example of this would be the sale of a patent that expires in 5 years instead of 25 years. It is debatable, however, whether cryptocurrencies are capable of being legally defective.[234] This might be different for each cryptocurrency as some altcoins have different protocols. What this may mean for bitcoin in terms of prior claims is as yet unclear.

However, it is possible to consider the entry of the transaction in the block chain as being legally unsound if the transaction is criminal.[235] This might happen if the bitcoin being transferred from a particular wallet arose out of an illegal transaction. If this occurs, the buyer of the stolen bitcoin has a right of revocation according to section 346 of the Civil Code. Where stolen bitcoins are involved in an exchange contract, the innocent person who received the bitcoin has a right to revoke the contract.[236]

---

[233] BÜRGERLICHES GESETZBUCH [BGB] [Civil Code], Aug. 18, 1896, RGBL., 195, as amended, §§ 280, 281, 325.
[234] Engelhardt & Klein, *supra* note 174, at 359 n. 62.
[235] Engelhardt & Klein, *supra* note 174, at 357.
[236] BÜRGERLICHES GESETZBUCH [BGB] [Civil Code], Aug. 18, 1896, RGBL., 195, as amended, §§ 346, 437, 488.

4.5. Damages for Breach of Duty

If a person breaches his or her obligations, the co-contracting party may have a claim in damages against the breaching party.[237] The most relevant breach of contract relating to cryptocurrencies might be that a person delivers the cryptocurrency payment later than was stipulated and the cryptocurrency loses value in the meantime, leading to a loss for the receiver.[238] This type of a contract breach would open the possibility for a damage claim.[239]

4.6. Tort Law

The favoured position is that cryptocurrencies are protected by the law of tort.[240] However, it is debatable whether the protection arises out of section 823(1) of the Civil Code or out of section 823(2) of the Civil Code in conjunction with the Criminal Code. According to section 823(1), a person who unlawfully injures the life, body, health, freedom, property or the rights of another person, be it intentionally or negligently, is liable to make compensation to the other party for the damage arising from this action. As cryptocurrencies (which are solely or mainly stored in the block chain) and the cryptocurrency key are not defined as property (as discussed above), cryptocurrencies are not protected by the term "property" under section 823(1) of the Civil Code.[241] However, the cryptocurrency key is indirectly protected if the key is saved, for example, on a disk or paper.[242] When this occurs, the disk or paper is the property that is protected by section 823(1). In the event that it is damaged or stolen, not only does the value of the disk or paper have to be restored, but the value of the saved data on the disk or paper must also be restored.[243] However, this gives no legal

---

[237] Bürgerliches Gesetzbuch [BGB] [Civil Code], Aug. 18, 1896, RGBL., 195, as amended, § 280 ff; Boehm & Pesch, *supra* note 150, at 78.
[238] Engelhardt & Klein, *supra* note 174, at 358.
[239] Bürgerliches Gesetzbuch [BGB] [Civil Code], Aug. 18, 1896, RGBL., 195, as amended, §§ 280(2), 286.
[240] Gerald Spindler & Martin Bille, *supra* note 5, at 1363; Engelhardt & Klein, *supra* note 174, at 358.
[241] Bürgerliches Gesetzbuch [BGB] [Civil Code], Aug. 18, 1896, RGBL., 195, as amended, § 823(1).
[242] Spindler & Bille, *supra* note 5, at 357.
[243] Oberlandesgericht Oldenburg [OLG] [Higher Regional Court] Nov. 24, 2011, Zeitschrift für Datenschutz [ZD] at 177, 2012;

protection if the key is copied by a third party while the disk or paper remains untouched.[244]

As this conclusion may not seem to offer a satisfactory legal protection, one view is that cryptocurrencies should be protected as "another right" as provided under section 823(1) of the Civil Code.[245] The main argument for this is that the Supreme Court created the constitutional right of "the confidentiality and integrity of information technology systems."[246] Therefore, there exists a right for the private key to remain confidential, unused, and uncopied. This right can therefore be considered to be "another right" within the meaning of section 823(1) of the Civil Code.[247]

Another view suggests that cryptocurrencies are protected by section 823(2) of the Civil Code.[248] According to this section, a person whose acts breach a statute that is intended to protect another person must compensate the other person for any resulting damages. Examples of such statutes are section 202a of the Criminal Code (pertaining to data espionage), section 263a of the Criminal Code (pertaining to computer fraud) and section 303a of the Criminal Code (pertaining to data tampering).[249] Therefore, a person who violates the aforementioned sections must compensate the victim who suffers any resulting damage. As stated previously, the unauthorized transaction of cryptocurrencies to another wallet fulfills the element of 263a of the Criminal Code, therefore, the victim of such an act would be able to claim damages from the cause of the action. It appears as though both of these views (i.e., that which considers contracts to pay in cryptocurrency as subject to the rule regarding tort law, and that which sees cryptocurrency as "another right") arrive at the same conclusion through different means. The victim of stolen cryptocurrencies therefore should have a claim against the wrongdoer.

---

[244] Spindler & Bille, *supra* note 5, at 1363.
[245] *Id.*; BÜRGERLICHES GESETZBUCH [BGB] [Civil Code], Aug. 18, 1896, RGBL., 195, as amended, § 823(1).
[246] Spindler & Bille, *supra* note 5, at 1363.
[247] BÜRGERLICHES GESETZBUCH [BGB] [Civil Code], Aug. 18, 1896, RGBL., 195, as amended, § 823(1).
[248] Engelhardt & Klein, *supra* note 174, at 358.
[249] Kammergericht Berlin [KG] [Higher Regional Court] Oct. 10, 2009, NEUE JURISTISCHE ONLINE ZEITSCHRIFT [NJOZ] at 2164, 2010; Engelhardt & Klein, *supra* note 174, at 358.

4.7. Calculation of Damages

As mentioned above, a claim for damages may arise out of a breach of contract or from the application of tort law principles (e.g., stolen bitcoin, similar to the tort of conversion). The damage is calculated according to section 249 *et seq.* of the Civil Code. As the values of cryptocurrencies tend to fluctuate, it can be problematic to calculate a claim for damages.[250] According to section 249 of the Civil Code, a person who is liable for damages must restore the injured party to the position that she would have been in if the circumstances obliging the liable party to pay damages had not occurred.

Thus, a person who steals cryptocurrency at a time when the per unit value of the currency is €100 might have to return the cryptocurrency at a time when the value is only €50 per unit. It is the prevailing view in Germany that the wrongdoer who has committed cryptocurrency theft must pay to the victim the higher of two values between the moment of theft and the moment when he or she is reprimanded, meaning that he or she is liable for the higher per unit value of the currency if it has increased or decreased.[251]

If there is a decrease of the value of the cryptocurrency, the creditor may also have another claim against the wrongdoer if the creditor could have sold the cryptocurrencies to avoid the loss of value of the cryptocurrency had the theft not been committed.[252] The calculation of the damage from this claim is similar to the calculation of the damage from the claim for delayed delivery of the cryptocurrency. The starting point for calculating the damages for the second claim is usually the moment at which the creditor receives damages for the first claim.[253] To make such a claim, the creditor must prove that she would have sold the cryptocurrency to avoid an enormous loss. It may be difficult to present evidence that he or she would have acted in a certain way, but if the behavior was an expected type of action, this may be sufficient.[254] Previous trading behavior might be an indicator of how a person would have dealt with a loss in the value of cryptocurrency. If, for example, the value of the cryptocurrency rose from €100 per unit to €200 per unit and then decreased back to €100 per unit, the

---

[250] Engelhardt & Klein, *supra* note 174, at 358.
[251] HARTMUT OETKER, MÜNCHENER KOMMENTAR BÜRGERLICHES GESETZBUCH (BGB) § 249 No. 311 (Franz Jürgen Säcker et al. eds., 6th ed. 2012).
[252] See Erman/Ebert no. 29; Soergel/Mertens § 249 no. 50.
[253] OETKER, *supra* note 251 § 249 no. 314.
[254] BÜRGERLICHES GESETZBUCH [BGB] [Civil Code], Aug. 18, 1896, RGBL., 195, as amended, § 252(2) ff; OETKER, *supra* note 251 § 249 no. 311.

moment at which the cryptocurrency would have been sold is to be estimated, according to section 287 of the Code of Civil Procedure.[255] If the cryptocurrency value increases from €100 per unit to €300 per unit, the wrongdoer can try to prove that the creditor would have sold the cryptocurrency at a price of €200. If the wrongdoer is able to present such proof, he or she only has to compensate for damages of approximately €100 per unit.[256]

4.8. Specific Performance of a Claim in Cryptocurrencies

Whether compulsory enforcement, also known as specific performance, can be applied to debts in the form of cryptocurrencies is disputed.[257] The prevailing view is that the relevant section on specific performance in the Code of Civil Procedure (i.e. section 808) does not apply to cryptocurrencies, as it only applies to moveable property (as discussed previously).[258] It is also the consensus that a compulsory enforcement on the basis of sections 829 and 835 of the Code of Civil Procedure is not possible because these sections only apply to payments of money.[259] The prevailing view is that cryptocurrencies are not money.[260]

It may be possible to enforce a claim in cryptocurrencies according to section 857 of the Code of Civil Procedure. According to this section, enforcement of a claim on "other rights" is possible. It is therefore necessary to assume that cryptocurrencies are "other rights" in the context of section 857 of the Code of Civil Procedure.[261] A denial that cryptocurrencies are "other rights" will negate the applicability of section 857 of the Code of Civil Procedure.[262] If the applicability of section 857 of the Code of Civil Procedure is refuted, compulsory enforcement is still possible under section 888 of the Code of Civil Procedure. It states that the debtor can be forced to take an action

---

[255] Zivilprozessordnung [ZPO] [Code of Civil Procedure], Oct. 10, 2013; BUNDESGESETZBLATT, Teil I [BGBL. I] at 3786, § 287; OETKER, *supra* note 251 § 249 no. 313.
[256] Engelhardt & Klein, *supra* note 174, at 358.
[257] Boehm & Pesch, *supra* note 150, at 78; Schroeder, *supra* note 174, at 111.
[258] Boehm & Pesch, *supra* note 150, at 78; Schroeder, *supra* note 174, at 111.
[259] Boehm & Pesch, *supra* note 150, at 78; Schroeder, *supra* note 174, at 111.
[260] Boehm & Pesch, *supra* note 150, at 78; Schroeder, *supra* note 174, at 111.
[261] Schroeder, *supra* note 174, at 111.
[262] Boehm & Pesch, *supra* note 150, at 78.

such as the disclosure of information[263] (which could involve providing the private key of the wallet and/or transferring cryptocurrency).[264]

5. Anti-Money Laundering Law

The German Financial Intelligence Unit (FIU) is affiliated with the Federal Criminal Police Office.[265] The function of the FIU is to receive and evaluate all notifications of suspicious transactions that could involve money laundering and/or financing of terrorism.[266] Prior to 2013, neither the FIU nor the cybercrime unit had focused explicitly on money laundering or financing terrorism using bitcoin or other cryptocurrencies.[267] In 2013, however, the FIU was notified at least 49 times regarding suspicious transactions related to electronic payment systems.[268] Furthermore, there are no special laws addressing money laundering, financing terrorism, and cryptocurrency specifically. However, the FIU has been monitoring electronic payment systems since 2008. As there is no special law addressing bitcoin, the general laws regarding the prevention and criminalization of money laundering and financing terrorism apply.

5.1. Money Laundering and Financing Terrorism as Crime

Money laundering is a crime according to section 261 of the Criminal Code and those who launder money shall be liable to imprisonment ranging from three months to five years. Financing terrorism is also a crime according to section 89a(2) no. 4 of the Criminal Code and is punishable by imprisonment ranging from six months to ten years. Money laundering occurs when a person tries to hide an object acquired through an unlawful act, either for himself or for a third person. An object, according to section 261 of the Criminal Code, is interpreted in a very broad manner and includes more than just

---

[263] MICHAEL STÜRMER, BECK'SCHER ONLINE-KOMMENTAR ZIVILPROZESSORDNUNG (ZPO), § 888 no. 6, (Volkert Vorwerk & Christian Wolf, 14th ed. 2014).
[264] Schroeder, *supra* note 174, at 114.
[265] BUNDESKRIMINALAMT, FINANCIAL INTELLIGENCE UNIT (FIU), *Jahresbericht 2013*, *available at* http://www.bka.de/nn_204308/SharedDocs/Downloads/DE/Publikationen/JahresberichteUndLagebilder/FIU/Jahresberichte/fiuJahresbericht2013,templateId=raw,property=publicationFile.pdf/fiuJahresbericht2013.pdf.
[266] Geldwäschegesetz [GwG] [Money Laundering Act] Aug. 13, 2008, BUNDESGESETZBLATT, Teil I [BGBL. I] at 1690, § 11.
[267] BUNDESKRIMINALAMT, *supra* note 265.
[268] *Id.*, at 30.

cash but also money in banks, rights, and even marketable positions.[269] Consequently, bitcoin is an object within the meaning of section 261 of the Criminal Code. A person procures an object, within the meaning of section 261 of the Criminal Code, if that person receives control over the object. In doing so, it is irrelevant whether the person has a claim to receive the object or not. Therefore, a person who receives bitcoin or money obtained out of illegal activities or bitcoin transactions may be guilty under the criminal provisions regarding money laundering.

5.2. Money Laundering Prevention

To prevent money laundering and terrorist financing, there are several laws that place obligations upon third parties to report the suspicious behavior of customers to the Financial Intelligence Unit. The main obligations to prevent money laundering and terrorist financing are in the Money Laundering Act. This law is also supplemented by the Banking Act, which creates some obligations that have the effect of preventing money laundering.

5.2.1. Businesses That Are Obligated under the Money Laundering Act

The Money Laundering Act places several obligations on certain types of businesses and individuals to avoid and prevent money laundering. Those with such obligations include credit or financial institutions, insurance companies, lawyers who administer assets (e.g., buying real estate), tax advisors, real estate agents, casinos (land-based and online) and persons trading goods within the meaning of section 2 of the Money Laundering Act. Some cryptocurrency-related business models will likely qualify as obligated parties pursuant to the Money Laundering Act. Relevant models are credit institutions or financial institutions within the meaning of the Banking Act, pursuant to section 2(1) no. 1 and no. 2 of the Money Laundering Act.[270] As the Money Laundering Act makes reference to the Banking Act, a person that trades cryptocurrencies as goods is likely considered to be a financial services institution according to section 1 (1a) 2 Nr.

---

[269] Strafgesetzbuch [StGB] [Criminal Code], Nov. 13, 1998, BGBL. I at 945, § 261; FELIX RUHMANNSEDER, BECK'SCHER ONLINE-KOMMENTAR STRAFGESETZBUCH (STGB) § 261 no. 8 (Bernd von Heintschel-Heinegg, 24th ed. 2014).

[270] Geldwäschegesetz [GwG] [Money Laundering Act] Aug. 13, 2008, BGBL. I at 1690, § 2(1) no. 1, § 2(1) no. 2.

4a of the Banking Act.²⁷¹ Therefore, such a person is obligated under the Money Laundering Act as a financial services institution, not as a trader of goods.

However, a merchant who accepts cryptocurrencies as payment will become an obligated party because all traders of goods are obligated parties according to section 2(1) no. 13 of the Money Laundering Act. This is different with respect to offering a service. A person who accepts cryptocurrencies as payment for a service does not become an obligated party within the meaning of the Money Laundering Act.²⁷² Furthermore, persons who operate an online wallet or who are mining cryptocurrencies do not become obligated parties within the meaning of the Money Laundering Act, as those activities do not qualify as financial services within the meaning of section 1 of the Banking Act.²⁷³

5.2.2. Obligations Without Incidents

Typically, all obligated persons have to take records of information related to customers and store them for five years.²⁷⁴ Furthermore, all obligated parties must take internal measures to prevent money laundering²⁷⁵ and must report all transactions that are suspicious.²⁷⁶ There is also the general obligation to monitor the business relationship on an ongoing basis, which includes close examination of transactions undertaken throughout the course of this relationship.²⁷⁷

5.2.3. Obligations With Incidents

Certain events will create anti-money laundering obligations for businesses. These obligations usually arise when a business relationship

---

[271] See section 1.4.3, above.
[272] PETER HÄBERLE, STRAFRECHTLICHE NEBENGESETZE GWG § 2 No. 18 (Georg Erbs et al. eds., 195th ed. 2013).
[273] Spindler & Bille, *supra* note 5, at 1367.
[274] Geldwäschegesetz [GwG] [Money Laundering Act] Aug. 13, 2008, BGBL. I at 1690, § 8.
[275] Geldwäschegesetz [GwG] [Money Laundering Act] Aug. 13, 2008, BGBL. I at 1690, § 9.
[276] Geldwäschegesetz [GwG] [Money Laundering Act] Aug. 13, 2008, BGBL. I at 1690, § 11.
[277] Geldwäschegesetz [GwG] [Money Laundering Act] Aug. 13, 2008, BGBL. I at 1690, § 3.

is established.[278] The obligation to report suspicious activity occurs whenever (i) whenever a transaction with a value of €15,000 or more is carried out outside of an existing business relationship;[279] (ii) factual circumstances exist to indicate that the assets or property connected with a transaction or business relationship are the product of an offence under section 261 of the Criminal Code or are related to terrorist financing;[280] or (iii) there is doubt as to the veracity of the information collected in relation to the identity of the contracting party or the beneficial owner.[281]

Investigations are required whenever there is a suspicious transaction, regardless of the volume of the transaction. When these incidents occur, the obligated parties have to identify the contracting partner, obtain information about the purpose and intended nature of the business, and clarify whether the contracting party is acting on behalf of a beneficial owner and identify the beneficial owner.[282] It is the duty of the FIU to inform the public and relevant businesses about new forms of money laundering and therefore assist in the identification of suspicious transactions. At the time of writing, the FIU has not mentioned that transactions involving bitcoin are necessarily suspicious, meaning that an obligated party who receives bitcoin does not need to become suspicious merely because the customer paid in bitcoin.

However, the obligation to identify the contract partner upon the establishment of the relationship is not required if the obligated party is a business that trades goods.[283] Furthermore, such businesses typically only incur this obligation in cases where they receive €15,000 or more in cash.[284] Accordingly, this usually means that no identification obligation is required if the trader receives the amount

---

[278] Geldwäschegesetz [GwG] [Money Laundering Act] Aug. 13, 2008, BGBL. I at 1690, § 3(2) no. 1.
[279] Geldwäschegesetz [GwG] [Money Laundering Act] Aug. 13, 2008, BGBL. I at 1690, § 3(2) no. 2.
[280] Geldwäschegesetz [GwG] [Money Laundering Act] Aug. 13, 2008, BGBL. I at 1690, § 3(2) no. 3.
[281] Geldwäschegesetz [GwG] [Money Laundering Act] Aug. 13, 2008, BGBL. I at 1690, § 3(2) no. 4.
[282] Geldwäschegesetz [GwG] [Money Laundering Act] Aug. 13, 2008, BGBL. I at 1690, § 3(1).
[283] Geldwäschegesetz [GwG] [Money Laundering Act] Aug. 13, 2008, BGBL. I at 1690, § 3(2) no. 1.
[284] Geldwäschegesetz [GwG] [Money Laundering Act] Aug. 13, 2008, BGBL. I at 1690, § 3(2).

in cryptocurrencies and not in euros.[285] However, when this occurs, section 3(2) 1 no. 3 of the Money Laundering Act might apply whereby a transaction is connected to an offence.

5.2.4. Obligations under the Banking Act

Credit and financial services institutions under section 1 of the Banking Act incur additional obligations.[286] For example, a credit service institute must investigate and gather additional information when money is transferred outside of the European Union. A credit institution is only allowed to transfer money when the receiving credit institution is undertaking all necessary measures to prevent money laundering.[287]

6. Conclusion

In this chapter, we reviewed the intersection of some of the more salient German laws and regulations with several aspects of cryptocurrencies. The laws of financial institutions, income taxation and VAT rules, criminal law provisions, the civil code of obligations, and anti-money laundering and counter-terrorist financing rules all touch on cryptocurrencies in Germany. The law is, as yet, highly undeveloped with few cases to rely upon, but it is also dynamic and attracting more attention. We shall have to wait to see how both the public and private law aspects of cryptocurrencies develop in Germany and in the European Union in the coming months and years.

---

[285] Spindler & Bille, *supra* note 5, at 1367.
[286] Kreditwesengesetz [KWG] [Banking Act], Jul. 10, 1961, BGBL. I at 2776, § 25 ff.
[287] Kreditwesengesetz [KWG] [Banking Act], Jul. 10, 1961, BGBL. I at 2776, § 25k.

THE UNITED KINGDOM

PAUL ANNING
MICHAEL TAYLOR
LORNA BRAZELL
MARK BRAILSFORD

ooooooooooooooooooooooooooooooooooooo

EXECUTIVE SUMMARY

The United Kingdom's response to the opportunities and challenges posed by cryptocurrencies has been, in common with many of its European neighbours, piecemeal. The first meaningful response by a UK governmental institution was the March 2014 publication on the tax treatment of bitcoin (the "**HMRC Briefing**") issued by the UK HM Revenue & Customs ("**HMRC**").[1] The view expressed in that publication—*viz.*, that income received from bitcoin mining activities and other associated activities will generally be outside the scope of VAT—is one that is broadly shared by other European tax authorities at the time of writing. Following HMRC's briefing, other responses were released by UK governmental institutions and figures, most notably, publications on cryptocurrencies from the Bank of England[2] which, amongst other things, discussed whether cryptocurrencies posed a material risk to the monetary and financial stability of the United Kingdom. The Chancellor of the Exchequer, the Rt. Hon. George Osborne, also gave a speech in which he expressed

---

[1] HM REVENUE & CUSTOMS, REVENUE AND CUSTOMS BRIEF 9 (2014): BITCOIN AND OTHER CRYPTOCURRENCIES (2014), *available at* https://www.gov.uk/government/publications/revenue-and-customs-brief-9-2014-bitcoin-and-other-cryptocurrencies/revenue-and-customs-brief-9-2014-bitcoin-and-other-cryptocurrencies.

[2] Robleh Ali et al., *The economics of digital currencies*, BANK OF ENGLAND QUARTERLY BULLETIN 2014 Q3 276 (2014), *available at* http://www.bankofengland.co.uk/publications/Documents/quarterlybulletin/2014/qb14q302.pdf [hereinafter *Economics*]; Robleh Ali et al., *Innovations in payment technologies and the emergence of digital currencies*, BANK OF ENGLAND QUARTERLY BULLETIN 2014 Q3 262 (2014), *available at* http://www.bankofengland.co.uk/publications/Documents/quarterlybulletin/2014/qb14q301.pdf [hereinafter *Innovations*].

his desire for the UK to become the world's leading FinTech hub.[3] The question of whether the current UK legislative and regulatory framework is suitable for cryptocurrencies such as bitcoin to prosper remains an issue for debate.

This chapter will consider three aspects of the legal and regulatory impact of bitcoin in the UK.

First, the treatment of bitcoin under UK intellectual property law will be reviewed. There have been few bitcoin-specific developments in the UK in respect of IP, and it is our view that it is unlikely that the systems governing the operation of bitcoin would be patentable in the United Kingdom.

Second, the UK tax matters concerning bitcoin will be analysed. While the issue of whether or not bitcoin constitutes e-money has been largely sidestepped by the UK's legal and regulatory bodies, the HMRC Briefing[4] expressly deals with the tax treatment of virtual currencies such as bitcoin. From this publication there are a number of insights to be drawn. HMRC takes a positive and common-sense approach to the taxation of transactions executed in bitcoin and is largely in line with other European jurisdictions.

Thirdly, the general UK regulatory response to bitcoin will be outlined. Bitcoin does not constitute "money" under any of the relevant legislation or regulations, and most bitcoin-related activities are unregulated, at least insofar as certain aspects of money and monetary instruments are concerned. Broadly, the UK has adopted a more libertarian approach than other European jurisdictions, placing a greater emphasis on encouraging innovation in the financial sector. This is in keeping with the UK's status as a pre-eminent world financial centre. However, the pressure from Europe to bring bitcoin within the scope of additional regulation may force the UK's hand in the near future.

THE INTERPLAY OF INTELLECTUAL PROPERTY RIGHTS WITH BITCOIN

The principles upon which the Bitcoin system was based were published in a paper authored by Satoshi Nakamoto in 2008.[5]

---

[3] Rt. Hon. George Osborne, MP, UK Chancellor of the Exchequer, Chancellor's speech at the launch of the new trade body for FinTech, 'Innovate Finance (Aug. 6, 2014), *available at* https://www.gov.uk/government/speeches/chancellor-on-developing-fintech.

[4] HM REVENUE & CUSTOMS, *supra* note 1.

[5] SATOSHI NAKAMOTO, BITCOIN: A PEER-TO-PEER ELECTRONIC CASH SYSTEM 1 (2008), https://bitcoin.org/bitcoin.pdf.

Transparency is the essence of the system; users have to work together to ensure that coins are spent only once, which requires a complete record to be kept of every transaction in which a coin has been used. Whilst this could still be achieved even with intellectual property rights being asserted over the technology and identity of the system, the intention of the system's inventor(s) and developers to date has been to maintain an open source approach to enable wider engagement with both using and developing the system.

This does not, however, mean that the Bitcoin universe is an intellectual property-free zone.

Bitcoin's fundamental components

Since the principles and fundamental components of the system— the nature of the bitcoins themselves and the block chain system for maintaining a distributed public ledger of transactions—were published as an article rather than a patent, those principles are now in the public domain and cannot themselves be the subject of a patent application anywhere in the world since, in order to be patentable, an invention must be novel.[6] It might still be possible to apply for a patent over alternative applications of the components of the system, such as the use of a block chain for date or time stamping purposes or digital verification rather than maintaining records of Bitcoin transactions, provided that such applications were not disclosed either expressly or implicitly in the original paper. Any such application-specific patent will be relatively narrow in that it will only monopolise the application of the component and not the component in any other context. Given the range and number of post-Bitcoin applications already available, the scope for future novel and so potentially patentable applications is steadily decreasing with time. But as the extent of Bitcoin-like products increases (such as the Trests, to be launched in India by Trestor Network in 2015), so also will the level of detail of operation at which patent applications will be aimed.

It is unlikely that either the system of miners verifying transactions and maintaining a distributed ledger or its components would be patentable in the United Kingdom. They would presumably consist of a series of principles which together constitute a business method. Such

---

[6] Agreement on Trade-Related Aspects of Intellectual Property, Apr. 15, 1994, Marrakesh Agreement Establishing the World Trade Organization, 1869 U.N.T.S. 299, art. 27, para. 1 [hereinafter TRIPS Agreement] (defining patentable subject matter, reflected in the national laws of all WTO contracting states).

methods are excluded from patentability pursuant to the Patents Act 1977,[7] albeit subject to the proviso that the exclusion applies only to applications to patent a business method "as such." In operational form, the system for creating and transacting in bitcoins consists of software, which is also excluded under the same provision and subject to the same proviso. These two exclusions derive from Article 52 of the European Patent Convention, and are common amongst the national patent laws of all EU Member States. There has been considerable debate over the point at which a computer program ceases to be a program "as such." Software controlling the operation of a physical machine (and claimed together with that machine) is patentable, whereas software simply moving value across a series of investment accounts is not. The precise boundary, however, is difficult to identify. An invention needs to have some technical effect over and above the ordinary interaction of software with a computer memory and processes in order to be patentable, with the English courts' approach to what constitutes such a technical effect having tended[8] to be somewhat narrower than that applied by the European Patent Office.[9] The English courts have become somewhat more liberal in recent decisions such as *HTC Europe Co Ltd v. Apple Inc.*[10] Despite this, software implementing a method of generating and transacting in a cryptographic currency is likely still to fall on the unpatentable side of the line since it would be difficult to identify a technical effect outside the computer suitable to bring the program into the realm of patentability.

Nevertheless, once a computer program is tied to a specific device or application, then it may well be patentable within that context. Accordingly, devices such as the Trezor hardware wallet (to enable ordinary users to transact in bitcoins with online and real world merchants) may well be patentable if the technology used meets the normal criteria—novelty and an inventive step—for patentability. As Bitcoin gains greater acceptance outside the cryptographic community, it is highly likely that exactly as with the currently emerging forms of payment technology, technology companies will patent the features and functions of their particular implementations that they hope will give them a market lead. Of course, many existing patents over aspects

---

[7] Patents Act, 1977, c. 37, § 1(2)(c) (U.K.).
[8] *See, e.g.*, Aerotel Ltd v. Telco Holdings Ltd, [2006] EWCA Civ 1371; Symbian Limited v. Comptroller Gen. of Patents, [2008] EWCA Civ 1066.
[9] *See, e.g.*, Case T 0931/95, Pension Benefit Systems Partnership, ECLI:EP:BA:2000:T093195.20000908 (2000).
[10] [2013] EWCA Civ 451.

such as contactless payment will apply to devices for transacting in bitcoins exactly as they do to devices transacting in traditional currency, if the same technology is used.

The analysis of the application of copyright to Bitcoins and the surrounding technology follows a similar line. The Nakamoto paper originally published is, of course, protected by copyright since this is a right which arises automatically upon creation of a literary work.[11] In theory, therefore, there could be scope for Satoshi Nakamoto to bring copyright infringement proceedings against anyone copying the material he disclosed in it. However, in practice copyright is unlikely to protect the ideas expressed in the paper,[12] and so any organisation wishing to establish its own virtual currency, or use components of the system described, using the same techniques, would be unlikely to infringe any copyright.

The source code subsequently released to bring Bitcoin itself into practice was declared to be open source. Therefore, despite also being a work in which copyright arose automatically upon its creation, the copyright is now effectively subject to a unilateral licence (granted by the copyright holders without requiring any act by or even identification of the licensees) enabling any developer who is interested to copy and expand upon it. As with patentability, there are likely to be many commercial organisations developing software to provide additional functionality—bitcoin wallets and the like—that will not be subject to any such licence. Similarly, bitcoin exchanges and other service providers will operate using copyright software which may be enforceable against any unlicensed users provided that it is the code, rather than the underlying principles or algorithms, that are copied. The Court of Justice of the European Union ruled in *SAS Institute Inc. v. World Programming Ltd*[13] that copyright does not subsist in mathematical functions since these abstracts cannot constitute any author's own intellectual creation, as required for the subsistence of copyright under the Copyright Directive.[14]

---

[11] Copyright, Designs and Patents Act, 1988, c. 48, § 1(a) Section 1(a) (U.K.).
[12] TRIPS Agreement, *supra* note 6, art. 9, para. 2.
[13] Case C-406/10, SAS Inst. Inc. v. World Programming Ltd, 2012 E.C.D.R. 22.
[14] Directive 2001/29, of the European Parliament and of the Council of 22 May 2001 on the Harmonisation of Certain Aspects of Copyright and Related Rights in the Information Society 2001 (L 167) 10 (E.C.).

Public/private keys

The public and private cryptographic key pairs that underlie the Bitcoin system are unlikely in themselves to qualify for copyright protection since they consist solely of a 256 character software-generated alphanumeric chain with no human-interpretable meaning, and therefore will not meet the current "author's own intellectual creation" standard for copyright protection. A collection of such keys may, however, be protected as a database under the *sui generis* database right[15] provided that the database has been created through an investment not in creating the keys but in collecting, verifying or presenting them.

Further, for as long as it is kept secret, each individual private key will be protectable as confidential information since the requirements as a matter of English law for the protection of confidential information by the law of equity—i.e., that the information is precisely identifiable, secret and has value (*Lansing Linde Ltd v. Kerr*[16])—will be met, the value being whatever the corresponding bitcoin account represents at the time. Protection under the laws of confidentiality has limits; accidental disclosure may lead to a total loss of confidentiality, so the value of a private key depends entirely upon it being inaccessible to other users of a shared computer, for instance, or even hackers. Best practice is to maintain the key in a hard copy form, or at least completely separate from any networked device. This is referred to as "cold storage," and has been the subject of a US patent application[17] by the founder of BitBills. The claim is limited to electronic devices capable of registering any tampering with the stored value and transferring the stored value to the digital domain, and does not appear to have been followed by any European filing, so even if granted in the US it will not have effect in the UK.

Characterising private keys as confidential information highlights one significant issue under English law, which is that the legal rights associated with confidential information are not of the same nature of property rights. Trade secrets cannot be owned, mortgaged, assigned or stolen (*Oxford v. Moss*[18]) in the strict legal sense of that term, engaging criminal law remedies. Instead, they are purely rights in

---

[15] Directive 96/9, of the European Parliament and of the Council of 11 March 1996 on the Legal Protection of Databases 1996 (L 77) 20 (E.C.).
[16] [1991] 1 All. E.R. 418.
[17] U.S. Patent App. 13/336779 (filed Jun. 27, 2013).
[18] (1979) 68 Crim. App. R. 183 (appeal taken from Eng.).

equity to prevent mishandling (unauthorised disclosure or use) of the information. Accordingly, private keys cannot be stolen, although any physical medium upon which they are recorded can be. This is relevant in the case of a private key being memorised rather than the medium itself being taken. Of course, the number of people capable of rapidly memorising a 256 bit alphanumeric string is fairly limited.

Bitcoin identifiers

The name "Bitcoin" itself is not protected by the community of Bitcoin developers and consequently trade marks have been filed over it by a number of different individuals and entities. The term Bitcoin for use in electronic commerce over the internet was registered as a Community Trade Mark in 2011 in the name of Tibanne Co. Ltd, a Japanese company, which also holds variants on it such as a yellow and black logo with the word bitCOIN across it. There is even a UK trade mark registration for the use of chocolate "Bitcoins."

The validity of registrations of the term Bitcoin, for use with genuine Bitcoin applications, may be vulnerable to challenge, since the word can be argued to be a generic term for all cryptocurrency generated using the Bitcoin algorithm (and verified by the nodes of the Bitcoin system) rather than distinctive of any service originating from a particular trader. Registration of such terms is prohibited under the Trade Marks Act 1994.[19] Alternatively or in addition, it could be argued that as a privately owned trade mark Bitcoin is of such a nature as to deceive the public as to the nature of the service since, as mentioned above, it is the essence of the Bitcoin system that it is open source and independent of private ownership. If so, registration would also be prohibited under section 3(3)(b) of the Act.

The Bitcoin logo is of course also protected by copyright, but has been made available for universal use on www.bitcoin.org. Consistent with the nature of the site, it includes no detail as to the authorship of the logo nor any terms and conditions for its use. It is therefore possible that at some future date a designer could come forward claiming to have designed the logo and own the copyright in it, but it is likely that, having consented to provision of the logo to all the world through the site, any organisation using it would be found to be impliedly licensed during that period of consent even if the licence could then be terminated (on reasonable notice).[20] Any visual representations

---

[19] Trade Marks Act, 1994, c. 26, § 3(1)(d) (U.K.).
[20] Fisher v. Brooker [2009] UKHL 41 (appeal taken from Eng.).

of Bitcoins, such as the BitBills or physical bitcoin wallets, will be protected by copyright over the graphics and layout, but since these aspects are independent of the actual functionality of the currency they do not present any barrier to independent development of other physical wallets. They function only as a means of recognition of particular organisations' bitcoin-related products.

WHAT IS THE TAX TREATMENT OF BITCOIN IN THE UK?

Introduction

This section considers the main taxes in the UK that would be of concern to those involved in bitcoin transactions and dealings. These are, firstly, income tax and capital gains tax, the concepts behind which will be familiar. Companies, however, are not subject to these taxes but to corporation tax on their income and capital gains and the regimes are moderately different (more so in the case of income than capital gains). Potentially of most concern is Value Added Tax ("**VAT**"). VAT is a turnover tax that is based upon principles laid down in Directives of the European Union,[21] with which the UK is required to comply. Broadly speaking, VAT is a tax levied on the full amount (i.e., not just the profit element) of supplies of certain goods and services made in the course of business. However, some services are exempt from VAT, principally in the financial arena (such as making loans, other dealings in money, share issuances, and, most relevantly for bitcoin and bitcoin-related services, payment processing). Although the tax is designed so that the tax is borne by the consumer of the relevant goods or services, the burden of accounting to HMRC for the VAT chargeable falls upon the supplier.

---

[21] *See, e.g.,* First Council Directive 1301/67, on the Harmonisation of Legislation of Member States Concerning Turnover Taxes, 1967 J.O. 70 (E.C.); Second Council Directive 67/228, on the Harmonisation of Legislation of Member States Concerning Turnover Taxes, 1967 J.O. 70 (E.C.); Sixth Council Directive 77/388 on the Harmonization of the Laws of the Member States Relating to Turnover Taxes—Common System of Value Added Tax: Uniform Basis of Assessment, 1977 O.J. (L 145) 1 (E.C.); Council Directive 2006/112, on the Common System of Value Added Tax, 2006 O.J. (L 347) 1 (E.U.).

HMRC Briefing 2014

The current treatment of bitcoin under the UK tax regime has been set out in the HMRC Briefing.[22] HMRC notes that its position is provisional and subject to any developments in this area, in particular in respect of the regulatory and EU VAT position. While the HMRC Briefing does not carry the force of law, the document makes it clear that taxpayers are able to rely on the treatment outlined within until HMRC announces any changes, with such changes not to apply retrospectively.[23]

VAT and bitcoin

The UK tax treatment as set out in this commentary is accordingly based on the HMRC Briefing. It starts by considering the VAT position, and this commentary follows that ordering, as the VAT position has the greatest potential for giving rise to unexpected tax costs and is determined by the nature of bitcoin transactions.

Noting that the HMRC Briefing is provisional, the tax treatment of bitcoin as set out by HMRC is relatively straightforward (and contrasts with a more complex and unhelpful viewpoint that HMRC was previously believed to take). HMRC's view is that for VAT purposes:

(A) income received from bitcoin mining activities will generally be *outside the scope of VAT* on the basis that the activity does not constitute an economic activity for VAT purposes because there is an insufficient link between any services provided and any consideration received [and]

(B) income received by miners for other activities, such as for the provision of services in connection with the verification of specific transactions for which specific charges are made, will be *exempt from VAT* under Article 135(1)(d) of the EU VAT Directive as falling within the definition of 'transactions, including negotiation, concerning deposit and current accounts, payments, transfers, debts, cheques and other negotiable instruments[.]'[24]

---

[22] HM Revenue & Customs, *supra* note 1.
[23] *Id.*
[24] *Id.* (emphasis added).

The treatment under both of these paragraphs is favourable as it leads in each case to the result that no VAT is payable. It is interesting that HMRC has found a means to arrive at this result without having to expressly address the question of whether bitcoin is treated as "money" for VAT purposes or not. To some extent, therefore, HMRC could be regarded as hedging its bets pending market developments and particularly the evolution of the EU's thinking on the subject.

With regards to the exchange of bitcoin for currency and related charges, HMRC's view is as follows:

> when bitcoin is exchanged for Sterling or for foreign currencies, such as Euros or Dollars, *no VAT will be due* on the value of the bitcoins themselves [and] charges (in whatever form) made over and above the value of the Bitcoin for arranging or carrying out any transactions in bitcoin (e.g., service charges and currency exchange fees) will be *exempt from VAT* under Article 135(1)(d) as outlined ... above.[25]

As would be expected, HMRC is also very clear that sales of goods and services in exchange for payment in bitcoin will be subject to VAT based on the sterling value of the bitcoin at the relevant time. No express guidance is provided as to how that sterling value is to be established. The assumption is that, as with any currency exchange objective, evidence of applicable exchange rates will be identified.

Income tax and capital gains tax

The income tax and capital gains tax treatment is relatively straightforward. Where a taxpayer is carrying on a trade that includes the bitcoin-related activities in question, it will be subject to income tax on the profits and losses of the business as set out in the accounts, and the profits from the bitcoin activities will be included in that. Where a transaction is not taxed as part of a trade, any profit arising would normally be taxed as a capital gain and subject to capital gains tax.

Corporation tax

For corporation tax, the complicating factor is that there are particular rules for taxing foreign exchange movements and debts. In this regard, HMRC appears to accept the bracketing of virtual

---

[25] *Id.* (emphasis added).

currencies with "real" currencies and states that "the profits or losses on exchange movements between currencies are taxable. For the tax treatment of virtual currencies, the general rules on foreign exchange and loan relationships apply."[26]

HMRC has therefore not published bespoke rules for transactions in bitcoin, but wishes to assimilate such transactions within the general provisions. It notes that for companies, exchange movements are determined between the company's functional currency (usually the currency in which the accounts are prepared, e.g., pounds sterling) and the other currency in question (bitcoin, for example). If there is an exchange rate between bitcoin and the functional currency, the transaction will be subject to tax in the normal way. The currency exchange element of transactions denominated in, producing, or involving bitcoin would be reflected in the company's accounts and those accounting results would (normally) be followed for tax purposes and any resulting profit taxed under normal corporation tax rules.

The HMRC position described above reflects what the position would be if the bitcoin transaction is entered into as part of a trade or falls under the loan relationship rules, as in both of those cases the tax treatment would be determined by the accounts. However, HMRC has also added a note to the effect that a bitcoin transaction that is not entered into as part of a trade and is outside the loan relationship rules would be taxed as a capital gain. It is to be hoped that this is not intended to undermine the general position that has been stated. A pessimist may take the view that as HMRC has not enacted any bespoke rules, they are still hedging their bets as to whether the bitcoin transactions do actually fall within the "general rules on foreign exchange and loan relationships,"[27] and that the statement set out above has been carefully crafted simply to say that the rules "apply." If HMRC then decides to interpret the way they "apply" as being to the effect that bitcoin transactions do not fall within them, then the result for a non-trading transaction would be capital gains treatment. It remains to be seen whether such a pessimistic viewpoint has any foundation.

Position in other EU member states

Although there have been a number of efforts to combat tax competition within the EU, tax is not currently harmonised across the

---

[26] *Id.*
[27] *Id.*

twenty-eight Member States. The current position in the EU remains the same as that outlined in a 2006 European Commission document, namely that "as Community law currently stands, Member States remain largely free to design their direct tax systems so as to meet their domestic policy objectives and requirements."[28]

However, broadly speaking, HMRC's approach is bolder than that of a number of other European states, with most states yet to publish definitive guidance on the tax treatment of bitcoin. The Finnish Tax Administration published guidance in August 2013 stating that where bitcoin is used as a form of payment for goods and services it is to be treated as a trade, and the increase in value that the currency might have gained after it was obtained is taxable.[29] Similarly, the Estonian Tax and Customs Board ruled that any supply arising from bitcoin trading is subject to VAT at the rate of 20%.[30] Further, the Danish National Bank has stated that "bitcoins have no actual utility value, bearing closer resemblance to glass beads,"[31] while the Danish Tax Authority has published a binding reply that invoices cannot be issued in bitcoin and that losses in bitcoin cannot be deducted as a cost of doing business.[32]

One potentially useful development is that the Swedish tax authority has referred a case to the European Court of Justice for a preliminary ruling as to the application of VAT to the exchange of

---

[28] *Communication from the Commission re: Co-ordinating Member States' Direct Tax Systems in the Internal Market*, at 3, COM (2006) 823 final (Dec. 19, 2006), *available at* http://eur-lex.europa.eu/legal-content/EN/TXT/PDF/?uri=CELEX:52006DC0823&from=EN.

[29] VERO SKATT [FINNISH TAX ADMINISTRATION], INKOMSTBESKATTNING AV VIRTUELLA VALUTOR [INCOME TAXATION OF VIRTUAL CURRENCIES] (2013) *available at* http://www.vero.fi/sv-FI/Detaljerade_skatteanvisningar/Inkomstbeskattning_av_personkunder/Inkomstbeskattning_av_virtuella_valutor%2828454%29.

[30] KPMG, *Estonia—Services From Bitcoin Trades Subject to VAT*, http://www.kpmg.com/global/en/issuesandinsights/articlespublications/taxnewsflash/pages/estonia-bitcoin-trades-vat-income-tax.aspx (last visited Jan. 15, 2015).

[31] Danmarks Nationalbank, *Bitcoins Are Not Money*, *available at* http://www.nationalbanken.dk/en/pressroom/Documents/2014/03/Presshistory_Bitcoins_UK.pdf (last visited Jan. 15, 2015).

[32] SKAT [TAX AUTHORITY OF DENMARK], BITCOINS, IKKE ERHVERVSMÆSSIG BEGRUNDET, ANSET FOR SÆRSKILT VIRKSOMHED [BITCOINS ARE CONSIDERED SEPARATELY FROM COMMERCIAL ACTIVITIES] (2014) *available at* http://www.skat.dk/SKAT.aspx?oId=2156173&vId=0.

virtual currency for traditional currency.[33] However it is likely to take approximately two years (if not more) before the case reaches the point where a decision is made, and then any ramifications from the case would need to be built into the legislative processes of the EU and individual member states.

WHAT IS THE REGULATORY TREATMENT OF BITCOIN IN THE UK?

The Financial Conduct Authority ("**FCA**") regulates the financial industry in the UK, and derives its rule-making, investigative and enforcement powers from statute. The FCA supervises the conduct of over 50,000 firms, the majority of which are regulated under the Financial Services and Markets Act 2000[34] ("**FSMA**") and its associated secondary legislation. The FCA also regulates firms caught by the Electronic Money Regulations 2011[35] (the "**EMRs**") and the Payment Services Regulations 2009[36] (the "**PSRs**"). Broadly, the FSMA states that any person carrying on a regulated activity (e.g., issuing e-money, accepting deposits and managing investments) must be either authorised by the FCA or exempted from the authorisation requirement.

Under current UK legislation, bitcoin falls outside the scope of the key UK regulatory regimes: electronic money ("**e-money**"); payment services; regulated activities and anti-money laundering and terrorist financing, by virtue of the fact that it is decentralised, i.e., is not issued nor redeemed by a central bank, and is not pegged to any fiat currency. This was confirmed in a December 2013 House of Lords written answer to a question by Lord Myners as to whether any authorised UK bank has been granted permission to make markets in bitcoin, in which the Commercial Secretary to the Treasury, Lord Deighton (Con) stated that "the Financial Conduct Authority are not aware of any authorised bank in the UK offering bitcoin trading or exchange

---

[33] Case C-264/14, Skatteverket v. Hedqvist, 2014, available at http://curia.europa.eu/juris/document/document.jsf?text=&docid=154888&pageIndex=0&doclang=en&mode=lst&dir=&occ=first&part=1&cid=184821.
[34] Financial Services and Markets Act, 2000, c. 8 (U.K.).
[35] Electronic Money Regulations, 2011, S.I. 2011/99 (U.K.).
[36] Payment Services Regulations, 2009, S.I. 2009/209 (U.K.).

services. *Bitcoin is currently unregulated in the UK*, and as such no permissions currently exist for making markets in bitcoins."[37]

We examine each of the e-money, payment services, anti-money laundering, consumer protection and wider financial regulation regimes in turn, and conclude by reviewing the legal and regulatory outlook for the UK.

E-money

The EMRs implement the European Parliament and European Council's second Electronic Money Directive[38] and govern the issue of e-money by specified institutions, including FCA-authorised e-money institutions ("**EMIs**"), credit institutions, and Member States or their regional or local authorities when acting in their capacity as public authorities. The EMRs set the standards by which e-money products such as prepaid cards and the e-money stored on them are issued and operated by EMIs.

Of the various regimes, one would expect bitcoin to be most similar in nature to e-money as both constitute electronically stored monetary value. However, when we look closer at the statutory definition of e-money, it becomes clear that bitcoin is not e-money and therefore falls outside the scope of the EMRs.

HM Treasury has described e-money as a means of payment that "derives its value not from any intrinsic worth, but from the expectation that it can be exchanged for its underlying value."[39] E-money is defined in the EMRs to mean:

> electronically (including magnetically) stored monetary value as *represented by a claim on the electronic money issuer* which—
>
> (a) is *issued on receipt of funds* for the purpose of making payment transactions;

---

[37] 572 PARL. DEB., H.L. (5th ser.) (2013) WA201 (U.K.) (emphasis added), *available at* http://www.publications.parliament.uk/pa/ld201314/ldhansrd/text/131218w0001.htm.

[38] Directive 2009/110, of the European Parliament and of the Council of 16 September 2009 on the Taking Up, Pursuit and Prudential Supervision of the Business of Electronic Money Institutions Amending Directives 2005/60/EC and 2006/48/EC and repealing Directive 2000/46/EC, 2009 O.J. (L 267) 7 (E.U.).

[39] HM TREASURY, LAYING OF REGULATIONS TO IMPLEMENT THE NEW E-MONEY DIRECTIVE (2010), § 2.10, *available at* https://www.gov.uk/government/uploads/system/uploads/attachment_data/file/81328/emoney_directive_consultation.pdf.

(b) is accepted by a person other than the electronic money issuer; and
(c) is not excluded by regulation 3[.][40]

Looking at each limb of this definition, bitcoin does not constitute e-money as it is fundamentally neither "represented by a claim on an electronic money issuer" nor "issued on receipt of funds."

A bitcoin does not represent a claim on any person for the purposes of the EMRs as it is not issued, backed or guaranteed by any central bank, financial institution, or state. Unlike the funds on a prepaid card which are a claim against the relevant EMI (essentially a liability of the EMI), bitcoin is neither an IOU nor a liability on any central bank or state. In terms of whether it is "issued," a bitcoin is essentially a chain of digital signatures *generated* upon the resolution of complex mathematical algorithms. It is not *issued* on the receipt of funds, for example, like a prepaid card where e-money is issued when the prepaid card is topped up in fiat currency. Hence bitcoin does not constitute e-money. This means that bitcoin is not subject to requirements of the EMRs such as regulation by the FCA, initial and minimum ongoing capital requirements, and "passporting rights" under which EMIs are entitled to establish a branch or provide services in another EEA state.

Payment services

We now turn from the application of the EMRs to bitcoin as a currency to the application of the PSRs on bitcoin-related activities. The PSRs implement the European Parliament and European Council's Payment Services Directive[41] and govern the carrying on of payment services by, amongst others, FCA-authorised payment institutions ("**PIs**"). The PSRs set conduct of business standards that apply to providers of payment services such as PIs, EMIs and credit institutions. For example, the PSRs regulate the timeframes within which payment transactions must be executed, information requirements regarding the provision of information both before a framework contract is entered into and during that contract, and provisions governing the termination of a framework contract.

---

[40] Electronic Money Regulations § 2(1) (definition of "electronic money") (emphasis added).
[41] Directive 2007/64, of the European Parliament and of the Council of 13 November 2007 on Payment Services in the Internal Market Amending Directives 97/7/EC, 2002/65/EC, 2005/60/EC and 2006/48/EC and Repealing Directive 97/5/EC, 2007 O.J. (L 319) 1.

The European Parliament and the European Council have proposed a new directive (known as "**PSD2**") that was first published in July 2013 concerning payment services in the Internal Market (i.e., the single market in the European Union in which the free movement of goods, services, capital and persons is ensured).[42] PSD2 will, if enacted, amend the second Electronic Money Directive and repeal the Payment Services Directive, and is seen as a necessary step if the legislative and regulatory framework governing PIs is to keep up with commercial developments. One key change from the 2009 Payment Services Directive is that the provisions relating to transparency and information requirements contained in the most recent available version of the draft text applies to all currencies, and not merely to EU currencies. While it is not clear whether this move is aimed at capturing cryptocurrencies such as bitcoin, this would appear to be consistent with the Commission's stated objective in its July 2013 proposal for PSD2 to address the legal vacuum for certain newly emerged internet service providers. However, it is not anticipated that PSD2 will be implemented in Member States until 2016 at the earliest.

The payment services listed in the PSRs are as follows:

(a) services enabling cash to be placed on a payment account and all of the operations required for operating a payment account;
(b) services enabling cash withdrawals from a payment account and all of the operations required for operating a payment account;
(c) the execution of the following types of payment transaction—
  (i) direct debits, including one-off direct debits;
  (ii) payment transactions executed through a payment card or a similar device;
  (iii) credit transfers, including standing orders;
(d) the execution of the following types of payment transaction where the funds are covered by a credit line for the payment service user—
  (i) direct debits, including one-off direct debits;
  (ii) payment transactions executed through a payment card or a similar device;
  (iii) credit transfers, including standing orders;
(e) issuing payment instruments or acquiring payment transactions;

---

[42] *Proposal for a Directive of the European Parliament and of the Council on Payment Services in the Internal Market and Amending Directives 2002/65/EC, 2013/36/EU and 2009/110/EC and Repealing Directive 2007/64/EC*, COM (2013) 547 final (Jul. 24, 2013), *available at* http://eur-lex.europa.eu/LexUriServ/LexUriServ.do?uri=COM:2013:0547:FIN:EN:PDF.

(f) *money remittance*; and
(g) the execution of payment transactions where the consent of the payer to execute the payment transaction is given by means of any telecommunication, digital or IT device and the payment is made to the telecommunication, IT system or network operator acting only as an intermediary between the payment service user and the supplier of the goods or services.[43]

Of this extensive list, we will consider "money remittance" in more detail. Bitcoin cannot fall within any of other types of "payment services" for the reasons outlined below.

Before we consider money remittance, by breaking down the definition of "payment services," it becomes clear that all of the payment services listed in the PSRs, other than money remittance, ultimately (through various definitions) turn upon:

(a) there being a "payment transaction" which is defined as "an act, initiated by the payer or payee, of placing, transferring or withdrawing funds, irrespective of any underlying obligations between the payer and payee;"[44] or
(b) there being "funds" which are defined as "banknotes and coins, scriptural money, and electronic money as defined in… the electronic money directive."[45]

The definition of "payment transaction" is structured so that placing, transferring or withdrawing bitcoin will only fulfil the definition if bitcoin can be construed as "funds." Turning to this definition, analysis of each limb in detail reveals that bitcoin will fall outside of the definition of payment transaction, as bitcoin is not:

(a) "banknotes," which are defined in the Currency and Bank Notes Act 1954 as "notes of the Bank of England payable to bearer on demand."[46] The Bank of England has the exclusive right of note issuance in England and as such only Bank of England notes are legal tender (i.e., a form of payment which, if paid into court in settlement of a debt, results in the creditor

---

[43] Payment Services Regulations, 2009, S.I. 2009/209, Sched. 1, § 1 (U.K.) (emphasis added).
[44] *Id.* § 2(1) (definition of "payment transaction").
[45] *Id.* § 2(1) (definition of "funds").
[46] Currency and Bank Notes Act, 1954, 2 & 3 Eliz. 2, c. 12, § 3 (U.K.).

being unable to sue the debtor for non-payment), in England and Wales; nor

(b) "electronic money" (as set out above); nor

(c) "coins" which are physical coins made and issued by the Crown in accordance with the Coinage Act 1971[47] and the Currency Act 1983;[48] nor

(d) "scriptural money" for which there is no statutory definition. However, our research appears to indicate that this means the recording of money units in a current bank account opened with a bank. This view is borne out by an opinion of the European Central Bank stating that "it is suggested that a definition of scriptural money should be established (in the definitions article), bearing in mind that only central banks and credit institutions (which include e-money institutions) may hold such funds."[49]

Although opinions of the European Central Bank are not binding, unlike regulations or decisions, it is regarded as representing best practice and may be taken into account by domestic and European courts. The opinion was given in response to a proposal by the Council of the European Union for what would later become the Payment Services Directive, with the opinion specifically referring to the need to align that directive with the first Electronic Money Directive; nor

(e) "cash" which, although not included in the definition of funds, features heavily in the definition of payment services. Cash is defined in the FCA Handbook by reference to the Consumer Credit Act 1974, which provides that cash, "includes money in any form."[50] In turn, money is defined as, "any form of money, including cheques and other payable orders."[51]

There is no formal or published guidance on whether bitcoin constitutes "funds" from the FCA. However, we understand informally that its present view is that bitcoin does not constitute

---

[47] Coinage Act, 1971, c. 24 (U.K.).
[48] Currency Act, 1983, c. 9 (U.K.).
[49] Opinion of the European Central Bank of 26 April 2006 on a Proposal for a Directive on Payment Services in the Internal Market, 2006 O.J. (C 109) 10, 18, § 12.10, *available at* https://www.ecb.europa.eu/ecb/legal/pdf/c_10920060509en00100030.pdf.
[50] Consumer Credit Act, 1974, c. 39, § 189(1) (U.K.).
[51] Financial Conduct Authority, Glossary—FCA Handbook (2014), at M22, *available at* http://media.fshandbook.info/content/FCA/Glossary.pdf.

"funds." Certainly, it is not generally used to or accepted as a means to discharge debts or pay for goods and services. Hence it is our view that bitcoin does not, presently, constitute "funds" for the purposes of the PSRs, but there is a risk that it might do so in the future, particularly as the text of the PSD2 undergoes the legislative scrutiny process and revisions are proposed.

Of the "payment services" listed in the PSRs, perhaps the closest fit to bitcoin is "money remittance" which is defined in the PSRs as:

> a service for the transmission of *money (or any representation of monetary value)*, without any payment accounts being created in the name of the payer or the payee, where—
>
> (a) funds are received from a payer for the sole purpose of transferring a corresponding amount to a payee or to another payment service provider acting on behalf of the payee; or
> (b) funds are received on behalf of, and made available to, the payee.[52]

Whether activities involving the exchange of bitcoin for national currency, or vice versa, constitute "money remittance" turns on whether bitcoin is "money (or any representation of monetary value)," separately from "funds."

In our view, bitcoin is not "money (or any representation of monetary value)." While there is no statutory definition of money, drilling down into the principal legal and economic principles of "money" reveals that "money" has three core characteristics, with bitcoin failing to satisfy all three:

1. it is a medium of exchange, i.e., at least two parties to a transaction are willing to treat bitcoin as payment for goods and services;
2. it is a store of value, i.e., its value can be saved, stored, retrieved and used to make purchases at some future date; and
3. it is a unit of account, i.e., it is used to measure/quantify the value of goods and services.

This view is supported by the Bank of Canada, which reported in April 2014 that, "using [the above] criteria for bitcoin and other cryptocurrencies, we see that they fall short of today's definition of

---

[52] Payment Services Regulations, 2009, S.I. 2009/209, § 2(1) (U.K.) (definition of "money remittance") (emphasis added).

'money.'"[53] The briefing highlighted that bitcoin falls short of the definition of money because (a) few retailers accept bitcoin as payment for goods and services; (b) bitcoin is highly volatile, with the value of bitcoin 40 times more variable than the value of the US dollar; and (c) even retailers who accept bitcoin advertise their prices in state currencies before converting to bitcoin at the point of sale, demonstrating bitcoin's unsuitability as a unit of measurement to be used to compare the value of a good or service.

Moreover, as the Bank of England noted in a 2014 article:

> In theory, digital currencies could serve as money for anybody with an internet-enabled computer or device. At present, however, digital currencies fulfil the roles of money only to *some* extent and only for a small number of people. They are likely at present to regularly serve all three purposes for perhaps only a few thousand people worldwide, and even then only in parallel with users' traditional currencies.[54]

The Bank of England's view that bitcoins do not meet the applicable criteria for money due to their limited usage is supplemented by statistics showing that bitcoin currently represents 0.1% of sterling notes and coin, and as few as 20,000 people in the UK currently hold bitcoin. The Bank of England estimates that there are fewer than 300 bitcoin transactions (among those people in the UK) per day.[55]

In addition, it is our view that other activities involving bitcoin, such as bitcoin exchanges and business technology management services, would not be caught by the PSRs. As explained above, the PSRs cover PIs, EMIs and credit institutions engaging in payment services, the definition of which does not capture a number of business models involving cryptocurrencies. In the case of money exchange businesses, these are specifically excluded by the PSRs.[56]

However, there has been movement towards recognising the similarities between businesses providing bitcoin exchange services and currency exchanges that exchange state-backed currencies. The Financial Crimes Enforcement Network, part of the US Department of the Treasury, has stated that providers of bitcoin exchange services

---

[53] BANK OF CANADA, DECENTRALIZED E-MONEY (BITCOIN) (2014), *available at* http://www.bankofcanada.ca/wp-content/uploads/2014/04/Decentralize-E-Money.pdf.
[54] *Economics*, *supra* note 2, at 279.
[55] *Id.* at 283.
[56] Payment Services Regulations, Sched. 1, § 2(f).

are considered money transmitters under the relevant legislation and, as such, are required to register as money transmitters.[57] The impetus provided by PSD2 may see European law-makers seeking to bring such activities within the scope of regulation.

Notwithstanding the foregoing analysis as to why bitcoin does not fall within the PSRs, the PSRs also list a number of exemptions, constituting a set of activities which are definitively not "payment services" within the meaning of the PSRs. However, on analysis, bitcoin does not easily or obviously fit within any of these exemptions. The below encompasses a non-exhaustive list of the exemptions:

(a) payment transactions executed wholly in cash and directly between the payer and the payee, without any intermediary intervention;

(b) payment transactions between the payer and the payee through a commercial agent authorised to negotiate or conclude the sale or purchase of goods or services on behalf of the payer or the payee;

(c) services where cash is provided by the payee to the payer as part of a payment transaction for the purchase of goods or services following an explicit request by the payer immediately before the execution of the payment transaction;

(d) payment transactions carried out within a payment or securities settlement system between payment service providers and settlement agents, central counterparties, clearing houses, central banks or other participants in the system;

(e) services provided by technical service providers, which support the provision of payment services, without the provider entering at any time into possession of the funds to be transferred, including—
  (i) the processing and storage of data;
  (ii) trust and privacy protection services;
  (iii) data and entity authentication;
  (iv) information technology;
  (v) communication network provision; and
  (vi) the provision and maintenance of terminals and devices used for payment services; and

---

[57] FINANCIAL CRIMES ENFORCEMENT NETWORK, REQUEST FOR ADMINISTRATIVE RULING ON THE APPLICATION OF FINCEN'S REGULATIONS TO A VIRTUAL CURRENCY TRADING PLATFORM 6–7 (Oct. 27, 2014), *available at* http://www.fincen.gov/news_room/rp/rulings/pdf/FIN-2014-R011.pdf.

(f) payment transactions executed by means of any telecommunication, digital or IT device, where the goods or services purchased are delivered to and are to be used through a telecommunication, digital or IT device, provided that the telecommunication, digital or IT operator does not act only as an intermediary between the payment service user and the supplier of the goods and services.[58]

While some of the above exceptions will clearly not capture bitcoin for the reasons discussed above, such as payment transactions executed wholly in cash, others may, on first glance, appear to capture those providing bitcoin-related services. Exemptions such as the exception for services provided by technical service providers are worded in a general manner to encompass entities providing technical support functions for payments, which may exempt a number of market participants such as payment gateway providers that accept payment in bitcoin.

However, the regulatory landscape may change with the implementation of PSD2. The FCA has also sought to strengthen the regulation of the payments industry with the creation of the Payment Systems Regulator, which will begin regulating in April 2015. The statute that created the Payment Systems Regulator[59] sets competition, innovation and service-user objectives for the Regulator when supervising a payment system, which is defined as: "a system which is operated by one or more persons in the course of business for the purpose of enabling persons to make transfers of funds, and includes a system which is design to facilitate the transfer of funds using another payment system."[60]

While it is impossible to state whether this may bring bitcoin within the scope of the Payment Systems Regulator's powers at this nascent stage, it is possible that the concerns surrounding cryptocurrencies generally and bitcoin in particular may see a shift towards increasing regulation in the forthcoming years. The Payment Systems Regulator's general functions consist of giving general directions and guidance and determining the general policy and principles by reference to which it performs particular functions.[61] The breadth of the powers granted to the Payment Systems Regulator, coupled with the generality of the

---

[58] Payment Services Regulations, Sched. 1, § 2.
[59] Financial Services (Banking Reform) Act, 2013, c. 33, § 40.
[60] Id. § 41(1).
[61] Id. § 49(4).

new defined term of "payment system" (a term that HM Treasury has the power to amend by order[62]), could result in bitcoin-related businesses falling under the Payment Systems Regulator's jurisdiction, particularly if bitcoin continues to grow in usage.

The wider UK regulatory regime

The FSMA sets out the rules that underpin the UK's core regulatory regime and defines what are considered to be activities for which firms must have the authorisation of the FCA (and in some cases, the Prudential Regulation Authority). FSMA states that authorisation must be sought by firms carrying on by way of business an activity of a specified kind relating to an investment of a specified kind in relation to property of any kind. Currently, bitcoin does not constitute a specified investment, resulting in providers of bitcoin-related services falling outside of regulation. As a consequence, users of such services are not protected by the FCA or Prudential Regulation Authority, and there is no way of opting in to the system.

Turning first to specified activities, the Financial Services and Markets Act 2000 (Regulated Activities) Order 2001, as amended (the "RAO") defines and describes each of these "regulated activities," and we now consider whether bitcoin may constitute a "regulated activity" within the meaning of the RAO. Of the various "regulated activities," the regulated activity of "accepting deposits" bears the closest resemblance to bitcoin.

"Accepting deposits" is defined in the RAO as an activity in which: "(a) money received by way of deposit is lent to others; or (b) any other activity of the person accepting the deposit is financed wholly, or to a material extent, out of the capital of or interest on money received by way of deposit."[63]

Bitcoin does not, presently, constitute the regulated activity of "accepting deposits". A "deposit" is defined in FSMA as "rights under any contract under which a sum of money ... is paid on terms under which it will be repaid,"[64] but the relevant legislation gives no definition, nor does the RAO contain any guidance, as to what constitutes "money," and specifically whether this includes bitcoin and other virtual currencies. The definition of "money" in the FCA

---

[62] *Id.* § 41(4).
[63] The Financial Services and Markets Act 2000 (Regulated Activities) Order, 2001, S.I. 544, § 5(1) (U.K.).
[64] Financial Services and Markets Act, 2000, c. 8, Sched. 2, § 22.

Handbook Glossary also does not provide any real detail: "any form of money, including cheques and other payable orders."

The position under FSMA and the RAO in respect of whether bitcoins fall under the definitions of "funds" and "money" reflects the position under the PSRs. Bitcoins do not conform easily to the definitions under the PSRs as they are currently drafted (a situation that is not likely to change with PSD2, as the latest text proposes no changes to these definitions). In addition, the nature of bitcoin is such that it would not naturally fall within the meaning of "deposit" as defined under the FCA Handbook, i.e., "a sum of money...paid on terms under which it will be repaid...in circumstances agreed by or on behalf of the person making the payment and the person receiving it."

Although other European jurisdictions have sought to regulate bitcoin exchanges in certain circumstances, notably in Germany in the case that exchanges change legal tender directly into bitcoin,[65] the current UK regulatory regime does not capture the vast majority of bitcoin exchanges as such exchanges tend to execute the sale of bitcoin at a spot price. Spot FX is not currently a specified investment in the UK and is to be contrasted with CFDs (contracts for differences), whereby buyers and sellers transact based on the expected value of a bitcoin at a specific time on a specific date without physical settlement of the underlying asset (which is likely to involve regulated activities under FSMA).

Many businesses providing bitcoin-related services will be excluded from the scope of regulation by the fact that bitcoin falls outside the definition of money under FSMA and the RAO (because, as noted above, it does satisfy the core characteristics of "money"). While it is not possible to state that all such businesses are excluded due to the high levels of innovation in this sector, bitcoin does not constitute a "specified investment" for the purposes of the RAO and as such would fall outside of the scope of FSMA.

Anti-Money Laundering

The UK's Money Laundering Regulations 2007[66] (the "**MLRs**") implement the European Commission's third Money Laundering

---

[65] JENS MÜNZER, BUNDESANSTALT FÜR FINANZDIENSTLEISTUNGSAUFSICHT [FEDERAL FINANCIAL SUPERVISORY AUTHORITY], BITCOINS: SUPERVISORY ASSESSMENT AND RISKS TO USERS (2014), *available at* http://www.bafin.de/SharedDocs/Veroeffentlichungen/EN/Fachartikel/2014/fa_bj_1401_bitcoins_en.html.

[66] The Money Laundering Regulations, 2007, S.I. 2007/2157 (U.K.).

Directive[67] and set out a system of internal controls and mechanisms that firms are required to implement as a means of combatting money laundering and terrorist financing, for example, the application of customer due diligence measures designed to identify and verify the identity of each customer.

The MLRs must also be read in conjunction with the guidance provided by the UK's Joint Money Laundering Steering Group ("**JMLSG**") and HMRC. The latter published updated anti-money laundering guidance for Money Service Businesses (defined below) in August 2014[68] (the "**HMRC MSB Guidance**"). While the guidance provided by both JMLSG and HMRC do not carry statutory force, HMRC and the English courts will consider whether a person has followed the guidance when deciding whether they have failed to comply with the MLRs.

The MLRs apply to a "financial institution" which is defined as an undertaking providing payment services, issuing and administering other means of payment, and issuing e-money.

As we have observed with our analysis of the treatment of bitcoin under the payment services and e-money regimes above, consideration of whether carrying out bitcoin-related activities means that a firm is a "financial institution" makes it clear that it is not. As with many of the issues discussed above, the matter turns on whether or not bitcoin can be considered as "money". Taking each of the relevant terms in turn:

(a) "*payment services*"—as discussed above, bitcoin does not fall within any of the categories of a "payment service;"

(b) "*issuing and administering other means of payments*"—this raises the same questions as we have seen in both the payment services and the e-money regimes: Is bitcoin a "means of payment?" If we consider this to mean is bitcoin generally regarded as means of payment, we would reflect the view of bodies such as the Bank of Canada, as discussed above, that it is not;

(c) "*money service business*"—defined to mean: "an undertaking which by way of business operates a currency exchange office, transmits money (or any representations of monetary value)

---

[67] Directive 2005/60, of the European Parliament and of the Council of 26 October 2005 on the Prevention of the Use of the Financial System for the Purpose of Money Laundering and Terrorist Financing, 2005 O.J. (L 309) 15.

[68] HM REVENUE & CUSTOMS, MONEY LAUNDERING REGULATIONS 2007: SUPERVISION OF MONEY SERVICE BUSINESS, (2014), *available at* https://www.gov.uk/government/uploads/system/uploads/attachment_data/file/387032/mlr_msb.pdf.

by any means or cashes cheques which are made payable to customers."[69] Again, the question cannot be answered without considering the question of whether bitcoin constitutes "money." For the reasons outlined above, we do not believe that this is the case; and

(d) *"issuing electronic money"*—again, it is clear from the above analysis that bitcoin is not e-money.

Accordingly, bitcoin is not presently legal tender nor a currency nor money nor any representation of money or e-money (for EMRs purposes) nor funds (for PSRs purposes), nor would bitcoin constitute a Money Service Business (for the purposes of the HMRC MSB Guidance). Therefore, it is unlikely that a firm carrying out activities related to bitcoin will fall within the meaning of a "financial institution" within the scope of the MLRs.

The MLRs are complemented by UK legislation such as the Proceeds of Crime Act 2002 ("**POCA**"), which contains three primary offences which any person, including businesses which are not within the regulated sector, may commit. These include:

(a) concealing, disguising, converting, transferring or removing the proceeds of crime from the jurisdiction;[70]
(b) entering into or becoming concerned in an arrangement known or suspected to facilitate (by whatever means) the acquisition, retention, use or control of criminal property;[71] and
(c) acquiring, using or possessing the proceeds of crime.[72]

Businesses engaging in transactions in bitcoin may be caught by POCA, as the three offences above apply to all legal persons, whether individual or corporate, and irrespective of whether they are acting in the course of business. In addition, the definition of "criminal property" has a wide scope, encompassing the obtaining of any benefit.[73] Benefit, in turn, is defined as obtaining property which includes money and all other forms of property, whether real, personal, heritable or moveable.[74] The breadth of this definition, which stands in

---

[69] Money Laundering Regulations, § 2(1) (U.K.) (definition of "money service business").
[70] Proceeds of Crime Act, 2002, c. 29, § 327 (U.K.).
[71] Id. § 328.
[72] Id. § 329.
[73] Id. § 340(3).
[74] Id. § 340(9).

contrast to the narrowness of the definitions of money in the payment services and e-money regimes, would encompass bitcoin. Businesses dealing in bitcoin should be aware of the real risk of criminal sanctions for money laundering offences involving bitcoin.

Consumer Rights Bill

The UK is in the process of adopting a Consumer Rights Bill ("**CRB**") which is intended to reform and consolidate the vast swathe of consumer laws in the UK. It is our view that the key pieces of consumer legislation in the UK, such as the Sale of Goods Act 1979[75] and the Unfair Contract Terms Act 1977,[76] are inadequate to deal with the challenges posed by consumers entering into contracts for or in bitcoin. For example, the definition of "goods" in the Sale of Goods Act 1977 specifically excludes things in action and money.[77]

At the time of writing, the CRB is in draft form and is working its way through the UK's legislative track. As well as consolidating existing consumer laws, the CRB introduces a definition of "digital content" and distinguishes "digital content" from "goods." It states that "goods" are "any tangible moveable items, but that includes water, gas and electricity if and only if they are put up for supply in a limited volume or set quantity"[78] "Digital content" on the other hand refers to "data which are produced and supplied in digital form."[79]

It has been suggested that bitcoin fits this definition of "digital content" and could inadvertently fall within the scope of the CRB as bitcoin is produced and supplied in digital form and as the CRB is intended to apply to:

(1) a contract for a trader to supply digital content to a consumer, if it is supplied or to be supplied for a price paid by the consumer.
(2) This Chapter also applies to a contract for a trader to supply digital content to a consumer, if—
   (a) it is supplied free with goods or services or other digital content for which the consumer pays a price, and
   (b) it is not generally available to consumers unless they have paid a price for it or for goods or services or other digital content.

---

[75] Sale of Goods Act, 1979, c. 54 (U.K.).
[76] Unfair Contract Terms Act, 1977, c. 50 (U.K.).
[77] Sale of Goods Act § 61(1).
[78] Consumer Rights Bill, 2014-15, H.L. Bill [64] cl. 2(8) (U.K.), *available at* http://www.publications.parliament.uk/pa/bills/lbill/2014-2015/0064/15064.pdf.
[79] *Id.* cl. 2(9).

(3) The references in subsections (1) and (2) to the consumer paying a price include references to the consumer using, by way of payment, any facility for which money has been paid.

(4) A trader does not supply digital content to a consumer for the purposes of this Part merely because the trader supplies a service by which digital content reaches the consumer.[80]

The Explanatory Notes published together with the CRB provide examples of the contracts intended to be covered by Chapter 3 of the CRB concerning digital content, flagging virtual currencies:

> This Chapter will apply to contracts between a trader and a consumer where a trader agrees to supply digital content that has been:
>
> - Paid for with money, or associated with any paid for goods, digital content or services (e.g. free software given away with a paid-for magazine) [and not generally available to consumers for free (that is, the consumer must pay something in order to get the digital content)], and/or
> - Paid for with a facility, such as a token, *virtual currency*, or gift voucher, that was originally purchased with money (e.g. a magic sword bought within a computer game that was paid for within the game using "jewels" but those jewels were originally purchased with money).[81]

The Explanatory Notes do not define what is meant by "virtual currency," only providing one example of a virtual currency: in-game currencies such as the magic sword discussed above. However, the Explanatory Notes do discuss what is intended by the term "digital content":

> "Digital content" is a key definition in Part 1 and as such is defined in clause 2 (Key definitions). It is defined as data which are produced and supplied in digital form and includes software, music, computer games and applications or "apps". In the case of digital content which is supplied under contract from a trader to a consumer, and

---

[80] *Id.* cl. 34(1)-(4).
[81] DEPARTMENT FOR BUSINESS INNOVATION & SKILLS, DRAFT CONSUMER RIGHTS BILL: EXPLANATORY NOTES, (2014), ¶ 170 (emphasis added) (discussing 2014-5, H.L. Bill [29] replaced by 2014-5 H.L. Bill [64], which largely maintains the original content of the former), available at http://www.publications.parliament.uk/pa/bills/lbill/2014-2015/0029/en/15029en.pdf.

largely or wholly stored and processed remotely, such as software supplied via cloud computing, some digital content will always be transmitted to the consumer's device so that they can interact with the digital content product that they have contracted for. This digital content falls within the scope of the definition of digital content as set out in clause 2 and as long as it is provided pursuant to the types of contract set out in clause 33 or 46, Chapter 3 applies. The definition of digital content would also cover the digital content supplied to a consumer as the result of a service which produced bespoke digital content, such as a website design service. The Chapter does not apply where a trader supplies a service merely to enable consumers to access digital content, such as Internet or mobile service provision."[82]

There is, however, very little guidance or commentary on whether bitcoin falls within the definition of "digital content" and therefore it is difficult to say with any certainty whether or not bitcoin will be, or is even intended to be, within the scope of the CRB. However, the mere fact of the inclusion of the new definition of "digital content" could indicate an increasing willingness to regulate transactions conducted in bitcoin. The Explanatory Notes, although only making a single reference to bitcoin, state that, "digital currencies (or cryptocurrencies) that can be used in a variety of transactions with a number of traders, and exchanged for real money, are much more akin to real money (e.g. bitcoins)."[83] This reflects the assumption latent in statements such as that of the Bank of Canada, as discussed above, that as bitcoin becomes accepted far more widely by retailers and consumers alike, it will become far more akin to money and may attract a concomitant level of scrutiny from legislators and regulators.

If bitcoin and other virtual currencies were to be included in the scope of the CRB, it would result in any contract with a consumer for the supply of digital content, whether conducted in state-backed currencies or virtual currencies, having certain terms implied into the contract. This would include implied terms as to the satisfactory quality of the digital content, that it is fit for a particular purpose notified in advance by the consumer, that it meets any given description, and that the trader has the right to supply the digital content in question.

There are also a number of non-legal advances which may improve the current perceived vulnerability of consumers who engage in bitcoin transactions. It is through technology that many businesses

---

[82] *Id.* ¶ 162.
[83] *Id.* ¶ 211.

seek to challenge the stance adopted by the Director of the Consumer Financial Protection Bureau, an organ of the US government, that "virtual currencies are not backed by any government or central bank, and at this point consumers are stepping into the Wild West when they engage in the market."[84] Innovations such as multi-signature approaches, also known as "multisig," provide a way for parties engaging in transactions to protect themselves from a failure to perform by the other party by making such transactions contingent on the collective agreement of multiple parties.[85] Under this approach, the bitcoin used to effect the transaction would be held in what is effectively an escrow and only released once any two out of the three private key-holders (the transacting parties and the escrow agent) authorise the transaction.

THE LEGAL AND REGULATORY OUTLOOK FOR THE UK

European Central Bank's October 2012 paper on virtual currencies

The European Central Bank (the "**ECB**") 2012 paper on virtual currencies,[86] while seeking to provide clarity, highlighted a number of key areas of uncertainty in the legal and regulatory treatment of virtual currencies.

The paper shares a number of characteristics with later publications that are discussed below, detailing risks posed by virtual currencies such as price stability, financial stability, payment system stability, the reputational risks to central banks, and the risks resulting from what it perceives as a lack of regulation. It is in respect of the latter that the ECB is most radical, contrasting with the later more pro-regulatory stance taken by the European Banking Authority (the "**EBA**").

Although the paper is clear in highlighting the real risks of a lack of regulation, including the ability of criminals to exploit the system and a lack of a finality of settlement concept, the paper takes the stance that due to the global scope of virtual currencies,

---

[84] Consumer Financial Protection Bureau, *CFPB Warns Consumers About Bitcoin* (Aug. 11 2014), *available at* http://www.consumerfinance.gov/newsroom/cfpb-warns-consumers-about-bitcoin/.

[85] *See, e.g.*, John Villasenor, *Could 'Multisig' Help Bring Consumer Protection to Bitcoin Transactions?*, FORBES, Mar. 28, 2014, *available at* http://www.forbes.com/sites/johnvillasenor/2014/03/28/could-multisig-help-bring-consumer-protection-to-bitcoin-transactions/.

[86] EUROPEAN CENTRAL BANK, VIRTUAL CURRENCY SCHEMES 13–15 (2012), *available at* http://www.ecb.europa.eu/pub/pdf/other/virtualcurrencyschemes201210en.pdf.

governments and central banks would face serious difficulties if they tried to control or ban any virtual currency scheme, and it is not even clear to what extent they are permitted to obtain information from them. In the particular case of Bitcoin, which is a decentralised peer-to-peer virtual currency scheme, there is not even a central point of access, i.e. there is no server that could be shut down if the authorities deemed it necessary.[87]

Although the paper moots the possibility of overcoming this hurdle by obtaining quantitative information on the funds moved between the virtual economy and the real economy, it also analyses the trajectory of PayPal from FinTech start-up to regulated financial institution and discusses it as a model to ensure a form of regulatory control over virtual currencies. However, there is a clear sense that this suggestion is proposed only tentatively, with the paper admitting that it "is not an easy step, but it looks like the only possible way to strike a proper balance between money and payment innovations on the one hand, and consumer protection and financial stability, on the other."[88]

EBA's July 2014 Opinion on 'Virtual Currencies'

Article 9 of the founding regulation of the EBA sets out that the EBA may adopt guidelines and recommendations with a view to promoting the safety and soundness of markets.[89] In July 2014, the EBA published an opinion making consumers aware of the risks of unregulated virtual currencies, building on a December 2013 paper which identified 70 risks in all.[90]

The paper continues in this spirit of caution, both advocating the required characteristics for an effective regulatory system and proposing a number of short- and medium-term steps that existing national supervisory authorities and EU legislators should take to mitigate the risks identified by the EBA.

---

[87] *Id.* at 42–43.
[88] *Id.* at 44.
[89] Regulation (EU) No 1093/2010, of the European Parliament and of the Council of 24 November 2010 Establishing a European Supervisory Authority (European Banking Authority), Amending Decision No 716/2009/EC and Repealing Commission Decision 2009/78/EC, 2010 O.J. (L 331) 12, 23, art. 9, para. 2 (E.U.).
[90] EUROPEAN BANKING AUTHORITY, EBA OPINION ON 'VIRTUAL CURRENCIES' (2014), *available at* http://www.eba.europa.eu/documents/10180/657547/EBA-Op-2014-08+Opinion+on+Virtual+Currencies.pdf.

The EBA states that a suitable regulatory response to the challenges posed by virtual currencies would require

> a substantial body of regulation, some components of which are untested. It would need to comprise, amongst other elements, governance requirements for several market participants, the segregation of client accounts, capital requirements and, crucially, the creation of 'scheme governing authorities' that are accountable for the integrity of a VC [virtual currency] scheme and its key components, including its protocol and transaction ledge.[91]

These scheme governing authorities are intended to address the risks that apply to virtual currencies given that anyone, including criminals, can create a virtual currency. The currency, once available to multiple users, can have changes made to its protocol or other core elements, breaking the chain of accountability between the originator of the currency and its users. The scheme governing authority would establish and govern the rules for the use of a virtual currency and maintain the central transaction ledger, the protocol, and other core functional components.

The EBA recognises that, at first glance, a scheme governing authority may appear to contradict the decentralised non-regulated appeal of virtual currencies, stating that the existence of the authority would not necessarily require currency units to be centrally issued. The paper explains that:

> This function can remain decentralised and be run through, for example, a protocol and a transaction ledger. If it is true that the decentralised VC schemes are secure, it should be possible for market participants to establish themselves as scheme governance authorities. However, if a legal person is not able to exercise authority over market participants and is therefore unaccountable to a regulator for compliance purposes, it would be unreasonable to expect a regulator to guarantee integrity in their place.[92]

The EBA also recommends giving national regulators the power to impose requirements relating to matters such as customer due diligence, fitness and probity standards, corporate governance, transparent price information, and a requirement that virtual currency market

---

[91] *Id.* at 5.
[92] *Id.* at 40.

participants, e.g., scheme governance authorities and exchanges, be incorporated in an EU Member State, which would allow such entities to more easily sue and be sued in the EU.

However, the EBA recognises that such a regulatory regime can only be viewed as a long-term goal, while some of the risks it identifies threaten current market participants. To this end, the EBA proposes a number of steps which would mitigate these risks in the short-term. While the EBA stops short of recommending the wholesale prohibition of financial institutions holding virtual currency, it does recommend that "national supervisory authorities discourage credit institutions, payment institutions, and e-money institutions from buying, holding or selling" them.[93]

It also recommends that the EU legislate so as to bring market participants within the ambit of the EU Anti-Money Laundering Directive.[94] The EBA claims that this approach will allow virtual currencies to "innovate and develop outside of the financial services sector,"[95] although this seems at odds with the EBA's general stance that virtual currencies are inherently high-risk for the financial sector. It is also questionable the extent to which financial institutions would respond to such discouragement, particularly if virtual currencies such as bitcoin were giving investors strong returns.

The disparity between the strongly pro-interventionist stance of the EBA in its July 2014 Opinion and the earlier ECB position (*viz.*, that technological and legal hurdles may prevent virtual currencies being regulated in the same way as other financial entities) could be seen as a response to the prevailing circumstances at the time of writing. At the time of the publication of the EBA's report, the Mt. Gox scandal, in which around $450,000,000 worth of bitcoin belonging to both Gox customers and Mt. Gox itself disappeared in February 2014, was still causing sizeable concerns for UK and European regulators and law-makers. This may have hardened the stance of the EBA in the face of unprecedented losses for holders of digital currency.

Bank of England's September 2014 Publications on Bitcoin

In its Quarterly Bulletin, the Bank of England published two papers that we have referred to already *(Innovations in Payment Technologies and the Emergence of Digital Currencies* and *The*

---

[93] *Id.* at 44.
[94] *Id.* at 43–44.
[95] *Id.* at 44.

Economics of Digital Currencies) and which provide some insight into potential future regulatory developments.[96]

The first paper argues that bitcoin is not a revolution in currency so much as a revolution in payment systems, highlighting the "distributed ledger" technology, i.e., a system in which "a user, wishing to make a payment, issues payment instructions that are disseminated across the network of other users," with certain users (i.e., miners) gathering together blocks of transactions and competing to verify them.[97] This system allows Bitcoin to operate in a decentralised manner without the involvement of intermediaries such as banks. The paper posits that this may engender wider changes in the financial system as transactions become increasingly digitised, e.g., the majority of financial assets such as shares and bonds are no longer recorded in paper form, and exist only as digital records. The distributed ledger system could result in any type of financial asset being recorded on a distributed ledger, doing away with the current tiered structure of record keeping (i.e., records of individuals' accounts held at their bank, and the bank's reserves held at a central bank).

The second paper provides a broader understanding of the underlying economic mechanics of digital currencies such as bitcoin, and presents an initial assessment of the risks that bitcoin may pose to the Bank of England's objectives for monetary and financial stability.

The Bank of England acknowledges that digital currencies do not currently pose such a risk but "could conceivably change ... if they were to grow significantly."[98] However, the article also casts doubt on whether this growth would ever occur, as the article argues that, "the incentives embedded in the current design of digital currencies pose impediments to their widespread usage."[99] The article identifies that low transaction fees are the principal driver for the uptake of digital currencies. The lower fees when compared with centralised payment systems stems from the fact that transaction verifiers, or miners, are paid for their services in the form of new currency, a system which the Bank of England terms a "subsidy." However, the paper questions the sustainability of low transaction fees, as it posits that in the long run, the eventual supply of digital currencies will remain fixed while the costs incurred by miners can be expected to rise as the use of bitcoin increases. Therefore:

---

[96] *The Economics of Digital Currencies, supra* note 2; *Innovations, supra* note 2.
[97] *Innovations, supra* note 2, at 266.
[98] *Economics, supra* note 2, at 276.
[99] *Id.*

Digital currencies with an ultimately fixed supply will then be forced to compete with other payment systems on the basis of costs. With their higher marginal costs, digital currencies will struggle to compete with centralised systems unless the number of miners falls, allowing the remaining miners to realise economies of scale. *A significant risk to digital currencies' sustained use as payment systems is therefore that they will not be able to compete on cost without degenerating—in the limiting case—to a monopoly miner, thereby defeating their original design goals and exposing them to risk of system-wide fraud.*[100]

Notwithstanding the Bank's view on the inherent limitations of cryptocurrencies, the paper goes on to note some of the legal and regulatory challenges that cryptocurrencies may pose to the stability of the UK financial system in the future.

First, the volatility of the prices of digital currencies is highlighted, and while the total value of bitcoin to the UK economy is currently relatively minimal, the paper suggests that "[i]f marked increases in prices were to occur, it is possible that the total valuation may become large enough such that a price crash might have implications for financial stability in this manner."[101]

The Bank also stresses the risks of systemic fraud, a situation that the Bank believes would be far more likely for cryptocurrencies given their reliance on technology and the inherent tendency towards monopolistic practices as outlined above. On the latter point, the bank posits the possibility of a scenario in which "a single miner, or coalition of miners, came to control a sustained majority of the computing power in a digital currency, that group would be able to control which payments were permitted or even to create fraudulent 'double spend' payments."[102]

The paper concludes by emphasising that despite the varied nature of the risks to financial stability that could be engendered by a vastly increased take up of digital currencies, "most of [the risks] could be addressed through regulatory supervision of relevant parties."[103] While acknowledging that not all of the risks and incentives of cryptocurrencies are fully understood, the paper stands for the

---

[100] *Id.* at 281.
[101] *Id.* at 283.
[102] *Id* at 283–4.
[103] *Id.* at 286.

proposition that traditional methods of maintaining stability through regulation would be able to combat new challenges.

The Chancellor's August 2014 Speech on FinTech in the UK, the FCA's October 2014 remarks, and the UK Government's November 2014 Call for Evidence

The Chancellor of the Exchequer, the Rt. Hon. George Osborne, gave a speech in August 2014 outlining the UK government's desire for the UK to be the global fintech capital.[104] The speech placed considerable weight on the government's desire to create a regulatory environment that allows such firms to flourish.

The speech also outlined a number of legal and regulatory developments that give insight into how the UK will respond to the regulatory challenges posed by cryptocurrencies such as Bitcoin. The key message of the speech was that, "[r]egulation has to be pro-innovation,"[105] with the FCA "committed to open[ing] its doors to financial service firms who are developing new approaches, to help them navigate the regulatory system and identify areas where the regulatory system needs to adapt to new technology."[106]

In order to identify such areas, the Chancellor announced a consultation on how to plan for the next generation of digital technology. This announcement was strengthened by remarks made by the CEO of the FCA in October 2014, in which the FCA's intention to investigate the ways in which the technology underpinning bitcoin can be used elsewhere in the formal financial services industry was outlined.[107] The remarks were made in a speech in which the regulator indicated that it has been tasked by the UK government to break down barriers for entry for firms using innovative technology that could pose a challenge to the existing banking industry. In particular, the FCA is interested in exploring the potential for the block chain technology used in bitcoin transactions to be exploited by financial services firms. This reflects a view shared by a number of financial services firms that, in time, large corporations may use the technology underpinning Bitcoin in place of existing settlement systems. The financial services sector perceives that it is currently witnessing (or it is anticipated that

---

[104] Osborne, *supra* note 3.
[105] *Id.*
[106] *Id.*
[107] Martin Wheatley, Chief Executive of the FCA, Speech at the Financial News Conference, London—Innovation: The Regulatory Opportunity, *available at* http://www.fca.org.uk/news/innovation-the-regulatory-opportunity.

it will witness), "the slow emergence of an ecosystem to accommodate a broader use of crypto-currencies in the real economy."[108]

The UK government's focus on the transformative power of virtual currencies for the financial system as a whole was emphasised further in a November 2014 Call for Information, published by HM Treasury, on the benefits and risks of digital currencies.[109] The Call for Information seeks views from fintech firms, the financial services industry, regulators and law enforcement agencies.

While the announcement highlighted the government's concerns that users of cryptocurrencies are not protected to the same extent as users of banks, and that cryptocurrencies could be used for illegal activities, the benefits that cryptocurrencies can bring to consumers and businesses were strongly emphasised, while the possibility of regulation of cryptocurrencies was mooted rather than insisted upon, in contrast with the approach of the EBA's 2014 paper.[110] This hints at a possible clash between the strongly pro-regulatory stance of European decision makers and the pro-innovation stance of the UK government. With the UK keen to cement its position as the European, if not global, centre for fintech businesses, the drive to regulate cryptocurrencies within the European Union may be met by strong resistance by a UK government that does not wish to restrict a burgeoning industry in its nascent stages.

WHERE NOW FOR THE REGULATION OF BITCOIN IN THE UK?

Following a number of high-profile scandals involving bitcoin, most notably the Mt. Gox bankruptcy, the widespread use of bitcoin on Silk Road for illicit activity and episodes of extreme volatility (such as that of the dramatic fall in value since December 2013, at least at the time of writing), global regulators are increasingly seeking to regulate Bitcoin and entities that deal in bitcoin.

Earlier attempts to tackle the challenges posed by bitcoin such as the ECB's 2012 paper sought to recognise the technological and legal limits to regulating a decentralised non-nationally-based digital currency. However, successive issues involving bitcoin and the

---

[108] Johann Palychata, *Cryptomania*, QUINTESSENCE, Autumn 2014, at 16, 17, available at http://securities.bnpparibas.com/files/live/sites/quintessence/files/Quintessence%20-%20Sept%202014/Files/p16-17%20BNPP%20Bitcoinv7.pdf.

[109] HM Treasury, *Digital Currencies: Call for Information* (2014), available at https://www.gov.uk/government/consultations/digital-currencies-call-for-information/digital-currencies-call-for-information.

[110] European Banking Authority, *supra* note 90.

increasing concern of national regulators as transactions carried out in cryptocurrencies constitute an ever greater proportion of financial activity, has resulted in a general hardening of positions.

Jurisdictions such as China and India have placed severe restrictions on the ability to buy and sell cryptocurrencies, while the European Banking Authority has expressly supported a policy of discouraging financial institutions from trading in bitcoin.

However, the UK, in keeping with its position as the pre-eminent financial centre in Europe, has instigated a Call for Information in order to investigate the benefits and risks posed by cryptocurrencies while signalling that any regulatory changes in respect of Bitcoin will seek to promote innovation in the fintech sector. (The results of this Call for Information were released with the 2015 Budget.) When this is coupled with a tax treatment afforded to bitcoin transactions following the HMRC MSB Guidance that is more favourable than a number of other European jurisdictions, this may suggest increasing tension between European law-makers and the UK government as to the appropriate reach and scope of regulation for cryptocurrencies. This may become particularly acute as the generally pro-regulation stance of European regulators contrasts ever more greatly with the UK government's efforts not to extend the scope of regulation to virtual currencies.

As with many other jurisdictions, more discussion and debate is required in this nascent area with its idiosyncratic legal and regulatory challenges. The nature of the debate will change as cryptocurrencies continue to grow in prominence and will alter as new challenges arise. What will remain constant is the need to engage consumers, market participants, retailers, legislators and regulators, both national and supranational, in the ongoing debate as how best to protect consumers and businesses alike. The question remains unanswered as to whether this is possible within the existing regulatory framework, as advocated by the Bank of England's most recent publications, or whether a radically new model is required.

THE UNITED STATES

RYAN J. STRAUS
MATTHEW J. CLEARY

oooooooooooooooooooooooooooooooooo

I. INTRODUCTION

Bitcoin was conceived as a "purely peer-to-peer version of electronic cash [that] would allow online payments to be sent directly from one party to another without going through a financial institution."[1] A detailed description of the technical specifications of the Bitcoin protocol is beyond the scope of this chapter. However, at its most basic level, Bitcoin is a system with a protocol for the allocation of permissions, which are denominated in arbitrary units (bitcoins) and tied to system-specific addresses. Anyone with knowledge of the access credentials associated with a particular address can request that the system disassociate the units from the subject address and reassociate units to different addresses. The decentralized manner, and the resulting data structure, in which these requests are publicly submitted, approved, recorded and stored is often referred to as the *block chain*. While many non-financial applications of Bitcoin and the underlying technology, the block chain, have been proposed, this chapter will focus primarily on the rules applicable to bitcoins as financial instruments in the United States.

At this point, a few notes on the terminology used in this chapter are in order. The term *Direct Bitcoin Holdings* refers to units associated with addresses where one has actual knowledge of the access credentials and *Indirect Bitcoin Holdings* means units where one has delegated the maintenance of the access credentials to another party. Similarly, an *On-Block Chain Transaction* is a peer-to-peer transaction where units are actually re-associated to other bitcoin addresses on the system and an *Off-Block Chain Transaction* is a private, intermediated transaction that is not reflected on the block chain. While Indirect and Direct Bitcoin Holdings and On- and Off-Block Chain Transactions

---

[1] Satoshi Nakamoto, Bitcoin: A Peer-to-Peer Electronic Cash System 1 (2008), http://bitcoin.org/bitcoin.pdf.

are often conflated in practice, these distinctions will be fundamental to the analysis in this chapter.

It should also be noted, at the outset, that the law of bitcoin—or of cryptocurrencies, more generally—involves the consideration of both private law and public law questions.[2] In addition, within public law, for example, the characterization of bitcoins by one agency for one purpose (for example, the classification of bitcoins as personal property for federal income tax purposes) is not necessarily indicative of the treatment of bitcoins by the same agency for another purpose (for example, the classification of bitcoins as a virtual currency under the Bank Secrecy Act[3]). Finally, due to the dual nature of the financial system in the United States, a separate analysis of bitcoins and intermediaries involved in bitcoin transactions at both the state and federal level is often required. For clarity, we have attempted to frame the various inquiries and conclusions separately. Unfortunately, any additional clarity comes at the expense of concision and may result in redundancy.

This chapter will begin in Part II by evaluating the private law implications of bitcoins. In Part III, we will look at the developing body of public law with respect to bitcoins. In Part IV, we will look at the case law applicable to parties involved in bitcoin transactions.

II. THE PRIVATE LAW OF BITCOIN

Considerable scholarly and regulatory attention has been devoted to public law and regulatory issues associated with Bitcoin, such as how bitcoins should be taxed or treated for purpose of compliance with anti-money laundering laws. However, many private law questions associated with Bitcoin remain entirely unexplored.[4] While countless new payment mechanisms and services have been proposed and introduced in recent years, most have been new ways to transfer the same types of underlying value. In addition, the financial laws and regulations of the United States often presuppose the involvement of

---

[2] As used herein, *private law* refers to the laws governing the relations among persons and is contrasted with *public law*, which governs the relations between persons and the state.

[3] Currency and Foreign Transactions Reporting Act, 12 U.S.C. § 1829b, 12 U.S.C. §§ 1951–1959, 31 U.S.C. §§ 5311–5314e, 31 U.S.C. §§ 5316–5330 (1970).

[4] For a notable attempt to analyze the private law implications of Bitcoin, *see* Shawn Bayern, *Dynamic Common Law and Technological Change: The Classification of Bitcoin*, 71 Wash. & Lee L. Rev. Online 22 (2014), http://scholarlycommons.law.wlu.edu/wlulr-online/vol71/iss2/2.

a financial intermediary. As a result, the applicability of existing laws and regulations to Indirect Bitcoin Holdings and Off-Block Chain Transactions is often more straightforward than with respect to Direct Bitcoin Holdings and On-Block Chain Transactions.

Since the purpose of this chapter is to describe the law as it is or, perhaps more accurately, as it appears to be, comparison with other financial instruments is necessary. However, since Bitcoin is, in some respects, *something new*, a purely formal, as opposed to functional, analysis is not appropriate as the similarities between bitcoin—Direct Bitcoin Holdings, in particular—and traditional financial instruments are often outnumbered by points of difference.[5] The first part of this section will evaluate the private law implications of Direct Bitcoin Holdings and the rules applicable to On-Block Chain Transactions. The second part of this section will engage in the same inquiry with respect to Indirect Bitcoin Holdings and Off-Block Chain Transactions.

1. Direct Bitcoin Holdings and On-Block Chain Transactions

Bitcoin was conceived as a "purely peer-to-peer version of electronic cash"[6] and is frequently referred to colloquially as *money* or *currency*. However, these terms, especially money and currency, have special importance in the private law context. In fact, the rules applicable to the transfer of Direct Bitcoin Holdings and the use of On-Block Chain Transactions in the payment context will depend upon whether bitcoins are properly characterized as money. This subsection will begin by defining the legal concepts of money and currency. Next, we will discuss the unique legal attributes of money and currency. We will continue by evaluating whether Direct Bitcoin Holdings can be properly characterized as money or currency or both. Finally, this section will conclude with a discussion of the proper private law classification of Direct Bitcoin Holdings.

1.1. Money and Currency

A universal definition of money has yet to be devised. On one hand, economists often define money by referring to its functions

---

[5] *Id.* at 33-34 ("Because Bitcoin is something new, it does not fit neatly into classical categories…The trend toward functional rather than formal analysis in the common law demonstrates the importance of not relying excessively on categorization when determining legal rules that will govern bitcoin ownership, bitcoin transactions, and so on.").

[6] NAKAMOTO, *supra* note 1, at 1.

as a medium of exchange, as a measure of value, as a store of value, and as a unit of account.[7] Lawyers, on the other hand, are primarily focused on the legal "framework within which money has a role and its use has specified legal consequences...[and] must necessarily focus upon money as a means of performance of contractual or other legally enforceable obligations."[8]

Money, as we use the term today, refers to both *monetary objects*, or money in its physical form, and *monetary value*, or the right to receive monetary objects. With respect to monetary objects, the U.S. Constitution confers upon Congress the exclusive power "to coin Money, [and] regulate the Value thereof."[9] This provision has been further interpreted by the U.S. courts:

> Thus, the Supreme Court has noted that 'to determine what shall be lawful money and a legal tender is in its nature and of necessity a governmental power. It is in all countries exercised by the governments'. It followed that Congress had the power (and, it may be added, the sole power) 'to issue obligations of the United States in such form, and to impress upon them such qualities of money...as accord with the usage of sovereign governments. The power...was a power universally understood to belong to sovereignty'...Of course, the exclusive right to issue banknotes enjoying legal tender status is now vested in the Federal Reserve...[10]

While it is clear that only the state can bestow legal tender status upon monetary objects, the modern concept of money is not limited to monetary objects that enjoy legal tender status in the United States.[11] Indeed, the Uniform Commercial Code (the "**UCC**") defines money as "a medium of exchange currently authorized or adopted by a domestic or foreign government."[12] As noted above, the legal definition of money is concerned with whether a particular asset or instrument can be used to satisfy legal or contractual obligations. As a result, monetary value, or rights to receive monetary objects held by a third

---

[7] MANN ON THE LEGAL ASPECT OF MONEY 10 (Charles Proctor, ed., 7th ed. Oxford U. Press 2012).
[8] *Id.* at 10–11.
[9] U.S. CONST. art. I, § 8, cl. 5.
[10] MANN ON THE LEGAL ASPECT OF MONEY, *supra* note 7, at 19-20 (citing *Hepburn v. Griswold*, 75 U.S. 603, 615 (1869) and *Juilliard v. Greenman*, 110 U.S. 421, 447 (1883)).
[11] *Id.* at 21.
[12] U.C.C. § 1-201(b)(24) (2013).

party, while not legal tender, can be considered money if available for the purpose of making immediate payment.[13] In sum, although the public law of the United States may indirectly induce a creditor to accept monetary objects that constitute legal tender, private law considerations suggest that because monetary value may be used as a means of payment, albeit subject to the creditor's consent, the modern, legal definition of money should include both monetary objects and monetary value.

1.2. Legal Attributes of Money

The fact that money includes both monetary objects and monetary value does not mean that they are the same for legal purposes. However, an asset or instrument's characterization as money, either as a monetary object or monetary value, does have special import.

1.2.1. Payment of Money

The concept of payment, at its most basic level, refers to any act that is offered and accepted in satisfaction of a monetary obligation. Generally, payments are made by physically delivering monetary objects or by initiating a payment mechanism to transfer monetary value, or the right to receive monetary objects from a third party. For ease of reference, payment by delivery of monetary objects that qualify as currency, that is legal tender, is referred to as a *cash payment* and payment by transfer of monetary value is referred to as a *non-cash payment*.

Cash payments are unique in that the underlying monetary obligation is discharged instantly upon delivery and, as a result, the payment recipient need not be concerned with the creditworthiness of the transferor. The mechanics of cash payments are relatively straightforward:

> If A wishes to make payment to B by means of currency, all that is required is a delivery of the currency. At the moment of delivery, the underlying obligation is satisfied and the recipient of the currency becomes the party entitled to it. Because the payment transaction is instantaneous, a currency recipient need not worry about the

---

[13] MANN ON THE LEGAL ASPECT OF MONEY, *supra* note 7, at 42.

credit-worthiness of the transferor...[and] also faces little, if any, risk of fraud by the transferor.[14]

Non-cash payments are considerably more complicated than cash payments. Transfers of monetary value generally constitute payment only at such time as the transferee is able to dispose of the value and apply it towards the discharge of its own obligations.[15] The advantages of cash payments can be illustrated by comparing the position of the currency recipient with that of a person who accepts a check, as follows:

> [S]uppose that A makes payment to B by delivery of a check. The physical delivery of the check is only the first step of the process. Payment does not occur until after B deposits the check and the process of check collection is completed. If—and this is a big if—nothing goes wrong, the collection process results in a debit to A's account at the payor bank and a credit to B's account at the bank where B deposited the check. Until that collection process is completed, the person who takes payment by check runs the risk of the creditworthiness of the person who makes payment.[16]

The risk assumed by the payment recipient is that the payor is not creditworthy. The same concerns apply to parties who accept other payment mechanisms such as credit cards, debit cards, automated clearing house transactions and wires.

In sum, unlike cash payments, which discharge monetary obligations upon delivery, the initiation of a payment mechanism to transfer monetary value merely suspends, but does not discharge, a monetary obligation. A non-cash payment only discharges a monetary obligation if and when the payment recipient is able to apply the monetary value to the discharge of its own monetary obligations. This represents a critical distinction between payment by delivery of legal tender and payment by transfer of monetary value.

---

[14] James S. Rogers, *The New Old Law of Electronic Money*, 58 SMU L. REV. 1253, 1255–56 (2005).
[15] MANN ON THE LEGAL ASPECT OF MONEY, *supra* note 7, at 48.
[16] Rogers, *supra* note 14, at 1255–56.

1.2.2. Title to Money

In addition to money's ability to discharge or suspend monetary obligations upon delivery, the property rules applicable to money are also unique legal characteristics of money. Monetary objects, or coins and bank notes, are chattels. The general rule applicable to the transfer of chattels is *nemo dat quod non habet*, or, one who has not cannot give.[17] Currency represents an exception to *nemo dat*:

> 'Currency' is an exception to the fundamental common law rule that a seller can transfer no better title than he himself has, or as it is expressed in Latin, *nemo dat quod non habet*. The operation and rationale of the currency exception pertaining to money is set forth and demonstrated by Lord Mansfield in *Miller v. Race*, where it was held that money "can not be recovered after it had passed in currency." Thus, "in case of money stolen, the true owner can not recover it, after it has been paid away [i.e. taken] fairly and honestly upon a valuable and bona fide consideration...." The *bona fide* taker for value from the thief (or from someone deriving title from the thief) gets a clear title to money. As explained by Lord Mansfield, the reason money cannot be followed into the hands of a *bona fide* taker for value is not a by-product of its being fungible, of it having "no earmark." "The true reason is, upon account of the currency of it: it can not be recovered after it has passed in currency." Currency thus facilitates the use of money as a universal medium of exchange in a given time and territory.[18]

Similarly, if a transferee of monetary value receives funds in good faith and for value, the transferee is entitled to retain the value and need not be concerned with the manner in which the transferor came into the underlying funds.

1.3. Bitcoin as Money

Bitcoin was devised as a new form of medium of exchange that could be delivered electronically "allowing any two willing parties to transact directly with each other without the need for a trusted third

---

[17] STEPHEN M. WADDAMS, INTRODUCTION TO THE STUDY OF LAW 146 (4th ed. 1992).
[18] Benjamin Geva, *From Commodity to Currency in Ancient History: On Commerce, Tyranny, and the Modern Law of Money*, 25 Osgoode Hall L.J. 115, 117–18 (1987).

party."[19] As discussed previously, a payment can be broadly defined as the delivery of monetary objects or the transfer of monetary value that discharges a monetary obligation. Cash payments are ill-suited for parties transacting remotely. As a result, payments on the Internet rely almost entirely on payments of monetary value, or the right to receive money from a third party. While non-cash payments can be fast, they necessarily rely on third party intermediaries and, as a result, speed and convenience come at the expense of increased costs and decreased privacy. Bitcoin purports to be a non-monetary payment instrument that functions as a monetary object. While, broadly speaking, anything that a creditor agrees to accept to discharge a monetary obligation could be considered a medium of exchange, not all media of exchange are treated equally in the eyes of the law. Significantly, currency, a medium of exchange that the sovereign has declared to be legal tender, automatically discharges the underlying monetary obligation.[20]

In the United States, the federal government has the sole power to bestow the status of legal tender upon monetary objects and has exercised this power with respect to Federal Reserve notes and coins minted by the United States Mint. Notably, similar action has not been taken with respect to bitcoins. As a result, one of the few things we can say with certainty in this chapter is that Direct Bitcoin Holdings are neither legal tender nor currency in the United States. Furthermore, while the distinction between On-Block Chain Transactions and Off-Block Chain Transactions is, in many respects, similar to the distinction between payments by delivery of monetary objects and payments of monetary value, there is one very important caveat: bitcoins are not monetary objects.

1.4. The Private Law Characterization of Direct Bitcoin Holdings

If Direct Bitcoin Holdings do not constitute money, then what, if anything, does it mean from a private law perspective to "own" bitcoins? At this point, it may be helpful to revisit our description of Bitcoin: Bitcoin is a system with a protocol for the allocation of permissions, which are denominated in bitcoins, and tied to system-specific addresses. In practice, a party with knowledge of the access credentials for a particular address is referred to as the 'owner' of any associated bitcoins. Ownership of a bitcoin thus refers to the ability to request that the system disassociate the units from the subject

---

[19] NAKAMOTO, *supra* note 1, at 1.
[20] Rogers, *supra* note 14, at 1275.

address and reassociate units to different addresses. However, what is the nature of this right? Is it an equity interest, a contractual right or a property interest?

Ownership of a bitcoin bears a passing resemblance to the ownership of a share of capital stock. Indeed, attempts to ascribe a value to a single bitcoin have often begun by assigning a value to Bitcoin as a whole. However, ownership of an equity security confers ascertainable and enforceable legal rights against the issuer of the security. Bitcoin is open source software and is not owned by a single person or entity. There is no issuer(s) of bitcoins. Ownership of a bitcoin, that is, the mere knowledge of address access credentials associated with a bitcoin, does not represent a fractional ownership interest in Bitcoin as a whole.

It is tempting to characterize ownership of bitcoin as a contractual right. However, one does not have to agree to abide by any terms of use or otherwise agree to take or refrain from taking any action to acquire ownership of a bitcoin. Likewise, the other participants in the system are not bound by any contract, express or implied:

> Those running the Bitcoin software are free to ignore my attempts to transfer bitcoins to a new bitcoin address. They have no contract with me, implied or otherwise. They are free to ignore me, to dispute my ownership of bitcoins on technological grounds, and so on. The Bitcoin system works only because there are mathematically verifiable ways to convince other honest users of the software that my own bitcoins represent a legitimate stake (and because there is a social trust that enough honest people will continue to run the Bitcoin software). But, for example, if all the current participants in Bitcoin chose not to run the Bitcoin software, or if individual participants ran modifications of the software that operated on rules different from those that I initially understood, it is unlikely I have any recourse. In this sense, a bitcoin is not a right against the other users (*qua* users) of the Bitcoin network.[21]

Ownership of bitcoin, or the ability to request that the system disassociate bitcoin from the subject address and reassociate bitcoin to different addresses, is not a contractual right. In fact, "ownership of a bitcoin does not itself confer a legal right against participants in the Bitcoin system."[22]

---

[21] Bayern, *supra* note 4, at 32–33.
[22] *Id.* at 31.

Some have argued that bitcoins are intangible personal property. Property law is concerned with the "relations among people with regard to things."[23] Property is a broad concept that is not limited to tangible 'things' but, rather, "includes every right and prerogative capable of possession or disposition."[24] However, are bitcoins, or arbitrary units used by a single system to denominate a system resource, capable of possession or disposition? In *Kremen v. Cohen*, the Ninth Circuit applied a three-part test to determine whether a property right exists:

> First, there must be an interest capable of precise definition; second, it must be capable of exclusive possession or control; and third, the putative owner must have established a legitimate claim to exclusivity.[25]

Bitcoins would appear to satisfy the first two criteria. Bitcoins can be precisely defined as arbitrary units used by the Bitcoin system to allocate and track a finite system resource. In addition, while bitcoins cannot be possessed it appears that they are capable of exclusive control by a person who has knowledge of the access credentials to the associated address. But how would a person establish a legitimate claim to exclusive ownership or control of bitcoins associated with a particular address?

This element was discussed by the court in *Kremen*, where the Ninth Circuit determined that a registrant of a domain name had a legitimate claim to exclusivity because "[r]egistering a domain name is like staking a claim to a plot of land at the title office. It informs others that the domain name is the registrant's and no one else's."[26] The association of bitcoin to a bitcoin address is functionally similar to the association of an IP address to a domain name. The putative owner's knowledge of the access credentials of an address associated with bitcoins should be sufficient to establish her control. However, there is no definitive mechanism for associating an address with a personal identity. Property is, after all, concerned with the relationship between people and things. Knowledge of access credentials may be sufficient to show that an identified person, in fact, controls an address. However, legitimate control must mean more than actual control. At this point,

---

[23] Joseph William Singer, Introduction to Property 2 (2d ed. 2005).
[24] Downing v. Mun. Court, 88 Cal. App. 2d 345, 350 (1948).
[25] 337 F. 3d. 1024, 1030 (9th Cir. Aug. 20, 2002).
[26] *Id.*

it would seem fair to ask whether the anonymity of actors in Bitcoin precludes bitcoins from being considered property:

> If a property system purports to enable transfers, it does so by conveying the information about who now owns the what. If the property system purports to enable exclusion—the most commonly discussed element of property systems—then it relates a *what* to a *not-who*, that is, the set of people who are barred from making use of a resource.[27]

While it is important to recognize the possibility that a court may find that bitcoin cannot be the subject of proprietary rights because actors are not identifiable, that cannot be the end of our inquiry. Bayern has shrewdly pointed out as follows:

> The trend toward functional rather than formal analysis in the common law demonstrates the importance of not relying excessively on categorization when determining legal rules that will govern bitcoin ownership, bitcoin transactions, and so on. In functional terms, a bitcoin is an important economic right to many who participate in the network. It is clearly proper to criminalize its theft. It matches parties' expectations if bitcoin is treated as intangible, moveable personal property.[28]

In other words, for private law purposes it is likely that, although bitcoins do not "fit neatly into classical categories,"[29] we cannot simply throw up our hands and say that something that is being valued in the market is really nothing at all. Therefore, we tentatively conclude, based on a purposive approach and as a matter of private law, that bitcoin will be deemed to be an intangible personal property.

1.5. Bitcoin as Property

If bitcoins are intangible personal property, we must return to our earlier discussion about *nemo dat quod non habet*, the default rule of property transfer. *Nemo dat* provides that title to property is derived from the predecessor in interest and, therefore, a transferee's interest in particular property is necessarily equal to or less than the transferor's

---

[27] Josh Fairfield, *BitProperty*, 88 S. Cal. L. Rev. 1, 54 (forthcoming 2015).
[28] Bayern, *supra* note 4, at 34.
[29] *Id.* at 33.

interest unless an exception applies. In this subsection, we will first identify the applicable exceptions to the *nemo dat* rule in the United States. We then evaluate whether any of the exemptions are applicable to intangible personal property, in general, or bitcoin, in particular, and, finally, we will conclude with a discussion about the resulting rules for transfer of bitcoins.

Nemo dat is ubiquitous in both common law and civil law jurisdictions. As we have seen, currency is an important common law exception to *nemo dat*. The U.C.C. also codifies the various situational exceptions to the rule with respect to negotiable instruments (§ 3-203(b), protecting holders in due course), documents of title (§ 7-504(a), where delivered but not duly negotiated), securities (§ 8-302(a)), and goods (§ 2-403(1), protecting good faith purchasers; § 9-320(a)–(b) respecting security interests).

Do any of the exceptions to *nemo dat* apply to the transfer of Direct Bitcoin Holdings in On-Block Chain Transactions? As discussed above, currency refers to monetary objects that the sovereign has deemed legal tender. As a result, the currency exception to *nemo dat* does not apply to Bitcoin. Likewise, Direct Bitcoin Holdings do not meet the definition of a negotiable instrument as a bitcoin is not an "an unconditional promise or order to pay a fixed amount of money."[30] While there is a good faith exception for bona fide purchasers of goods, this is simply an exception, not the rule. However, this exception is strengthened where there is a seller that trades in the good in question. A purchaser is less likely to be required to give back her purchase if bought from a dealer known to trade in such goods. This gives implied credibility to the sale, enhancing the perception of good faith purchase. With respect to bitcoin, this sort of exception could be applied to bitcoins received from reputable exchanges or wallet providers. Such providers are in the business of buying and selling bitcoins and, therefore, have an implicit level of trust in performing that business. This will only apply if bitcoins are found to be goods under the U.C.C.; otherwise the exception would not be relevant to the transaction.

---

[30] Lary Lawrence, *What Would Be Wrong with a User-Friendly Code: The Drafting of Revised Articles 3 and 4 of the Uniform Commercial Code*, 26 Loy. L. A. L. Rev. 659 (1993).

2. Indirect Bitcoin Holdings and Off-Block Chain Transactions

It may be helpful to review the distinction made at the beginning of this chapter between Direct Bitcoin Holdings, or units associated with addresses where one has actual knowledge of the access credentials, and Indirect Bitcoin Holdings, i.e., units where one has delegated the maintenance of the access credentials to another party. Section 1 of Part II was concerned solely with Direct Bitcoin Holdings and the nature of the rights, if any, that one has with respect to bitcoin associated with an address for which one has actual knowledge of the access credentials. It was determined that, while Direct Bitcoin Holdings are not currency, Direct Bitcoin Holdings are likely intangible personal property.

This section is concerned with Indirect Bitcoin Holdings, or the rights one has when another party is entrusted to maintain the address(es) and access credentials associated with bitcoin. As Bayern puts it,

> [M]any and perhaps most people who "hold" (or "own" or "buy") bitcoins have done so without running a copy of Bitcoin software that directly participates in the Bitcoin network and without setting up the cryptographic framework that would be necessary to safeguard the private numbers [i.e., access credentials]—"keys"—that confer the ability to transfer bitcoins on the Bitcoin network. Instead, many people who have purchased bitcoins simply keep an account on a website that operates as a kind of informal bank or broker. The website reports a financial balance to the investor…[31]

While the idea of entrusting another party to 'hold' bitcoins, which were designed to allow parties to transact on a peer-to-peer basis without an intermediary, seems like a strange concept, most commercial transactions are facilitated by intermediaries in a similar manner. Indeed, intermediaries exist with respect to other forms of intangible property such as funds, securities and commodities. Furthermore, the rights and obligations of customers and their respective intermediaries in these markets are relatively well settled. This section will focus on the nature of the relationship between intermediaries and their customers, and their attendant rights and obligations, with respect to Indirect Bitcoin Holdings. We begin by looking at traditional financial intermediaries and account-based systems. We then examine the nature

---

[31] Bayern, *supra* note 4, at 25.

of bitcoin intermediaries. The licensing and regulatory requirements of intermediaries will be addressed elsewhere.

2.1. Financial Intermediaries

All modern financial intermediaries are rooted in the law of regular deposits and irregular deposits. Indeed, the starting point for determining the nature of the relationship between intermediaries and their customers involves determining whether they are engaged in the acceptance of regular or irregular deposits. The critical distinction between the two types is whether title to the subject property passes to the depository (*irregular deposit*) or remains with the depositor (*regular deposit*):

> Under the irregular deposit, ownership rights to deposited assets were transferred from the depositor to the depository, and this deposit became the basis of modern bank account relationships. In contrast, under the regular deposit, the depositor remains the owner and the depository obtains 'naked' possession, without rights to dispose of the object deposited.[32]

The modern bank provides a helpful illustration of the relationship between regular and irregular deposits. A customer at a bank branch may, subject to the terms of the customer's agreement with the bank, make an irregular deposit by handing monetary objects to the teller. Alternatively, a customer may make a regular deposit by placing monetary objects in a designated safe deposit box. From the customer's perspective, the regular deposit (the placement of monetary objects in a safe deposit box) and the irregular deposit (passing monetary objects to the bank teller) are superficially similar as both involve the customer's relinquishment of possession of monetary objects. However, the legal and accounting effects of the transactions are very different. Prior to making either a regular or irregular deposit, the customer has a property interest in the specific monetary objects that will be deposited. The customer making an irregular deposit relinquishes both possession of *and title to* specific monetary objects deposited in the bank. As a result of an irregular deposit, title to the specific monetary objects deposited passes from the customer to the bank. As explained by Dubovec,

---

[32] Marek Dubovec, The Law of Securities, Commodities and Bank Accounts: The Rights of Account Holders 11 (2014).

> A [irregular] deposit is essentially a loan transaction whereby the depositor lends funds to the bank in exchange for receiving credit to this bank account. Under the [irregular] deposit, customers transfer ownership and the right use the funds to the bank and the relationship between the depositor and the bank is that of a creditor and debtor.[33]

In exchange for title to the specific monetary objects deposited, the customer receives monetary value, or the right to receive the same number of monetary objects from the bank. The depository that accepts irregular deposits is not obliged to return the specific monetary objects the customer deposited because, after an irregular deposit, the specific monetary objects deposited are owned by the bank, not by the depositor.[34] The bank enters a liability on its accounts to the depositor, which can be discharged by legal payment of the amount owing, but not necessarily the specific monetary objects deposited.[35]

The depositor making a regular deposit also relinquishes possession of the specific monetary objects deposited but retains title to the property:

> Under the regular deposit the relationship between the depositor and the bank is that of a bailor and a bailee. It is not a relationship based on contract but is instead based on property. The depositor does not surrender ownership rights to the bank and the bank does not acquire any rights to use or commingle the object of the deposit.[36]

Since the regular depositor retains title to deposited property, the depository that accepts regular deposits of monetary objects is obligated to return, on demand, the same monetary objects deposited. To ensure the return of the deposited property, the subject property cannot be commingled with the depository's own property or that of other depositors.

While the preceding illustration deals with money, the distinction between regular and irregular deposits is relevant to all financial intermediaries. Intermediaries originally engaged only in regular deposit–taking:

---

[33] *Id.* at 121.
[34] Scammon v. Kimball, 92 U.S. 362, 369-370 (1875).
[35] *Id.* at 370.
[36] DUBOVEC, *supra* note 32, at 120.

For centuries, securities, money and commodities were placed with intermediaries for regular deposits (custody)...Gradually, it became common practice for intermediaries to commingle the property of their customers. Once commingled, the depositor could no longer trace his rights to specific securities, banknotes or commodities. The inability to trace rights to specific objects transformed the ownership into a different kind of right. For funds deposited to a bank account, the ownership became a contractual claim against the bank for repayment of the funds. The bank account has become a credit relationship. For commodities, ownership right became a co-ownership interest in the bulk belonging to multiple depositors, and eventually a contractual claim against the intermediary. Holders of securities have been granted a special right (security entitlement) that does not fit into any of the existing categories of property rights.[37]

The duties owed to an irregular depositor are contractual in nature. As a result, the irregular depositor is concerned with any conduct of the depository that jeopardizes the ability of the depository to repay the depositor the amount deposited. In other words, the irregular deposit necessarily exposes the depositor to the risk that the depository is or becomes insolvent. The duties owed to a regular depositor, on the other hand, are proprietary in nature. The regular depositor is not concerned with the financial health of the intermediary so long as the deposited property is stored safely, segregated from the depository's own property, and not commingled with other depositor's property or otherwise exposed to the claims of creditors (other than the depositor's own creditors). The different risks posed by intermediaries engaging in regular and irregular deposit-taking is reflected in the nature and the extent of the regulation of various intermediaries. While the regulation of financial intermediaries will be discussed in greater detail later in this chapter, government mandated insurance is the primary regulatory safeguard for irregular depositories and segregation is the primary safeguard for regular depositories.

2.2. Bitcoin Intermediaries

How should Indirect Bitcoin Holdings be characterized? As we have discussed, it is common practice for intermediaries to be entrusted with the maintenance of addresses and associated access credentials. However, what is the nature of the relationship between

---
[37] *Id.* at 11-12.

the intermediary (the entrusted party) and its customer (the entrusting party)? The answer depends on whether and how the depository framework developed for physical objects applies to bitcoin. In other words, if the depositor does not relinquish title to the specific property deposited, the depositor will remain the owner of the specific property deposited, somewhat in the manner of a regular deposit. If, on the other hand, the depositor relinquishes title to the specific property deposited, the ownership right will transform into a contractual right, conceptually similar to an irregular deposit. The contractual right between the depositor and the depository will likely be a debtor-creditor relationship.

While it is unclear what rights one holds with respect to Indirect Bitcoin Holdings, it does seem clear that any rights, including title, in specific bitcoin addresses, and the units associated therewith, would be extinguished upon transfer to a bitcoin address to which the depositor does not have knowledge of the access credentials. If the depositor does not have the access credentials, the depositor likely does not *own* the specific bitcoins deposited.[38]

Since title to the bitcoins deposited with an intermediary passes to the intermediary, the deposit should likely be characterized as an irregular deposit. As a result, the property right held in the Indirect Bitcoin Holdings is transformed into a contractual right to repayment (a debtor-creditor relationship).

III. THE PUBLIC LAW OF BITCOIN

While private law is concerned with the interactions among persons, public law relates to interactions between persons and the government. This part is concerned with the public law and regulatory matters associated with bitcoin, exclusively at the federal level in the United States. Enforcement and regulatory agencies are still in the process of clarifying the extent to which existing laws and regulations apply to Bitcoin. The various financial laws and regulations can be categorized by their primary purpose and the primary federal agencies responsible for their administration. The *Monetary Regime* refers to a set of anti-counterfeiting statutes and laws relating to competing currencies. The *AML Regime*, the group of laws and regulations designed to prevent money laundering and terrorist financing and the use of financial products for illicit purposes, is primarily administered by the Financial Crimes Enforcement Network ("**FinCEN**"), a bureau

---

[38] Bayern, *supra* note 4, at 22.

of the U.S. Treasury (the "**Treasury**"). The *Investment Regime*, the category of potentially applicable laws and regulations designed to protect investors and the financial markets, is the responsibility of the Securities Exchange Commission (the "**SEC**") and the Commodity Futures Trading Commission (the "**CFTC**"). The *Consumer Protection Regime*, the set of federal laws and regulations intended to protect consumers from the potential dangers associated with financial products and institutions, is governed by the Bureau of Consumer Financial Protection (the "**CFPB**") and the Federal Trade Commission (the "**FTC**"). For ease of reference, this section is subdivided into subsections for each potentially applicable regulatory regime.

1. Monetary Regime

1.1. The Stamp Payments Act of 1862

The Stamp Payments Act of 1862[39] criminalizes making, issuing, circulating, or paying out "any note, check, memorandum, token, or other obligation for a less sum than $1, intended to circulate as money or to be received or used in lieu of lawful money of the United States."[40] Despite its superficial breadth, judicial decisions appear to limit the law's application considerably. In *United States v. Monogahela*, the law was found to be inapplicable to "paper tickets to be received for toll" because the tickets had "no resemblance or similitude in shape, design or material, to the coin of the United States, nor to the postage currency, the free and untrammeled circulation of which it was the design of the act to advance and protect."[41] The Supreme Court similarly held the law inapplicable to a bearer instrument redeemable for goods at a store.[42] Even though the value of a bitcoin, or a fraction thereof, may be less than one U.S. dollar, it does not appear likely that a currency denominated in something other than dollars could be found to violate the Stamp Payments Act.

---

[39] 18 U.S.C. § 336 (1948). For notable background on this subsection, *see, e.g.*, Reuben Grinberg, *Bitcoin: An Innovative Alternative Digital Currency*, 4 HASTINGS SCI. & TECH. L.J. 159 (2012).

[40] 18 U.S.C. § 336 (1948).

[41] United States v. Monongahela Bridge Co., 26 F. Cas. 1292 (W.D. Pa. 1863) (No. 15796).

[42] United States v. Van Auken, 96 U.S. 366 (1878).

1.2. Anti-Counterfeiting Statutes

There are several federal laws applicable to "counterfeiting and forging of U.S. coins, currency, and obligations."[43] It is unclear whether bitcoin could be prosecuted under these statutes.[44]

2. AML Regime

Money laundering is generally defined as the processing of criminal proceeds to disguise their illegal origin.[45] Money laundering systems traditionally have three basic elements: (1) placement, (2) layering and (3) integration.[46] In the placement stage, the launderer introduces illegal profits into the financial system.[47] This is traditionally done by breaking up large amounts of cash into smaller sums that are then deposited into a bank or other financial institution account. Alternatively, cash may be used to purchase a series of small monetary instruments (money orders, checks, etc.). In the layering stage, the funds are moved from one account to another at various banks to distance them from the original source.[48] The funds might also be channeled through the purchase and sales of investment instruments or the transfers may be disguised as payments for goods or services. In the final stage, integration, the funds re-enter the legitimate economy.[49]

2.1 The Bank Secrecy Act

The United States's primary anti-money laundering and counter-terrorism financing legislative and regulatory framework is commonly known as the Bank Secrecy Act (the "**BSA**").[50] FinCEN issues regulations and interpretive guidance as the delegated administrator

---

[43] *See* CRAIG K. ELWELL ET AL., CONG. RESEARCH SERV., R43339, BITCOIN: QUESTIONS, ANSWERS, AND ANALYSIS OF LEGAL ISSUES (2014), *available at* http://fas.org/sgp/crs/misc/R43339.pdf (citing 18 U.S.C. §§ 470–477 and §§ 485–489 criminalizing "counterfeiting and forging of U.S. coins, currency, and obligations").
[44] *See id.*
[45] FINANCIAL ACTION TASK FORCE, WHAT IS MONEY LAUNDERING?, *available at* http://www.fatf-gafi.org/pages/faq/moneylaundering/.
[46] *Id.*
[47] *Id.*
[48] *Id.*
[49] *Id.*
[50] Currency and Foreign Transactions Reporting Act, 12 U.S.C. § 1829b, 12 U.S.C. §§ 1951–1959, 31 U.S.C. §§ 5311–5314e, 31 U.S.C. §§ 5316–5330 (1970).

of the BSA.[51] The BSA applies to banks and certain non-bank financial institutions that offer financial services such as casinos, securities and commodities firms and money service businesses.[52] A money service business (an "**MSB**") is a person, wherever located, doing business, wholly or in substantial part within the United States, in one or more of the following capacities: (1) a dealer in foreign exchange; (2) a check casher; (3) an issuer or seller of travelers checks or money orders; (4) a seller or provider of prepaid access; (5) the United States Postal Service; or (6) a money transmitter.[53] With few exceptions, MSBs are required to register with FinCEN, develop and implement an anti-money laundering program, file suspicious activity and currency transaction reports and create and maintain certain records.

A money transmitter is a person that accepts currency, funds, or other value that substitutes for currency and transmits currency, funds, or other value that substitutes for currency to another location or person by any means.[54] The regulations promulgated by FinCEN under the BSA stipulate that whether a person is a money transmitter is a matter of facts and circumstances.[55] The regulations identify several specific circumstances under which a person's activities would not make such person a money transmitter including: (1) the provision of delivery, communication or network access services used by a money transmitter; (2) acting as a payment processor by agreement with the creditor or seller of goods or services; (3) operating a clearance and settlement system or other intermediary solely between BSA regulated institutions; (4) physically transporting currency, other monetary instruments, other commercial paper, or other value that substitutes as currency; (5) providing prepaid access; and (6) accepting and transmitting funds only integral to the provision of services, other than money transmission services.[56]

In March 2013, FinCEN issued interpretive guidance to clarify the applicability of the BSA to certain parties dealing in *convertible*

---

[51] Treas. Order 180-01, 67 Fed. Reg. 64,697 (Oct. 21, 2002), *available at* http://www.gpo.gov/fdsys/pkg/FR-2002-10-21/pdf/02-26656.pdf.
[52] 31 C.F.R. §1010.100 (2014).
[53] 31 C.F.R. § 1010.100(ff) (2010).
[54] 31 C.F.R. § 1010.100(ff)(5) (2010).
[55] 31 C.F.R. § 1010.100(ff)(5)(ii) (2010).
[56] *Id.*

*virtual currencies.*⁵⁷ As that term is used by FinCEN, a convertible virtual currency is "a medium of exchange that operates like a currency in some environments, but does not have all the attributes of real currency" and "has an equivalent value in real currency, or acts as a substitute for real currency."⁵⁸ FinCEN identifies two types of convertible virtual currencies: *centralized virtual currencies*, or virtual currencies with a centralized repository;⁵⁹ and *de-centralized virtual currencies*, or virtual currencies without a central repository or single administrator that can be obtained through computing or manufacturing effort.⁶⁰ The guidance clarifies that a user who obtains convertible virtual currency and uses it to purchase real or virtual goods or services is not an MSB.⁶¹ However, FinCEN opined that *administrators* or *exchangers* of centralized virtual currencies and exchangers of de-centralized virtual currencies are money transmitters and are therefore subject to the BSA.⁶²

FinCEN characterizes bitcoin as a decentralized virtual currency for purposes of the BSA.⁶³ As a result, unless an exception applies, a person engaged as a business in the exchange of bitcoin for real currency, funds, or other virtual currency is required to register with FinCEN as a money transmitter; assess the money laundering risks involved in its transactions, if any; and implement an anti-money laundering program to mitigate such risks and comply with the BSA's record-keeping, reporting, and transaction monitoring requirements. As of December 1, 2014, FinCEN has published five rulings relating to virtual currency matters.

---

57   FINANCIAL CRIMES ENFORCEMENT NETWORK, APPLICATION OF FINCEN'S REGULATIONS TO PERSONS ADMINISTERING, EXCHANGING, OR USING VIRTUAL CURRENCIES (Mar. 18, 2013), *available at* http://fincen.gov/statutes_regs/guidance/pdf/FIN-2013-G001.pdf.
58   *Id.*
59   *Id.* at 4.
60   *Id.* at 5.
61   *Id.* at 2.
62   *Id.* at 3. An administrator is a person engaged as a business in issuing (putting into circulation) a virtual currency, and who has the authority to redeem (to withdraw from circulation) such virtual currency. An exchanger is a person engaged as a business in the exchange of virtual currency for real currency, funds, or other virtual currency. *Id.* at 2.
63   *Beyond Silk Road: Potential Risks, Threats, and Promises of Virtual Currencies: Hearing before the S. Comm. on Homeland Security & Governmental Affairs*, 113th Cong. (2013) (statement of Jennifer Shasky Calvery, Director, Financial Crimes Enforcement Network), *available at* http://www.hsgac.senate.gov/hearings/beyond-silk-road-potential-risks-threats-and-promises-of-virtual-currencies.

On January 30, 2014, FinCEN released two administrative rulings clarifying the status of miners of bitcoins and of bitcoin software development and investment activity. In the first ruling, FinCEN reiterated that the mining of bitcoins does not, by itself, make the miner a money transmitter for the purposes of the BSA.[64] FinCEN confirmed that a miner may be a user, and thus may not be required to register as an MSB, if the miner uses mined bitcoins for her own purposes and not for the benefit of another.[65] In addition, FinCEN concluded that a business would be a user of bitcoins, and not an MSB, even if it uses bitcoins it has mined: (1) to pay for the purchase of goods or services or pay debts that it previously incurred (including paying debts to its owners); (2) to make distributions to its owners; or (3) to purchase real currency or another virtual currency, so long as such virtual currency is used solely to make payments or for investment purposes.[66] The second ruling clarified that a business that provides software to facilitate the sale of virtual currency is not an MSB by virtue of distributing such software.[67] The second ruling also provided guidance on bitcoin investments. To the extent that a person, either natural or legal, purchases and sells convertible virtual currency as investments for and on her own account, she is not an MSB as she is not engaged in the business of exchanging convertible virtual currency for other persons.[68]

On April 29, 2014, FinCEN issued another administrative ruling, this one on the rental of computer systems for mining virtual currency.[69] FinCEN ruled that a company is not functioning as an exchanger of virtual currency merely because it rents computer systems to third parties for the mining of virtual currency.[70] As support, FinCEN cited the exemption for a person that only provides the delivery,

---

[64] FINANCIAL CRIMES ENFORCEMENT NETWORK, APPLICATION OF FINCEN'S REGULATIONS TO VIRTUAL CURRENCY MINING OPERATIONS 3 (Jan. 30, 2014), *available at* http://www.fincen.gov/news_room/rp/rulings/pdf/FIN-2014-R001.pdf.
[65] *Id.*
[66] *Id.*
[67] FINANCIAL CRIMES ENFORCEMENT NETWORK, APPLICATION OF FINCEN'S REGULATIONS TO VIRTUAL CURRENCY SOFTWARE DEVELOPMENT AND CERTAIN INVESTMENT ACTIVITY 3 (Jan. 30, 2014), *available at* http://www.fincen.gov/news_room/rp/rulings/pdf/FIN-2014-R002.pdf.
[68] *Id.* at 4.
[69] FINANCIAL CRIMES ENFORCEMENT NETWORK, APPLICATION OF MONEY SERVICES BUSINESS REGULATIONS TO THE RENTAL OF COMPUTER SYSTEMS FOR MINING VIRTUAL CURRENCY (Apr. 29, 2014), *available at* http://www.fincen.gov/news_room/rp/rulings/pdf/FIN-2014-R007.pdf.
[70] *Id.* at 2–3.

communication, or network data access services used by a money transmitter.[71] Although paying real currency to rent computer systems to mine virtual currency technically results in an exchange of real currency for virtual currency, FinCEN declined to treat such businesses as exchangers subject to the BSA.

On October 27, 2014, FinCEN issued its two most recent (at the time of writing) administrative rulings. In both, FinCEN determined that the party operating the platform was a money transmitter and illustrated the application of several of the money transmission exemptions described above. The first ruling was in response to an unnamed party's request for an administrative ruling regarding the application of the BSA to a virtual currency trading platform.[72] The second addressed whether the operator of a virtual currency payment system is deemed to be a money transmitter.[73] The rulings held that, in order for money transmission to be exempt as integral to the provision of a service: (1) the money transmission must be part of the provision of goods or services distinct from money transmission itself; (2) the exemption must be claimed by the person that is engaged in the provision of goods or services; and (3) the money transmission must be necessary for the provision of the goods or services.[74] FinCEN also reiterated, in both rulings, the four requirements of the so-called payment processor exemption: (1) the payment processor must facilitate the purchase of goods or services or the payment of bills for goods and services (other than the money transmission itself); (2) the entity must operate through clearance and settlement systems that admit only BSA-regulated institutions; (3) the entity must provide the service pursuant to a formal agreement; and (4) the agreement must, at the minimum, be with the seller or creditor that provided the goods or services and receives the funds.[75]

---

[71] *Id.* at 2.
[72] FINANCIAL CRIMES ENFORCEMENT NETWORK, REQUEST FOR ADMINISTRATIVE RULING ON THE APPLICATION OF FINCEN'S REGULATIONS TO A VIRTUAL CURRENCY TRADING PLATFORM (Oct. 27, 2014), *available at* http://www.fincen.gov/news_room/rp/rulings/pdf/FIN-2014-R011.pdf.
[73] FINANCIAL CRIMES ENFORCEMENT NETWORK, REQUEST FOR ADMINISTRATIVE RULING ON THE APPLICATION OF FINCEN'S REGULATIONS TO A VIRTUAL CURRENCY PAYMENT SYSTEM (Oct. 27, 2014), *available at* http://www.fincen.gov/news_room/rp/rulings/pdf/FIN-2014-R012.pdf.
[74] *See, e.g., id.* at 4.
[75] *See, e.g., id.*

2.2 Economic and Trade Sanctions/Office of Foreign Assets Control

In addition to the BSA, the AML Regime includes economic and trade sanctions based on U.S. foreign policy and national security programs that are administered by the Office of Foreign Assets Control ("**OFAC**") of the Treasury. OFAC, under authority from both presidential national emergency powers and Congressional legislation, enforces economic and trade sanctions against targeted foreign countries, regimes, and groups of individuals such as terrorists and narcotics traffickers.[76] Sanctions can be either comprehensive or selective and the prohibitions vary for each specific sanctions program.[77] U.S. persons are prohibited from engaging in prohibited transactions, or trade or financial transactions defined by the sanctions program, unless authorized by OFAC or expressly exempted by statute.[78] Penalties for engaging in a prohibited transaction are severe and typically based upon "strict liability," i.e., it does not matter whether a person knows that she is conducting or facilitating a prohibited transaction with a prohibited person. The fact of the conduct or facilitation of a prohibited transaction is sufficient. It is conceivable that Bitcoin could be used to transfer funds to sanctioned countries, groups, or individuals, and thus evade sanctions. Since bitcoins can be sent to or from anywhere, bitcoins may be attractive to people attempting to evade OFAC sanctions, although research appears to indicate that Bitcoin may not be the optimal way to evade law enforcement and the block chain itself provides a high degree of value traceability.

3. Investment Regime

Securities and commodities regulation focus on two different legal issues involving bitcoin: (a) investments purchased with bitcoins; and (b) investing in bitcoins.[79] Both federal and state courts have determined for some purposes that investments purchased with bitcoins can be

---

[76] See TREAS., RESOURCE CENTER, FREQUENTLY ASKED QUESTIONS AND ANSWERS (last visited Dec. 7, 2014), http://www.treasury.gov/resource-center/faqs/Sanctions/Pages/answer.aspx#1.
[77] Id.
[78] Id.
[79] CRAIG K. ELWELL ET AL., CONG. RESEARCH SERV., R43339, BITCOIN: QUESTIONS, ANSWERS, AND ANALYSIS OF LEGAL ISSUES 14 (2014), available at http://fas.org/sgp/crs/misc/R43339.pdf.

securities.⁸⁰ The fact that such securities are purchased with bitcoins rather than currency is irrelevant to the determination of whether the underlying offering involves a security. The SEC and the CFTC have yet to formally opine on whether a purchase of bitcoins is a securities or commodity transaction.

1.1. Securities Exchange Commission

The SEC has the authority to regulate securities and securities-based derivatives as well as their respective markets. The definition of "security" under the Securities Act of 1933 includes a wide variety of instruments including notes, stocks, evidence of indebtedness, and investment contracts.⁸¹ In responding to an inquiry from the Senate Committee on Homeland Security and Government Affairs, SEC Chair Mary Jo White suggested that the bitcoin equivalent of monetary value (i.e., claims to bitcoins held by a third party) could constitute a security:

> Whether a virtual currency is a security under the federal securities laws, and therefore subject to our regulation, is dependent on the particular facts and circumstances at issue. Regardless of whether an underlying virtual currency is itself a security, interests issued by entities owning virtual currencies or providing returns based on assets such as virtual currencies likely would be securities and therefore subject to our regulation.⁸²

To date, SEC enforcement actions involving bitcoins have been largely focused on the investment of bitcoins into schemes by investors rather than the purchase of bitcoins.

In 2013, the SEC brought an action against Bitcoin Savings and Trust and Trendon T. Shavers for undertaking an alleged Ponzi scheme.⁸³ The defendants claimed that since they received bitcoins from investors, there was never an investment of money, which is a requirement for the purposes of determining whether an investment is an investment contract under the *Howey* test. Under *Howey*, an

---

80 *See, e.g.*, SEC v. Shavers, No. 4:13-CV-416, mem. op. (E.D. Tex. Aug. 6, 2013).
81 15 U.S.C. § 77b(a)(1) (1933).
82 Letter from Mary Jo White, Chair, Securities and Exchange Commission, to Thomas R. Carper, Chairman, Senate Committee on Homeland Security and Governmental Affairs (Aug. 30, 2013), *available at* http://online.wsj.com/public/resources/documents/VCurrenty111813.pdf.
83 *Shavers*, No. 4:13-CV-416 (E.D. Tex.).

investment contract involves: (1) the investment of money (2) in a common enterprise (3) with the expectation of profits (4) from the efforts of others.[84] If these factors are met, the investment sold will be considered an investment contract subject to SEC regulation. The court in *Shavers* found that bitcoin was money for purposes of the test, making the investments sold by Bitcoin Savings & Trust investment contracts.[85] However, this conclusion was only drawn to allow the court to determine (and find) subject matter jurisdiction and was not part of the holding of the case.

The Eastern District of Texas only concluded that bitcoins could be considered money under the *Howey* test. However, it may be argued that bitcoins are investment contracts under the *Howey* test and, therefore, securities in and of themselves.[86] The first *Howey* factor is an investment of money. There are three typical paths to obtain bitcoins: they can be generated through the mining process, they can be purchased through exchanges, or they can be obtained as gifts or as consideration from the provision of goods and services. As to the first two of these, bitcoins purchased through an exchange are clearly a money investment. It has also been estimated that the mining process costs approximately US$2.50 for each bitcoin mined in terms of electricity and processing power, which may be an investment of money.[87]

The second factor is common enterprise. Three tests have been put forward by different Circuits to determine when an investment involves a common enterprise: (1) horizontal commonality, (2) narrow vertical commonality, and (3) broad vertical commonality.[88] Horizontal commonality is the pooling of investor contributions by a promoter where profits and losses are distributed proportionally.[89] Narrow vertical commonality is a relationship between the investor and the promoter such that the investor's profits are tied to the promoter's profits, i.e., they must rise and fall together.[90] Finally, broad vertical commonality is a relationship between investors and a promoter where the investors rely on the expertise and efforts of the promoter to receive

---

[84] SEC v. W.J. Howey Co., 328 U.S. 293, 298–299 (1946).
[85] *Shavers*, No. 4:13-CV-416, mem. op. at 3 (E.D. Tex. Aug. 6, 2013).
[86] An excellent analysis of this issue is in Grinberg, *supra* note 39, at 196–99.
[87] Paul H. Farmer, Jr., *Speculative Tech: The Bitcoin Legal Quagmire & the Need for Legal Innovation*, 9 J. Bus. & Tech. L. 85, 101 (2014).
[88] *Id.* at 102. *See also* James D. Gordon III, Defining a Common Enterprise in Investment Contracts, 72 Ohio St. L.J. 59, 66–70 (2011).
[89] Farmer, *supra* note 87, at 102–03.
[90] *Id.* at 103.

a profit.[91] The Bitcoin network is supported by miners that devote their computer processing power to both the generation of new bitcoins and the confirmation of transaction on the block chain.[92] It may be said that the miners are the promoters of Bitcoin because their efforts are what keep the market alive and generates value.[93] Similar to a narrow vertical commonality, the profits of both investors and miners are tied together in the value of the bitcoins they create or transact with.[94] Further, Bitcoin would cease to exist without the miners moving the block chain forward, so profits for investors come from the efforts of the promoters (i.e., the miners).[95] In vertical commonality jurisdictions, bitcoin may satisfy the common enterprise factor.[96]

Third, the investment must be made with the expectation of profit. The primary use of bitcoins in the current market is arguably not as a medium of exchange; it is more often bought or sold for speculative investment purposes.[97] This means that purchasers are expecting to buy low and sell high in order to realize a profit.[98] If the market shifts and users primarily obtain bitcoins to purchase goods or services then this factor may fail, but for now most users may be investing with the goal of realizing profits.

Finally, the fourth factor requires the profits to come solely from the efforts of the promoter or a third party. As discussed under the common enterprise factor, bitcoin users are at the mercy of the miners for the continued availability of the marketplace. After obtaining bitcoins, users are not required, nor are they expected, to make any further effort to further the cause.[99] Independent network developers and promoters work to increase the acceptance and use of bitcoins, adding value to all of the users.[100] Therefore, under this analysis Bitcoin could be considered an investment contract, as such, as it passes the four factors of the *Howey* test.

---

[91] *Id.*
[92] *Id.*
[93] *Id.*
[94] *Id.*
[95] *Id.*
[96] *Contra* Grinberg, *supra* note 39, at 197–98.
[97] Farmer, *supra* note 87, at 102.
[98] *Id.*
[99] *Id.*
[100] *Id.*

1.2. Commodity Futures Trading Commission

The Commodity Futures Trading Commission (the "**CFTC**") is the regulatory body responsible for overseeing the on- and off-exchange trades of futures contracts. The mission of the CFTC is to "protect market participants and the public from fraud, manipulation, abusive practices and systemic risk related to derivatives...and to foster transparent, open, competitive and financially sound markets."[101] The primary statute that gives the CFTC power over these markets is the Commodity Exchange Act (the "**CEA**").[102]

The threshold question for determining whether bitcoin falls under the purview of the CEA is whether it meets the CEA's definition of a "commodity." The definition of "commodity" in the CEA includes a laundry list of goods such as wheat, cotton and rice as well as the catch-all "all services, rights, and interests...in which contracts for future delivery are presently or in the future dealt in."[103] This provision expands the definition of a commodity from tangible goods to include intangible constructs.

The CEA further subdivides commodities into three subparts: (1) exempt commodities, (2) excluded commodities and (3) agricultural commodities. An excluded commodity is, generally, any financial instrument such as a security, currency, interest rate, debt instrument, or credit rating; any economic or commercial index other than a narrow-based commodity index; or any other value that is out of the control of participants and is associated with an economic consequence.[104] Agricultural commodities include, among other things, the enumerated commodities listed in section 1a of the CEA. Finally, an exempt commodity is "a commodity that is not an excluded commodity or an agricultural commodity."[105] The CFTC provides two examples of exempt commodities: energy commodities and metals.[106]

As previously noted, bitcoins are an intangible, purely digital construct with no physical form. Accordingly, in order for bitcoin to be subject to the CFTC's jurisdiction under the CEA, it must be a 'right'

---

[101] COMMODITY FUTURES TRADING COMMISSION, MISSION AND RESPONSIBILITIES, *available at* http://www.cftc.gov/About/MissionResponsibilities/index.htm.
[102] 7 U.S.C. § 1 (1936).
[103] *Id.* § 1a(9) (2010).
[104] *Id.* § 1a(19) (2010).
[105] *Id.* § 1a(20) (2010).
[106] COMMODITY FUTURES TRADING COMMISSION, CFTC GLOSSARY—A GUIDE TO THE LANGUAGE OF THE FUTURES INDUSTRY, *available at* http://www.cftc.gov/ConsumerProtection/EducationCenter/CFTCGlossary/glossary_e

or 'interest' in which contracts for future delivery are presently or in the future dealt in." While we are confident that bitcoin will not be considered a currency for the purposes of CEA, the Internal Revenue Service (the "**IRS**") guidance released early in 2014 classifies bitcoin as property for tax purposes.[107] As property, bitcoin may be more closely equated to the trade of metals than securities; that could make it an exempt commodity. The CFTC has not decided how to classify bitcoin thus far, but it is clear that further guidance would be salutary.

Excluded commodities are not regulated by the CFTC other than to prevent fraud and market manipulation.[108] Exempt commodities will not be subject to regulation if agreements, contracts, or transactions are: "(1) [e]ntered into on a principal-to-principal basis solely between persons that are eligible commercial entities...and (2) [e]xecuted or traded on an electronic trading facility."[109] In other words, exempt commodity transactions are only truly exempt if they take place between institutional investors on a certified trading platform. Finally, if the CFTC finds that bitcoin falls under the definition of a commodity under the catch-all "rights and interests" phrase, bitcoin will be subject to full CFTC regulation.

The CFTC has not yet released guidance about their treatment of bitcoin but they have already approved a bitcoin derivatives market plan put forward by TeraExchange. TeraExchange is a Swap Execution Facility (an "**SEF**") that markets to large institutional buyers in an attempt to reduce the volatility of bitcoin.[110] TeraExchange was granted a temporary registration as an SEF in September 2013.[111] An SEF is a registered entity under the Dodd-Frank Act, which was created to provide greater pre-trade and post-trade transparency to the swaps markets.[112] As an SEF, TeraExchange is required to comply with all CEA provisions as well as any future CFTC regulations,

---

[107] I.R.S. Notice IR-2014-21 (Mar. 25, 2014), *available at* http://www.irs.gov/pub/irs-drop/n-14-21.pdf.

[108] However, many excluded commodities are also within the purview of the SEC, which has priority over any alleged violations of the CEA.

[109] 17 C.F.R. § 36.3(a) (2009).

[110] Stan Higgins, *TeraExchange Receives US Approval to Launch First Bitcoin Derivative*, CoinDesk (Sept. 12, 2014 21:20 GMT), http://www.coindesk.com/teraexchange-bitcoin-derivative-cftc/.

[111] Commodity Futures Trading Commission, CFTC Issues Notice of Temporary Registration as a Swap Execution Facility to TeraExchange, LLC, PR6698-13 (Sept. 19, 2013) *available at* http://www.cftc.gov/PressRoom/PressReleases/pr6698-13.

[112] *Id.*

guidance, interpretations, and amendments.[113] As of October 9, 2014, TeraExchange has begun offering bitcoin derivatives after months of work with the CFTC to ensure the quality of the swaps.[114]

4. Consumer Protection Regime

The Consumer Protection Regime includes several laws and regulations that may potentially apply to Bitcoin. While neither the FTC nor the CFPB have made definitive public statements indicating that they intend to regulate bitcoin-related activities, a recent Notice of Proposed Rulemaking from the CFPB suggests that the CFPB will act pursuant to its authority under the Electronic Funds Transfer Act and regulations promulgated thereunder (the "**EFTA**"). In addition, it is possible that the FTC could act under Section 5 of the Federal Trade Commission Act (the "**FTCA**"). A brief description of EFTA and Section 5 of the FTC Act and the possible application of each to bitcoin-related activities is provided below.

4.1 Electronic Funds Transfer Act/Regulation E

EFTA, and Regulation E promulgated thereunder, establishes a federal consumer protection framework for electronic transfers of funds. Generally, EFTA imposes fee disclosures and error-resolution procedures on financial institutions that enable consumers to electronically initiate funds transfers to or from the consumer's account at financial institutions.[115] The CFPB also has specific requirements for those performing "remittance transfers" which are electronic transfers from a U.S. consumer to someone outside the U.S. Similar to the framework outlined above, parties performing remittance transfers are required to make certain disclosures about a transaction, provide error-resolution procedures, and permit a sender to cancel the remittance transfer within thirty minutes after the transfer's request.[116] Due to the nature of the Bitcoin system, these error-resolution and cancelation requirements may be difficult to implement without important changes

---

[113] *Id.*
[114] *TeraExchange Completes First Bitcoin Derivatives Trade on Regulated Exchange*, MARKETWATCH (Oct. 9, 2014 11:01 EST), *available at* http://www.marketwatch.com/story/teraexchange-completes-first-bitcoin-derivatives-trade-on-regulated-exchange-2014-10-09.
[115] 15 U.S.C. §§ 1693c, 1693f (2010).
[116] 15 U.S.C. §§ 1693(o)–(o-1).

by intermediaries (for example) in how their customers interact with the Bitcoin protocol.

On November 13, 2014, the CFPB issued a Notice of Proposed Rulemaking that applies Regulation E to certain prepaid accounts and, if enacted, may cover Indirect Bitcoin Holdings.[117] The proposed rule would create a new definition of prepaid account:

> A prepaid account is a card, code, or other device, not otherwise an account under paragraph (b)(1) of this section, which is established primarily for personal, family, or household purposes, and which:
>
> (A) is either issued on a prepaid basis to a consumer in a specified amount or not issued on a prepaid basis but capable of being loaded with funds thereafter;
> (B) is redeemable upon presentation at multiple, unaffiliated merchants for goods or services, usable at automated teller machines, or usable for person-to-person transfers; and
> (C) is not: (1) a gift certificate as defined in § 1005.20(a)(1) and (b); (2) a store gift card as defined in § 1005.20(a)(2) and (b); (3) a loyalty, award, or promotional gift card as defined in § 1005.20(a)(4) and (b); or (4) a general-use prepaid card as defined in § 1005.20(a)(3) and (b) that is both marketed and labeled as a gift card or gift certificate.[118]

The CFPB acknowledges that the proposed rule may cover virtual currencies:

> The Bureau also recognizes that the proposed rule may have potential application to virtual currency and related products and services. As a general matter, however, the Bureau's analysis of mobile financial products and services, as well as and virtual currencies and related products and services, including the applicability of existing regulations and this proposed regulation to such products and services, is ongoing.[119]

---

[117] Prepaid Accounts, 79 Fed. Reg. 77,101 (Dec. 23, 2014) (to be codified at 12 C.F.R. pt. 1005, 12 C.F.R. pt. 1026).
[118] *Id.* 77,297.
[119] *Id.* 77,121.

4.2 Section 5 of the FTC Act

Although a thorough analysis of the FTC's authority and enforcement powers is beyond the scope of this chapter, section 5(a) of the FTCA, which prohibits unfair and deceptive acts and practices in or affecting commerce, warrants attention.[120] The FTC has frequently used its broad enforcement powers under Section 5(a) to 'fill the gaps' in the financial regulatory scheme to apply, by analogy, regulations applicable to traditional financial institutions to other enterprises.

The legal standards for unfairness and deception are distinct. Depending on the facts, an act or practice may be unfair, deceptive, neither or both. An act or practice is generally unfair where it: (1) causes or is likely to cause substantial injury to consumers; (2) cannot be reasonably avoided by consumers; and (3) is not outweighed by countervailing benefits to consumers or to competition.[121] An act or practice is deceptive where: (1) a representation, omission, or practice misleads or is likely to mislead the consumer; (2) a consumer's interpretation of the representation, omission, or practice is considered reasonable under the circumstances; and (3) the misleading representation, omission, or practice is material.[122]

Given the FTC's broad authority, it appears likely that FTC enforcement actions with respect to bitcoin will increase, especially in areas where the nature of bitcoin conflicts with the typical consumer's expectations based on the regulation of other payment methods. Expected areas of focus include liability for unauthorized transactions, inaccurate or unclear fee disclosures, data security and privacy and the failure to adequately explain the distinctions between On-Block Chain Transactions and Off-Block Chain Transactions.

5. Campaign Contributions

5.1. Federal Election Commission

The Federal Election Commission (the "**FEC**") has defined money as "currency of the United States or of any foreign nation, checks, money orders, or any other negotiable instruments payable on

---

[120] 15 U.S.C. § 45 (2006).
[121] 12 U.S.C. § 5531(c) (2010).
[122] Consumer Financial Protection Bureau, Bulletin 2013-07, 3 (Jul. 10, 2013), *available at* http://files.consumerfinance.gov/f/201307_cfpb_bulletin_unfair-deceptive-abusive-practices.pdf.

demand."[123] In November 2013, a draft advisory memorandum was published by the FEC giving preliminary guidance as to the treatment of bitcoins for political campaign contributions.[124] The draft advisory states that bitcoins do not fall within the FEC's definition of money and, therefore, cannot be accepted as money for campaign contributions.[125] However, the guidance goes on to suggest that bitcoins could be allowed as "in-kind contributions" which are defined as "anything of value," or as "non-monetary contributions" which are equated to stocks and commodities.[126]

The FEC released another advisory opinion dated May 8, 2014.[127] Make Your Laws PAC, Inc. ("**MYL**") had sent the FEC a request to determine MYL's proposed acceptance, purchase, and disbursement of bitcoins under the Federal Election Campaign Act of 1971. MYL proposed to receive donations of $100 or less in bitcoin and then to then sell, retain, or disburse those bitcoins to pay for various administrative expenses.[128] The FEC concluded that MYL could accept bitcoin contributions subject to valuation and reporting requirements.[129] Further, MYL could also purchase bitcoins with campaign funds for investment purposes. However, MYL may not disburse those bitcoins because FEC regulations require the funds to be returned to a campaign depository before they are to be used for disbursements.[130]

MYL's proposal included a series of disclosures they would require from contributors, such as a contributor's name, address, occupation, and employer as well as representations that the contributor is the owner of the bitcoins and that she is not a foreign national.[131] The FEC requires that if a contribution cannot be determined to have come from a legal source, the treasurer must refund the contribution within thirty days of receipt or discovery of illegality.[132] The precautions included in MYL's plan were designed to meet the regulations and overcome Bitcoin's private nature.

---

[123] 11 C.F.R. § 100.52(c) (2013).
[124] Conservative Action Fund, 13-45 Draft Advisory Op. (2013), *available at* http://saos.nictusa.com/aodocs/201315.pdf.
[125] *Id.* at 5-6.
[126] *Id.* at 6-7; *see also* 11 C.F.R. § 100.52(d)(1) (2009).
[127] Make Your Laws PAC, Inc., 2014-02 Advisory Op. (2014).
[128] *Id.* at 2-3.
[129] *Id.* at 6.
[130] *Id.* at 3-4.
[131] *Id.* at 4-5.
[132] *Id.*; *also see* 11 C.F.R. §§103.3(b)(1)-(2) (1980).

The FEC generally requires contributions to be put into a campaign repository within ten days of receipt if the contribution is not being returned.[133] However, contributions of "stocks, bonds, art objects, and other similar items" are not required to be liquidated and deposited the same way.[134] The FEC concluded that contributions of bitcoins will be considered pari passu with stocks, bonds, art objects, and other like items, and do not need to be deposited in a campaign depository within ten days of receipt.[135]

The advisory opinion also included the FEC's policy on bitcoin valuation. Like the IRS, the FEC concluded that political committees should value contributions based on the market value of bitcoins at the time the contribution is received.[136] The FEC also recognized that there are multiple bitcoin exchanges with different exchange rates so the policy will be to use the exchange rate listed on whatever processing service the committee is utilizing to receive the contribution.[137] However, if the political committee receives its contribution through an On-Block Chain transaction, one without the use of an intermediary, the committee should determine the value based on a reasonable exchange rate from a publicly available, high-volume exchange.[138]

6. Internal Revenue Code

In late March 2014, the IRS issued guidance that explained how existing general tax principles apply to virtual currencies like bitcoin.[139] The IRS has determined that bitcoins are not "currency" for tax purposes. Instead, bitcoin is taxed as "property," like gold or shares of a corporation's capital stock.[140] The guidance was developed after a May 2013 report of the Government Accountability Office (the "GAO") identified five tax compliance risks associated with virtual currencies and economies: (1) taxpayer lack of knowledge of tax requirements; (2) uncertainty over how to characterize income; (3) uncertainty about tax (cost) basis calculation; (4) challenges with

---

[133] 11 C.F.R. § 103.3(a).
[134] 11 C.F.R. § 104.13(b) (2014).
[135] Make Your Laws PAC, Inc., 2014-02 Advisory Op., 6 (2014).
[136] *Id.*
[137] *Id.* at 6–7.
[138] *Id.* at 7.
[139] I.R.S. Notice IR-2014-21, *supra* note 107.
[140] *Id.* at 2.

third-party reporting; and (5) evasion.[141] While the IRS had, prior to the March 2014 guidance, issued general information regarding "closed-flow" or "in-game currencies" used inside virtual worlds, the GAO recommended that the IRS develop guidance on "the basic tax reporting requirements for transactions using virtual currencies developed and used outside of virtual economies."[142]

The 2014 IRS guidance focuses predominantly on how 'virtual currency' should be treated for income tax purposes. The guidance uses the term 'virtual currency,' a term also used by FinCEN, to refer to "a digital representation of value that functions as a medium of exchange, a unit of account, and/or a store of value...[that] operates like 'real' currency [in some environments]...[but that] does not have legal tender status in any jurisdiction."[143] The guidance specifically notes that Bitcoin is a 'convertible virtual currency' and focuses on the tax compliance risks cited in the GAO report.[144]

According to the IRS, the use of virtual currency is a realization event and the amount realized is the fair market value of the property received.[145] In addition, the sale of virtual currency results in a taxable gain or loss that is calculated by subtracting the seller's basis from the amount realized in any sale.[146] The characterization of the gain or loss is based on whether the seller is an investor holding virtual currency as a capital asset (capital gain or loss) or engaged in a trade or business where the seller holds the virtual currency as inventory or other property (ordinary income or loss).[147]

Individual virtual currency miners are required to include the fair market value of the mined virtual currency as of the date of receipt in their gross income.[148] Furthermore, if the miner engages in the mining activity in course of its trade or business and not as an employee, the taxpayer is required to pay self-employment tax on the net-earnings from such earnings.[149]

With respect to information reporting, a person who, in the course of trade or business, makes a payment using virtual currency worth

---

[141] U.S. Gov't Accountability Office, GAO-13-516, Virtual Economies and Currencies: Additional IRS Guidance Could Reduce Tax Compliance Risks (2013).
[142] *Id.* at 17.
[143] I.R.S. Notice IR-2014-21, *supra* note 107, at 1.
[144] *See, e.g., id.* at 2–3.
[145] *Id.* at 3-4.
[146] *Id.* at 3.
[147] *Id.* at 3–4.
[148] *Id.* at 4.
[149] *Id.*

$600 or more to an independent contractor is required to file an information return (1099-MISC) and deliver the 1099-MISC to the payment recipient.[150] Other information returns are required to the same extent as if they were made using any other property.[151]

With respect to third-party reporting, the IRS notice provides that the third-party settlement organization (the "**TPSO**") rules apply to third parties that contract "with a substantial number of unrelated merchants to settle payments between the merchants and their customers."[152] A TPSO is required to report payments made to a merchant on a Form 1099-K if the number of transactions settled for that merchant exceeds 200 in a calendar year and the gross payments made to the merchant exceeds $20,000 in either real currency or virtual currency (calculated based on the fair market value on the date of payment).[153]

IV. CASE LAW

Bitcoin is a relatively new construct, having only gained prominence towards the end of 2013. Bitcoin has been around since 2009 but the extent of its use has been limited until recently. Due to the slow nature of the American legal system, it can take years for cases to be resolved. In high technology fields, these cases can take even longer while the parties seek to learn enough about the technology to make adequate arguments. As such, very few cases have actually gone to trial with resulting decisions relating to Bitcoin. This section is meant to detail some of the few decisions that have been released by American courts to give an idea of how the judiciary perceives Bitcoin.

The most prominent of these is *SEC v. Shavers*, referenced earlier. This case was launched in the federal court for the Eastern District of Texas in response to the defendant's fraudulent business. Trendon Shavers, the first defendant, was founder and operator of the Bitcoin Savings and Trust, the second defendant, which purported to give investors a 7% weekly return on their investment in Bitcoin by arbitraging the market.[154] In reality, the business was a Ponzi scheme defrauding its investors. The SEC argued that offering bitcoins as investments with rates of return made them appear to be securities or

---

[150] *Id.* at 5.
[151] *Id.*
[152] *Id.* at 6.
[153] *Id.*
[154] SEC v. Shavers, No. 4:13-CV-416, mem. op. & order, 1–2 (E.D. Tex. Sept. 18, 2014).

investment contracts.[155] Shavers claimed that since the business received bitcoins from investors there was never an investment of money which is a required element of the *Howey* test for investment contracts.[156] The court found that bitcoins acted as money or funds as they were accepted to purchase goods and services from specific vendors.[157] Bitcoins can also be converted to conventional currencies giving them a clear monetary value. The court further found an investment in a common enterprise because all investors were giving Shavers their bitcoins due to his supposed expertise in the Bitcoin markets.[158] Finally, the court found that the investors had an expectation of profits, and in fact Shavers promoted his investment services based on their return on investment.[159] Having met each factor of the *Howey* test, the court concluded Bitcoins could be the basis for an investment contract.[160]

While the SEC case against Shavers is pending appeal and post judgment motions have been filed with the court, another action has sprung up against Shavers and Bitcoin Savings and Trust. Shavers is, at the time of writing, being sued privately by those who invested in Bitcoin Savings and Trust and lost their investment. The complaint in *Liquid Bits, Corp. v. Shavers* alleges a number of violations of Florida state law,[161] including breaches of the Deceptive and Unfair Trade Practices Act, the Civil Theft Statute, and the Securities and Investor Protection Act.[162] This action could lead to interesting arguments and decisions about how a U.S. state will handle fraud in bitcoin. This action will also depend on the future of *SEC v. Shavers* as it continues to define how the federal courts think about Bitcoin.

In the realm of criminal law, *US v. Faiella* is one of the first cases to address the nature of bitcoin as it applies to money transmitter and money laundering laws. Robert Faiella and Charlie Shrem were allegedly acting as unlicensed bitcoin exchangers for the purposes of providing users with access to Silk Road, an online marketplace providing access to illicit goods, services and contraband[163] Faiella would purportedly receive cash deposits, exchange them for bitcoins,

---

[155] *Shavers*, No. 4:13-CV-416, mem. op., 2 (E.D. Tex. Aug. 6, 2013)
[156] *Id*. at 2–3.
[157] *Id*. at 3.
[158] *Id*.
[159] *Id*. at 4.
[160] *Id*.
[161] Liquid Bits, Corp. v. Shavers, No. 1:14-CV-22869-JAL, complaint (S.D. Fla. Aug. 4, 2014).
[162] *Id*. at 7–13.
[163] United States v. Faiella, No. 14-CR-243, complaint (S.D.N.Y. Jan. 24, 2014).

and then transfer those funds to the user accounts on the Silk Road site.[164] Shrem was alleged to have assisted in this enterprise through his position as the Chief Compliance Officer of BitInstant.[165] The criminal complaint was in the Southern District of New York. The court decided that "[t]hese were, in essence, transfers to a third party agent, Silk Road, for Silk Road users did not have full control over the Bitcoins transferred into their accounts."[166] Faiella argued in a motion to dismiss that Bitcoin is not money, that operating a Bitcoin exchange does not constitute transmitting, and that he was not a money transmitter.[167] The judge rejected the motion request, holding that bitcoin clearly qualifies as money under the plain meaning of the word.[168] Further, the court found that Faiella performed money transmitting services as he took cash from customers, converted it into bitcoins, and then transmitted the bitcoins to user accounts.[169] Finally, the court held that Faiella is clearly a money transmitter under the guidance put forward by FinCEN.[170]

Faiella ultimately pleaded guilty to operating an unlicensed money transmitting business. At the time of writing, he has just been sentenced to a prison term of not more than forty-eight months.[171] Shrem pleaded guilty to one count of aiding and abetting the operation of an unlicensed money transmitting business and was sentenced to federal prison for a term of not more than twenty-four months.[172]

The federal court in the Southern District of New York made a very similar order in *United States v. Ulbricht*. While Faiella was acting primarily as an exchanger for Silk Road, taking cash and returning bitcoins, Ulbricht is believed to be the leader of Silk Road known as the Dread Pirate Roberts. Ulbricht also claimed that, as bitcoins are not "money" or "funds," he cannot be guilty of money laundering.[173] The court found that bitcoin falls under the category of "funds" in 18 U.S.C. §1956.[174] Funds are used to pay for things and Bitcoin is used either as a medium of exchange or it can be used directly as a form of

---

[164] *Id.* at 4–5.
[165] *Id.*
[166] *Faiella*, mem. order, 47 (S.D.N.Y. Aug. 18, 2014).
[167] *Id.* at 1.
[168] *Id.* at 2.
[169] *Id.* at 3–4.
[170] *Id.* at 4–5.
[171] Faiella, judgment, 2 (S.D.N.Y. Jan. 26, 2015).
[172] *Faiella*, judgment, 2 (S.D.N.Y. Dec. 23, 2014).
[173] United States v. Ulbricht, No. 14-CR-68, op. and order, 5 (S.D.N.Y. Jul. 9, 2014).
[174] *Id.* at 49–50.

payment. The court concluded that finding Bitcoin to be outside the money laundering statutes would be nonsensical.[175]

While there is only a small amount of case law thus far that has directly commented on Bitcoin, there is one conclusion each court has made: Bitcoin is "money" and "funds" for certain purposes under federal law. This was the case in both the SEC proceedings in Texas and in federal criminal proceedings in New York. Much room for debate remains, but at least it is clear that courts will find bitcoin to be money in discrete cases.

---

[175] *Id.* at 50.

Printed in Germany
by Amazon Distribution
GmbH, Leipzig